Energy-Efficient Computing and Data Centers

*Series Editor*
*Serge Petiton*

# Energy-Efficient Computing
# and Data Centers

Luigi Brochard
Vinod Kamath
Julita Corbalán
Scott Holland
Walter Mittelbach
Michael Ott

WILEY

First published 2019 in Great Britain and the United States by ISTE Ltd and John Wiley & Sons, Inc.

ISTE Ltd
27-37 St George's Road
London SW19 4EU
UK

www.iste.co.uk

John Wiley & Sons, Inc.
111 River Street
Hoboken, NJ 07030
USA

www.wiley.com

Library of Congress Control Number: 2019940668

British Library Cataloguing-in-Publication Data
A CIP record for this book is available from the British Library
ISBN 978-1-78630-185-7

# Contents

# Introduction

As shown by a recent news article in *Nature* (Jones 2018), data centers consume about 1% of the total electricity demand while information and communication technology (ICT) as a whole, including personal devices, mobile networks and TV consumes about 10%. It shows also that the demand will grow exponentially in the near future leading in 2030 to a ratio of electricity demand varying depending on the estimations between 3% and 8% for data centers and between 8% and 21% for ICT An article in the *Guardian* (2017) shows a similar accelerating trend.

The energy consumed by a data center during a given period is the sum of the energy consumed by all the workloads that have been executed, plus the energy consumed when devices are idle, plus the energy loss to convert the electricity from the power lines down to the IT devices, plus the energy to cool the IT devices. This book will tackle of all four aspects of energy.

The energy consumed by a workload when running on a system is the integral of its power consumption over its execution time from beginning to end. If the power consumed by the workload is constant, it would simply be:

Energy = Power × Time

One trivial way to minimize the power of a workload while running on a system is to reduce the frequency of the processor. But this can be counterproductive since the elapsed time will very often increase to a point where the total energy is constant or has increased. From a return on investment perspective, it is also obvious that a system and a data center have to be used as much as possible and run as many workloads as possible. That is why energy efficiency, and not only power efficiency, is critical.

Existing data centers have two physical limits they cannot exceed: floor space and power supply. They also have an economical limit, which is their budget for operational costs.

To keep up as much as possible with Moore's law, power consumption of IT devices is also on the rise, so that existing data centers are facing the dilemma of either keeping the same density of servers per rack (leading to a tremendous power and cooling challenge) or giving up on the density. That is one reason why numerous new data centers are being built around the world by hyperscale, cloud and high-performance computing data centers.

This increasing energy demand impacts not only the planet's ecosystem but also the ICT business as increasing electricity demand leads to even more increased energy cost since the price of electricity itself is on the rise.

According to the U.S. Bureau of Labor Statistics, prices for electricity were 66% higher in 2018 versus 2000 which is 21% higher than inflation during the same period (Official Data Foundation 2018). A similar trend is seen in Europe (Eurostat n.d.).

Figure I.1 shows the wide range of electricity prices in 2018 around the world.

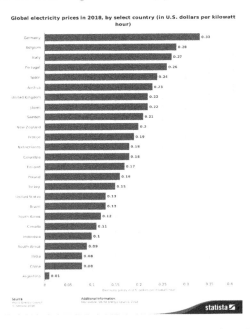

**Figure I.1.** *Price of electricity around the world in 2018, from Statisca.com*

These prices are average price across different locations in a country. For example, the average price of electricity in the United States is $0.13 per kW/h, but it differs widely across the different states with locations where it can be as low as $0.06 per kW/h in Colorado. This variability of electricity price associated with the environmental conditions (temperature, humidity, etc.) of the location does play a very important role in the power and cooling design of a data center.

Power usage effectiveness (PUE) is a measure of how efficiently a computer data center uses its power. PUE is the ratio of total energy used by a data center facility to the energy used by the IT computing equipment. The ideal value is 1.0.

$$PUE = \frac{Total\ energy}{IT\ equipment\ energy} \qquad\qquad [I.1]$$

In the following, we will use PUE as the cooling efficiency not taking into account the power conversion losses. Legacy data centers usually have a PUE of about 2 and with a careful design it is possible to get around 1.1. Table I.1 shows the numbers of years needed for the energy cost to power and cool a server to equal the server acquisition cost with various PUE and electricity prices.

| PUE = | 2 | 1.1 |
|---|---|---|
| electricity price | number of years | number of years |
| $0.06 | 12.7 | 23.1 |
| $0.21 | 3.6 | 6.6 |
| $0.33 | 2.3 | 4.2 |

**Table I.1.** *Impact of PUE on price of electricity versus price of server*

It shows how the energy costs can quickly equal the acquisition cost with a high PUE and medium to high electricity price. With a low electricity price, even with a high PUE, this will take more than 10 years and even close to 20 with a low PUE. This illustrates the importance of the data center location that impacts both PUE (through the possible use of free cooling) and electricity cost on the cooling infrastructure design.

Although PUE is an important metric, it does not take into account how much power the IT device is consuming and its power efficiency.

IT energy effectiveness (ITUE) measures how the IT equipment energy is optimized where voltage regulator (VR), PSU and fan are the energy consumed by the voltage regulator, power supply and fan. The ideal value is 1.0.

$$ITUE = \frac{IT\ equiment\ energy\ +VR+PSU+fan\ power}{IT\ equipment\ energy} \qquad [I.2]$$

We will study all ITUE components not in isolation, but in relation to the type of workload the server is running since the server power consumption depends on the workload running on it.

But even with a low PUE and ITUE, the heat produced by the systems in the data center is still lost without any waste heat reuse.

Energy reuse effectiveness (ERE) measures how efficient a data center reuses the energy dissipated by the computer. ERE is the ratio of total energy used by the facility minus the waste heat energy reuse divided by the energy used by the IT computing equipment.

$$ERE = \frac{Total\ facility\ energy\ -\ energy\_reuse}{IT\ equipment\ energy} \qquad [I.3]$$

An ideal ERE is 0.0. With no heat reuse, ERE = PUE and we have always:

$$ERE \leq PUE \qquad\qquad\qquad\qquad [I.4]$$

Many articles have been focusing on the PUE of data centers but very few have been looking at the global equation ITUE + PUE + ERE.

This is what we will address in this book.

Chapter 1 presents the different IT devices in a data center and the different components in a server from a power consumption perspective.

Chapter 2 presents the different cooling technologies in a server, their evolution and the trade-off between density and cooling.

Chapter 3 presents the different cooling technologies in the data center based on air cooling and liquid cooling, the ASHRAE standards and how waste heat can be reused in particular with adsorption chillers.

Chapter 4 presents the Xeon processor and NVIDIA accelerator evolution over the last 15 years in terms of performance and power consumption with reference to Moore's and Dennard's laws. It also presents the impact of microarchitecture evolutions and how the evolution in microprocessor design is power driven.

Chapter 5 analyzes the power, thermal and performance characteristics of a server when running different types of workloads in relation with the type of instruction executed. It also compares these metrics depending on the server cooling technologies.

Chapter 6 presents hardware and software to measure, model, predict and control power and performance in a server and in a data center in order to optimize their energy consumption.

Chapter 7 analyzes the PUE, ERE and total cost of ownership (TCO) of existing and new data centers with different cooling designs and the impact of power consumption, electricity price, free cooling and waste heat reuse. Through two data center examples it highlights also how a careful data center design, free cooling and waste heat reuse can reduce PUE, ERE and TCO and save up to 50% of energy. It concludes showing how renewable energy can be used to provide the remaining energy needed by the data center.

## Acknowledgments

This book is the result of a 12-year experience with IBM and Lenovo designing energy-efficient servers and data centers in collaborations with high-performance customers around the world. I would like to mention and thank in particular the Leibniz Supercomputing Center in Munich (LRZ) for the work we did since 2011 to design and deliver the most energy-efficient solutions. This book would not have been possible without the help of colleagues at Lenovo Data Center Group, with the application team (Eric Michel, Peter Mayes, Christoph Pospiech), with the power management team (Robert Wolford) and with the data center team (Jerrod Buterbaugh), at Intel (Andrey Semin), NVIDIA (François Courteille), IBM (Ingmar Meijer, Vadim Elisseev) and LRZ (Herbert Huber). Special thanks also to Peter Mayes for his rereading.

# 1

# Systems in Data Centers

There are different types of IT equipment that serve different functions depending on customer application. This chapter provides an overview of servers, storage arrays, switches and their components.

## 1.1. Servers

A server is a broad term describing a specific piece of IT equipment that provides computing capability and runs software applications in an environment networked with other IT equipment, including other servers. Most servers contain the following major hardware building blocks: processors, memory, chipset, input/output (I/O) devices, storage, peripherals, voltage regulators (VRs), power supplies and cooling systems. Additional application-specific integrated circuits (ASICs) may be necessary, such as an onboard redundant array of independent disks (RAID) controller and a server management controller.

Volume rack-mounted servers are designed to fit within commonly available rack sizes, such as the 19 in. (0.5 m) rack form factor defined by EIA/ECA Standard 310-E specification[1]. The vertical dimension is expressed in terms of rack units or just units (U). One U or 1U represents 1.75 in. (44.45 mm) of vertical height within a rack. Servers used for computing are available in standard rack-mount and custom configurations. Typical dimensions and sizes for standard rack-mount compute servers are full-width 1U, 2U or 4U. A single-server chassis may contain multiple server

---

1 Available at: https://www.server-racks.com/eia-310.html [Accessed May 7, 2019].

nodes. Each node is defined as containing all key components, except power supplies, needed to make up a complete server. These nodes simply share the larger chassis infrastructure to conserve data center space. For more dense servers, there are 1U and 2U server enclosures that house several 1U ½-width servers.

Microservers are an emerging technology. They are based on system on a chip (SOC) design where all the functions, which are located on a motherboard for a classic server, are integrated on a single chip with the exception of memory, boot flash and power circuits. SOC are usually less power hungry than usual microprocessors leading to microservers that are more dense than classic servers. Although microservers and SOC are not analyzed in the following chapters, they are worth mentioning. These servers generally provide sufficient, targeted performance with optimized performance-per-watt capability, while being easily scalable with shared power and cooling infrastructure for individual servers.

To achieve even higher compute density than the 1U form factor, blade servers are another option. Each manufacturer designs their blades based on their own packaging and design goals. These blade chassis range from 3U to 10U tall and can house many blades. Blade servers are the result of technology compaction, which allows for a greater processing density in the same equipment volume. The greater processing density also results in greater power and heat density, further complicating data center cooling. Server components that had previously been packaged inside the tower/ pedestal or rack-mounted server (e.g. fans and power supplies) are still required, but these components are now located within a chassis (or enclosure) that is designed to house multiple blade servers in a side-by-side or stacked configuration. Most of the time, the blade chassis includes networking, management and even storage functions for the blade servers, while the blade server integrates at least one controller (Ethernet, fiber channel, etc.) on the motherboard. Extra interfaces can be added using mezzanine cards.

Figure 1.1 illustrates 1U, 2U, 4U full width servers, a 2U chassis hosting four ½-width nodes and a 5U blade chassis hosting eight blades.

Examples of such servers will be given in Chapter 2.

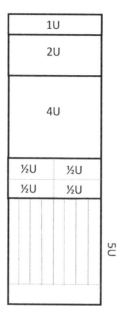

**Figure 1.1.** *1U, 2U, 4U full width servers, 2U chassis with four ½-width nodes and a 5U blade chassis with eight blades including a 1U base for power supplies*

## 1.2. Storage arrays

Disk arrays are enclosures that provide ample non-volatile storage space for use by servers. Like servers, and depending on the scale of deployment required, the storage configuration may be a standard rack-mounted system with varying unit height or possibly a custom stand-alone piece of equipment. Disk storage arrays are typically designed for use in EIA/ECA Standard-310-E-compliant racks. The enclosure contains the storage in either small or large form factor drives in addition to the controllers, midplane and batteries for cache backup. The storage array enclosure typically uses redundant power supplies and cooling in the event of component failures. One of the more challenging aspects of storage arrays is the design of a battery backup system to prevent data loss in case of a power interruption or loss. For an in-depth discussion of storage array thermal guidelines, please consult the ASHRAE storage equipment white paper (ASHRAE TC 9.9 2015).

While disk storage arrays are typically used for online storage, backup and disaster recovery, tape storage is known for its low cost and longevity for archiving purposes. Tape systems come in a variety of different formats based on the type of tape media.

## 1.3. Data center networking

A computer network, or simply a network, is a collection of computers and other hardware interconnected by communication channels that allow sharing of resources and information. Networking equipment facilitates the interconnection of devices and the sharing of data both within the data center and beyond. Networks tend to be designed in a hierarchical manner, with many devices (such as servers and storage devices in the case of a data center) connected to a switch that is connected to another switch at the next level of the hierarchy, and so on. Another common topology is a mesh configuration in which many peer network switches are connected to one another to form a single level of the hierarchy. We will consider three different levels of a network hierarchy: core, distribution and top of rack (TOR). More elaborate configurations will not be covered. The core network function can be thought of as the gateway through which all data entering and exiting the data center must pass. As such, the core network equipment is connected either directly or indirectly to every device in the data center. The core switch is also connected to a service provider, which is the "pipe" through which all data passes from the data center to the Internet. The distribution level of the network acts as an intermediate level between the core and edge levels of the network, and as such can offload some of the work the core network equipment needs to do.

Specifically, the distribution level is useful for passing data between machines inside the data center or aggregating ports to reduce the number of physical ports required at the core. The TOR network level consists of switches that connect directly to devices that are generating or consuming the data, and then pass the data up to the distribution or core level. A data center network implementation may have all three of these levels, or it may combine or eliminate some of the levels. In large data centers, the load on the networking equipment can be substantial, both in terms of port count and data throughput. The end-of-row (EOR) distribution equipment offloads the core equipment in both throughput and port count. The TOR edge networking equipment offloads the distribution equipment in both throughput and port count, in the same way as the distribution networking equipment offloads the core networking equipment. Switches enable communication between devices connected on a network. In the case of a data center, servers and storage arrays are connected to multiple switches in a hierarchical manner.

The ASIC chip decides where that data need to go and sends it back out through the correct port. The central processing unit (CPU) controls both the PHY and the ASIC. The CPU can take data from the network, process it and then send it back out onto the network.

## 1.4. Components

### 1.4.1. *Central processing unit*

The processor, also referred to as the CPU, is one of the greatest sources of heat generation within a server. Aside from the basic processing of data and instructions to provide an output result, processors may also have many more features for managing data and power throughout a system. The processor die is generally housed in a package that includes a substrate (i.e. a small printed circuit board, or PCB, for bringing out signals) and a lid, as shown in Figure 2.1. The lid, or case, more evenly distributes heat to an attached cooling component such as a heat sink (air-cooled) or cold plate (liquid-cooled), as shown in Figure 2.1. In most cases, a socket is used to enable removal and replacement of the processor on the motherboard. Some lower powered processors are lidless using direct attachment of a heat sink on top of the die. In the volume server segment, limitations of low-cost thermal solutions and a greater focus on performance per watt have slowed the generational increases in thermal design power (TDP). The transition to multicore processors has maintained Moore's law (a doubling of the transistors on a chip every 18 months), an improvement even within this limited power envelope. However, recent trends, which include the integration of functions previously implemented in a chipset or external devices, greater numbers of high-performance I/O interfaces and memory channels, larger internal caches and incorporation of specialty processing units, are pushing power up despite significant improvements in power management features. Although integration of additional features into the processor provides an overall improvement in server efficiency, a greater percentage of the overall server power is concentrated in a smaller volume, creating new cooling challenges. Over the last several years, customer demand and regulatory requirements have driven vendors to increase server efficiency across their portfolios. Power management features within the processor have become prevalent, with increasing capability to optimize performance within power, acoustical and thermal limits. Processor, subsystem and system level power-capping features are also expected to continue improving, enabling more options for system designers to tailor servers to the customer's power and cooling constraints. Microserver processors have appeared with power and die area is optimized for smaller, simpler and targeted/limited workloads. As this technology has evolved, it has improved its performance, capacity and reliability, availability, serviceability (RAS) features required for enterprise applications. These processors use fine-grain power optimizations developed for the mobile market and as such can be computationally efficient. Although the power of these individual micro-servers is quite low, system designers typically place many of them on a single board or in a single chassis (tens to hundreds). From a total power-per-unit-volume standpoint, aggregate power may be equivalent or higher than a traditional volume server but with a more even power distribution (versus concentration of power in traditional volume server CPU sockets). CPU power continues to slowly increase from generation to generation. Higher performance processors, typically used in high-performance computing applications, have TDP ranging from 100 to 200 W, with the prospect that over the next few years it will increase. For telecommunications and lower performance volume servers, the TDP has historically been in the 50–100 W range and will likely increase to the 150 W range over the same period of time. Historically, it has been difficult to extrapolate today's processor power into the future, and this remains the case today.

Table 1.1 presents a power summary of different Intel Xeon Scalable Skylake processors available in mid-2018.

| CPU | Idle Power (W) | Max Power (W) |
|---|---|---|
| Intel Skylake CPU (205W) | 16.2 | 205.0 |
| Intel Skylake CPU (200W) | 15.6 | 200.0 |
| Intel Skylake CPU (165W) | 19.0 | 165.0 |
| Intel Skylake CPU (150W) | 18.0 | 150.0 |
| Intel Skylake CPU (145W) | 18.0 | 145.0 |
| Intel Skylake CPU (140W) | 17.6 | 140.0 |
| Intel Skylake CPU (135W) | 17.9 | 135.0 |
| Intel Skylake CPU (130W) | 17.9 | 130.0 |
| Intel Skylake CPU (125W) | 18.1 | 125.0 |
| Intel Skylake CPU (115W) | 22.0 | 115.0 |
| Intel Skylake CPU (105W) | 16.8 | 105.0 |
| Intel Skylake CPU (85W) | 13.6 | 85.0 |
| Intel Skylake CPU (75W) | 13.7 | 75.0 |
| Intel Skylake CPU (70W) | 13.7 | 70.0 |

**Table 1.1.** *Power summary of different Intel Xeon Scalable Skylake processors*

## 1.4.2. *Graphics processing unit*

Graphics processing units (GPUs), also called general purpose GPUs (GPGPUs) in the industry, enable heterogeneous computing (multiple CPU types within one server) when installed into a server. A common example of this system is a server that has both GPUs, which have their own processor, and the server's CPU(s). This application is used for high-throughput computing with a more mainstream CPU for latency-sensitive computing. This model offers significant performance and capability improvements in computing while creating challenges in data center thermal management and planning.

Originally designed for computer graphics, GPUs are increasingly being used for other computational purposes that benefit from the massively parallel architectures of these devices. Today GPUs are designed to address parallel, high-throughput computing problems (e.g. rendering a screen's worth of data). This is similar to single instruction, multiple data (SIMD) vector processors used in old supercomputers. The aggregate compute capability of these small processors exceeds that of general-purpose processors. Memory bandwidth is also higher in GPUs compared to CPUs. Several companies have invested in this new paradigm, with GPU products currently available. Others are pursuing a somewhat different heterogeneous computing strategy, offering many integrated core (MIC) processors using a core architecture more similar to standard x86 CPUs. While both GPUs and MIC processors are similar in that they consist of a much higher number of smaller cores than in a typical CPU, there are also significant differences in their specific architecture and programming models. Each has its particular advantages and disadvantages and computational applicability, but these differences are beyond the scope of this book and will not be covered.

A downside to increased compute capability is a surge in power usage. GPUs and MICs that are relevant to servers typically draw between 75 W and 300 W, depending upon the application, with future solutions likely to draw greater than 400 W. While GPUs and MICs are usually more efficient in terms of performance per watt, the large increase in performance often results in server designs with different and larger power requirements compared to CPU-only nodes. Thus, while the overall server count and power draw of the solution may decrease, the power draw of individual servers and racks may increase, therefore making it more challenging to cool.

These GPUs can typically be deployed in a peripheral component interconnect express (PCIe) form factor; however, many manufacturers are developing products that integrate these processors on the main system board. They can have thermal solutions that are passive (no dedicated fans, instead relying on the base server air movers and heat sinks) or active (dedicated fans onboard the PCIe card itself). An active solution generally supports increased processor power and performance and has a lower platform fan power requirement for cooling than a passive solution. However, an active GPU/MIC thermal solution typically does not support fan redundancy, may increase airflow resistance and may not integrate as tightly with the host server base board thermal management strategy. Passive thermal solutions have been developed to support fan redundancy requirements and provide better integration with server management. Airflow and temperature requirements for passive solutions require custom shrouding/baffling to better manage airflow.

Table 1.2 presents a power summary of different GPUs available in mid-2018.

| GPU PCIe Cards | Idle Power (W) | Max Power (W) |
|---|---|---|
| ThinkSystem NVIDIA Quadro P2000 | 20.0 | 75.0 |
| ThinkSystem NVIDIA Tesla P100 PCIe 16GB | 20.0 | 250.0 |
| ThinkSystem NVIDIA Quadro P6000 PCIe Active GPU | 20.0 | 250.0 |
| ThinkSystem Intel Xeon Phi 7240P | 20.0 | 275.0 |
| NVIDIA Tesla M60 GPU, PCIe (passive) | 20.0 | 300.0 |
| NVIDIA Tesla M10 | 20.0 | 225.0 |
| NVIDIA Tesla P40 24GB | 20.0 | 250.0 |
| NVIDIA Quadro P4000 8GB | 11.1 | 105.0 |
| NVIDIA Tesla P4 8GB PCIe Passive | 20.0 | 75.0 |
| NVIDIA Quadro P600 2GB PCIe Passive | 4.4 | 40.0 |
| NVIDIA Tesla V100 16GB PCIe Passive | 20.0 | 250.0 |
| NVIDIA Tesla V100 16GB FHHL PCIe | 20.0 | 150.0 |
| AMD Radeon Instinct MI25 16GB PCIe Passive | 35.0 | 300.0 |

**Table 1.2.** *Power summary of different GPUs*

### 1.4.3. *Volatile memory*

Memory temporarily stores data that have been processed or are to be processed. Multiple dynamic random-access memory (DRAM) chips are packaged with many devices on one PCB. An example of form factor is the dual in-line memory module (DIMM). These PCBs have card edge connectors that allow them to be installed in sockets mounted on the board. The memory hierarchy is driven by the latency to access the data and the capacity to store the data. Onboard memory (i.e. DIMMs) is one step removed from the on-processor memory that stores data more directly in the execution path (with lower latency) and may be integrated on the processor die or packaged on the processor substrate. As processor core count and performance continue to increase, memory channel count has also been increasing. Each memory channel provides a link to a group of connected DIMMs on that channel and can effectively expand both throughput and capacity. DRAM device density has been doubling every 24–30 months for over a decade, but that trend is expected to start to slow over the coming decade. Despite the doubling of the number of storage cells and incremental frequency for each density generation, DRAM manufacturers have previously been able to hold per-device power relatively stable through process shrinks, improved power management features and lower core and I/O operating voltages. This power is now less likely to stay the same due to less efficient process scaling. As double data rate (DDR) memory operating frequency has increased, the quantity of DIMMs per channel (DPC) is more difficult to maintain, potentially decreasing capacity. To counter the loss of supportable DPC, server DIMMs have been increasing the number of ranks per DIMM, where a rank is a set (row) of DRAMs that are accessed simultaneously to provide the channel's full width in bits of data. To accommodate so many DRAMs, manufacturers have resorted to stacking multiple DRAM dies per DRAM package. Today's commodity DRAMs have a single die package (SDP), and premium packaging provides a dual die package (DDP). In the future, four and eventually eight DRAM stacking will be possible using a method called 3D stacking thru-silicon-via (3DS, TSV), where vertical die-to-die connections are made directly in the silicon. These stacked die packages will be roughly of the same height as an SDP but will consume greater power. Although only one rank per DIMM can be active at a time, all of the inactive ranks still consume idle power. DIMM buffer devices (mounted on each DIMM) are also expected to consume higher power as the operating frequency increases over time. Thus, as the number of ranks per DIMM increases, the worst case and typical power of the DIMM will increase. The expected trend is that single- and dual-rank DIMMs will gradually increase their current power envelopes with DRAM frequency increases and DIMMs with four or more ranks will increase in power, introducing new cooling challenges. DIMM volatile memory power typically ranges from 4 to 15 W, depending on the number of DIMMs per channel, capacity and speed.

Table 1.3 presents a power summary of different DIMMs available in mid-2018.

| MEMORY | Idle Power (W) | Max Power (W) |
|---|---|---|
| 8GB  DDR4 RDIMM (1DPC) | 0.9 | 4.5 |
| 8GB  DDR4 RDIMM (2DPC) | 0.8 | 3.8 |
| 16GB  DDR4 RDIMM (1DPC) | 0.9 | 4.8 |
| 16GB  DDR4 RDIMM (2DPC) | 0.8 | 3.8 |
| 32GB DDR4 RDIMM (1DPC) | 2.0 | 8.0 |
| 32GB DDR4 RDIMM (2DPC) | 1.3 | 4.8 |
| 64GB DDR4 LRDIMM (1DPC) | 3.2 | 11.7 |
| 64GB DDR4 LRDIMM (2DPC) | 3.5 | 7.3 |
| 128GB DDR4 RDIMM with 3DS DRAMs (1DPC) | 3.0 | 10.5 |
| 128GB DDR4 RDIMM with 3DS DRAMs (2DPC) | 2.8 | 7.0 |
| 128GB  DDR4 LRDIMM (1DPC) | 2.5 | 9.0 |
| 128GB  DDR4 LRDIMM (2DPC) | 3.8 | 7.0 |

**Table 1.3.** *Power summary of different DIMMs*

### 1.4.4. *Non-volatile memory*

Non-volatile-memory-based (NVM) DIMMs are becoming more commonplace, demonstrating the crossover between memory and storage and the potential for more than one usage for the same device. These devices, coupled with a system backup battery, have the capability to provide the server with the ability to capture volatile memory data, despite system power loss, to be saved to adjacent NVM. The downside to this added capability is higher power consumption than volatile memory. An example of such technology is Intel Optane DC Persistent Memory, which will be supported in Cascade Lake, the 14 nm evolution of Skylake that will be described in Chapter 4. Optane DIMMs should be pin compatible with DDR4 pins and provide capacity of 128, 256 and 512 GB.

### 1.4.5. *Non-volatile storage*

Solid-state devices (SSD) use the NVM technology and are incorporated into several different form factors. One common size is the spinning disk's small form factor (SFF). This SFF SSD typically consumes 9 to 12 W, but some models have the capability to reach 25 W. An alternative form factor is a PCIe card. These cards can vary in length, which will determine how many components can be placed on its printed circuit board assembly (PCBA), and will range from less than 25 W up to 300 W. Yet another more thermally challenging form factor is the M.2. There are two types of M.2 devices. Currently, the serial advanced technology attachment (SATA) M.2 has a maximum consumption of 5 W, while the PCIe M.2 consumes up to 8.25 W. At first, these power levels appear to be small until their power density is examined. Comparing the storage power as a function of length, M.2 easily doubles power density when compared to an SFF SSD drive. To compound the problem, these small devices are located in low airflow areas within the server, making them more challenging to cool. Historically, any components over 5 W are likely to have a heat spreader/sink, but these M.2s often do not have space to add heat sinks. M.2 devices come in multiple lengths and widths, with some of the more common examples being 60 mm, 80 mm and 110 mm lengths. The power that a NVM device consumes in operation is a function of its performance design point, capacity and the workload placed upon it. Ranking the performance of these storage solutions, the classical SATA and the serial attached SCSI (SAS) products would fall on the low end, the emerging PCIe and MultiLink SAS SFF products would fall in the mid-range and PCIe add-in cards would align with the high end. Finally, power will vary widely based on the workload as well, and some general rules of thumb apply:

– Sustained 100% write operations generate the maximum sustained power profile.

– Sustained 100% read operations generate the lowest sustained power profile, which in general will be about 60–80% of the maximum write power profile.

– Mixed workloads will range somewhere in-between, proportional to the read-to-write ratio.

Table 1.4 presents a power summary of different M.2 and SSD-NVMes available in a server in mid-2018.

| STORAGE | Idle Power (W) | Max Power (W) |
|---|---|---|
| (M.2) | | |
| M.2 SSD: 1x 32GB SATA Boot | 0.2 | 0.9 |
| M.2 SSD: 1x 128GB SATA Boot | 0.7 | 2.2 |
| M.2 SSD: 1x 480GB SATA Boot | 1.8 | 4.3 |
| M.2 SSD: 2x 32GB SATA Boot (RAID) | 2.6 | 3.4 |
| M.2 SSD: 2x 128GB SATA Boot (RAID) | 3.7 | 6.1 |
| M.2 Module ACHI | 0.1 | 0.1 |
| M.2 Module HW RAID | 0.1 | 1.8 |

| STORAGE | Idle Power (W) | Max Power (W) |
|---|---|---|
| **SSD-NVMe** | | |
| SSD: 240GB 2.5/3.5" 6Gbps SATA G4HS | 5.3 | 6.5 |
| SSD: 480GB 2.5" 6Gbps SATA G4HS Entry | 1.3 | 2.9 |
| SSD: 400GB 2.5" 6Gbps SATA G4HS Mainstream | 3.6 | 6.7 |
| SSD: 800GB 2.5" 6gbps SATA G4HS Mainstrm | 1.1 | 6.6 |
| SSD: 960GB 2.5/3.5" 6Gbps SATA G4HS Entry | 0.9 | 2.5 |
| SSD: 960GB 2.5/3.5" 6Gbps SATA G4HS Mainstream | 1.3 | 6.7 |
| SSD: 1.92TB 2.5/3.5" 6Gbps SATA G4HS | 1.3 | 6.7 |
| SSD: 3.84TB 2.5/3.5" 6gbps SATA G4HS Entry | 3.9 | 7.4 |
| SSD: 3.84TB 2.5/3.5" 6gbps SATA G4HS Mainstream | 1.5 | 4.0 |
| SSD: Samsung PM883 2.5" (240, 480, 960, 1.92, 3.84TB) | 1.3 | 4.0 |
| SSD: 400GB 2.5" 12Gbps SAS G4HS Mainstream | 4.5 | 6.4 |
| SSD: 800GB 2.5" 12Gbps SAS G4HS Mainstream | 5.0 | 6.6 |
| SSD: 400GB 2.5" 12Gbps SAS G4HS Perf | 5.0 | 6.4 |
| SSD: 800GB 2.5" 12Gbps SAS G4HS Perf | 4.6 | 6.0 |
| SSD: 1.6TB 2.5" 12Gbps SAS G4HS | 4.6 | 6.2 |
| SSD: 3.84TB 2.5" 12Gbps SAS G4HS Capacity | 4.6 | 6.2 |
| SSD: 7.68TB 2.5" 12Gbps SAS G4HS Capacity | 4.7 | 8.1 |
| SSD: 15.36TB 2.5" 12Gbps SAS G4HS Capacity | 4.7 | 8.1 |
| SSD: 1.92TB PCIe x8 Enterprise HHHL card | 3.8 | 5.1 |
| SSD: 3.84TB PCIe x8 Enterprise HHHL card | 3.9 | 7.4 |
| SSD: 400GB 2.5" 6gbps SATA, Intel S3610 | 0.8 | 5.2 |
| SSD: 480GB 2.5/3.5" 6gbps SATA, Intel | 0.8 | 3.7 |
| SSD: 800GB 2.5" 6gbps SATA, Intel S3610 | 0.8 | 6.7 |
| SSD: 240GB 2.5" SATA 6gbps, Samsung PM863a | 1.3 | 2.3 |
| NVMe: 960GB 2.5" Enterprise G4HS | 4.6 | 14.1 |
| NVMe: 1.92TB 2.5" Enterprise G4HS | 2.2 | 5.9 |
| NVMe: 3.84TB 2.5" Enterprise G4HS | 2.4 | 6.7 |
| NVMe: Samsung PM983 | 2.5 | 10.2 |
| NVMe: 375GB PCIe 3.0 x4 Hot Swap SSD | 4.6 | 14.2 |
| NVMe: 750GB PCIe 3.0 x4 Hot Swap SSD | 4.6 | 14.2 |
| NVMe: 1.0TB Intel P4500 PCIe3.0 HS | 4.6 | 14.2 |
| NVMe: 1.6B Intel P4600 PCIe3.0 HS | 2.2 | 5.9 |
| NVMe: 2.0TB Intel P4500 PCIe3.0 HS | 2.2 | 5.9 |
| NVMe: 3.2TB Intel P4600 PCIe3.0 HS | 2.4 | 6.7 |
| NVMe: 4.0TB Intel P4500 PCIe3.0 HS | 2.4 | 6.7 |
| NVMe: 800GB, 1.6, 3.2, 6.4TB Toshiba CM5 2.5/3.5" | 6.0 | 18.0 |
| NVMe: 6.4TB Intel P4600 PCIe3.0 HS | 25.0 | 25.0 |
| NVMe: 8TB Intel P4600 PCIe3.0 HS | 25.0 | 25.0 |
| SSD/NVMe: AVERAGE (avg of all above drives) | 4.2 | 8.2 |
| SSD/NVMe: MAX (max of all above drives) | 25.0 | 25.0 |

**Table 1.4.** *Power summary of different SSD-NVMes*

In the years ahead, as modern manycore processors evolve, providing adequate I/O performance will remain a challenge. One can expect enterprise NVM solutions to remain focused first on performance, thereby saturating the power of target form factors. This will lead to some unpredictability in projecting overall NVM subsystem trends at the server and data center levels.

## 1.4.6. *Spinning disks and tape storage*

While NVM offers low-latency permanent storage, spinning disks (hard disk drives, or HDDs) provide data storage for several years. Tape is the only medium rated for archival data storage (30 years).

Over the past 55 years, HDD size has reduced and settled on two common form factors. The large form factor (LFF) is also known as the 3.5″ drive, while the SFF is referred to as the 2.5″ drive.

An HDD is an electromechanical device containing two motors, resulting in a strong mechanical influence on power consumption. Operation at high I/O per second (IOPS) performance levels and/or high data transfer rates can cause power consumption to increase above idle.

The HDD is made up of several components. Internal to the HDD are a set of one or more rotating disks mounted on a spindle motor at a constant speed. While a second motor (voice coil motor, or VCM) drives the magnetic heads back and forth from the disk inner to outer diameter reading and writing data. The PCBA contains the firmware to control drive operation. The host interface is either SAS or SATA.

Over the past decade, HDD power has remained fairly constant. As shown in Table 1.5, LFF, 7,200 rpm drives have a measured idle power that ranges from 7 to 9 W, while when active the drive power ranges from 10 to 13 W. An SFF, 10,000 rpm measured idle power varies from 4 to 6 W, while in an active state these drives can consume between 6 and 9 W. All power consumed by the drive is eventually converted to heat and must be removed through the IT equipment cooling system.

In an effort to reduce HDD power consumption, SAS and SATA standards have been created. With these standards, these modes allow underused drives (idle or standby) to reach lower power states with short, but non-zero additive response times. These methods include management of the host interface, moving the actuator to the unloaded position and reducing spindle revolutions per minute to a fractional value.

Tape drives offer an inexpensive, long-term storage solution that is still being used today. The most common tape format is linear tape-open (LTO). This tape format is optimized for high capacity and performance with high reliability. Available in either single or multiple drive configurations, the

LTO format is ideally suited for enterprise-level backup, restore and archive applications. LTO is the open standard alternative to proprietary tape technologies, which results in interoperability across vendors and can be a more economical product line for the user.

Table 1.5 presents a power summary of different HDDs available in a server in mid-2018.

| STORAGE | Idle Power (W) | Max Power (W) |
|---|---|---|
| **(HDD, 2.5")** | | |
| HDD: 300GB 2.5" 15K 12Gbps SAS G4HS 512n | 8.3 | 10.0 |
| HDD: 600GB 2.5" 15K 12Gbps SAS G4HS 512n | 5.0 | 7.4 |
| HDD: 900GB 2.5" 15K 12Gbps SAS G4HS 512e | 5.7 | 8.1 |
| HDD: 300GB 2.5" 10K 12Gbps SAS G4HS 512n | 3.5 | 3.9 |
| HDD: 600GB 2.5" 10K 12Gbps SAS G4HS 512n | 4.0 | 6.2 |
| HDD: 900GB 2.5" 10K 12Gbps SAS G4HS 512n | 5.2 | 6.1 |
| HDD: 1.2TB 2.5" 10K 12Gbps SAS G4HS 512n | 5.9 | 6.6 |
| HDD: 1.8TB 2.5" 10K 12Gbps SAS Hot Swap 512e | 11.6 | 11.6 |
| HDD: 2.4TB 2.5" 10K 12Gbps SAS Hot Swap 512e | 7.3 | 6.4 |
| SED: 300GB 2.5" 10K 12Gbps SAS G4HS | 5.5 | 5.9 |
| SED: 600GB 2.5" 10K 12Gbps SAS G4HS | 5.3 | 5.8 |
| HDD: 1TB 2.5" 7.2K 12Gbps SAS G4HS 512n | 7.5 | 8.2 |
| HDD: 2TB 2.5" 7.2K 12Gbps SAS G4HS 512n | 4.7 | 5.8 |
| HDD: 8TB 2.5" SAS, WD Vela-AP | 8.6 | 12.9 |
| HDD: 10, 12 TB 2.5" SAS, Seagate MobulaBP | 6.5 | 10.0 |
| HDD: 1TB 2.5" 7.2K 12Gbps SATA G4HS | 7.3 | 7.8 |
| HDD: 2TB 2.5" 7.2K 12Gbps SATA G4HS | 4.0 | 4.3 |
| HDD: 1TB 2.5" 7.2K SATA 6Gb Hot Swap 512n | 8.6 | 9.3 |
| HDD: 2TB 2.5" 7.2K SATA 6Gb Hot Swap 512e | 9.3 | 9.7 |
| HDD: 8TB 2.5" SATA, WD Vela-AP | 7.4 | 11.9 |
| HDD: 10, 12 TB 2.5" SATA, Seagate MobulaBP | 6.5 | 10.0 |
| HDD: 2.5" AVERAGE (avg of all above drives) | 6.6 | 8.0 |
| HDD: 2.5" MAX (max of all above drives) | 11.6 | 12.9 |
| **HDD, 3.5"** | | |
| HDD: 900GB 3.5" 15K 12Gbps SAS HS 512e | 5.7 | 8.1 |
| HDD: 1TB 3.5" 7.2K 12Gbps SAS G4HS | 9.0 | 9.5 |
| HDD: 2TB 3.5" 7.2K 12Gbps SAS G4HS | 6.2 | 7.5 |
| HDD: 4TB 3.5" 7.2K 12Gbps SAS G4HS | 9.1 | 9.6 |
| HDD: 6TB 3.5" 7.2K 12Gbps SAS G4HS | 8.8 | 9.4 |
| HDD: 8TB 3.5" 7.2K 12Gbps SAS G4HS | 11.5 | 11.3 |
| HDD: 10TB 3.5" 7.2K 12Gbps SAS G4HS | 6.6 | 8.6 |
| HDD: 12TB 3.5" 7.2K 12Gbps SAS G4HS | 6.6 | 8.6 |
| HDD: 12TB 3.5" 7.2K 6Gbps SAS G4HS | 5.8 | 7.2 |
| SED: 4TB 3.5" 7.2K 12Gbps SAS G4HS | 7.5 | 8.4 |
| SED: 6TB 3.5" 7.2K 12Gbps SAS G4HS 512e | 8.8 | 9.4 |
| SED: 8TB 3.5" 7.2K 12Gbps SAS G4HS 512e | 6.6 | 8.6 |
| HDD: 1TB 3.5" 7.2K 6Gbps SATA G4HS | 9.3 | 9.5 |
| HDD: 2TB 3.5" 7.2K 6Gbps SATA G4HS | 5.7 | 9.2 |
| HDD: 4TB 3.5" 7.2K 6Gbps SATA G4HS | 6.0 | 8.7 |
| HDD: 6TB 3.5" 7.2K 6Gbps SATA G4HS | 7.8 | 9.2 |
| HDD: 8TB 3.5" 7.2K 6Gbps SATA G4HS | 8.7 | 10.8 |

| STORAGE | Idle Power (W) | Max Power (W) |
|---|---|---|
| HDD: 10TB 3.5" 7.2K 6Gbps SATA G4HS | 5.8 | 7.2 |
| HDD: 6TB 3.5" 7.2K 6Gbps SATA Non-hotswap 512e | 7.8 | 9.2 |
| HDD: 8TB 3.5" 7.2K 6Gbps SATA Non-hotswap 512e | 8.7 | 10.8 |
| HDD: 10TB 3.5" 7.2K 6Gbps SATA Non-hotswap 512e | 5.8 | 7.2 |
| HDD: 1TB 3.5" 7.2K 6Gbps SATA G4SS | 5.8 | 6.4 |
| HDD: 2TB 3.5" 7.2K 6Gbps SATA G4SS | 5.9 | 6.4 |
| HDD: 4TB 3.5" 7.2K 6Gbps SATA G4SS | 7.6 | 8.0 |
| HDD: 2TB 3.5" 7.2K 6Gbps SATA G4HS | 5.9 | 6.4 |
| HDD: 2TB 3.5" 7.2K 6Gbps SAS G4HS | 4.7 | 5.0 |
| HDD: 300GB 3.5" 10k 12Gbps SAS G4HS 512n | 5.7 | 8.1 |
| HDD: 3.5" AVERAGE (avg. of all above drives) | 7.2 | 8.4 |
| HDD: 3.5" MAX (max. of all above drives) | 11.5 | 11.3 |

**Table 1.5.** *Power summary of different HDDs*

## 1.4.7. *Motherboard*

The board (or motherboard) provides interconnections between the various active components of the servers. Typically, the boards themselves are multilayered with interconnects and circuitry residing on power and signal layers separated using dielectric layers.

VRs that convert power supply voltages to the required silicon voltages are placed on the board. With Haswell, Intel introduced an on-die (or on-package) VRM, which is usually referred to as a fully integrated voltage regulator (FIVR) or simply an integrated voltage regulator (IVR).

Table 1.6 presents a power summary of the different components on a Xeon board available in a server in mid-2018.

| PLANAR Misc | Idle Power (W) | Max Power (W) |
|---|---|---|
| Lewisburg PCH (LWB-1) | 2.0 | 15.0 |
| Lewisburg PCH (LWB-2) | 2.0 | 17.0 |
| Lewisburg PCH (LWB-4) | 2.0 | 19.0 |
| 2x1GbE LOM | 0.2 | |
| USB 2.0 | 0.0 | |
| USB 3.0 | 0.0 | |
| Emulex Pilot 4 | 2.8 | |
| 1GbE Mangement Port | 0.1 | |
| EMMC | 0.8 | |
| FPGA | 1.1 | |
| TPM | 0.0 | |
| Miscellaneous | 3.2 | |

**Table 1.6.** *Power summary of the different components on a board*

### 1.4.8. *PCIe I/O cards*

Network adapter and storage controller cards are projecting significant power increases over the next several years. For those not familiar with a network adapter card have media choices of either Ethernet, twisted-pair copper, or fiber. Their speed capability ranges from 1 to 100 GB/s. If fiber media is used, an active optical connector can be used. These connectors will drive up power as their performance increases, as much as 100% over the next couple of years.

Table 1.7 presents a power summary of different PCIe network cards available in a server in mid-2018.

| Network- PCIe | Idle Power (W) | Max Power (W) |
|---|---|---|
| PCIe:  1x 1GbE PCIe, Intel I350-F1 | 2.9 | 5.1 |
| PCIe:  2x 1GbE PCIe | 1.1 | 4.8 |
| PCIe:  4x 1GbE PCIe | 1.1 | 5.9 |
| PCIe:   2 x10GbE SFP+ | 9.2 | 12.3 |
| PCIe:  4 x10GbE SFP+, Emulex Oce14104B-NX | 11.2 | 11.9 |
| PCIe:  2 x10GbE Base-T | 4.6 | 13.0 |
| PCIe:  OmniPath, Intel | 7.4 | 14.9 |
| PCIe:  1x 16/32 Gb FC HBA (QLogic, Emulex) | 8.5 | 9.4 |
| PCIe:  2x 16/32 Gb FC HBA (QLogic, Emulex) | 8.7 | 10.2 |
| PCIe:  1x 25GbE NetXtreme-E, Broadcom | 8.3 | 15.0 |
| PCIe:  2x 25GbE ConnectX-4, Mellanox | 9.5 | 14.0 |
| PCIe:  2x 25GbE QLogic QL41232 | 5.0 | 15.0 |
| PCIe:  1x 40GbE ConnectX-4 (Patty) | 10.2 | 13.1 |
| PCIe:  1x100GbE (QSFP28) ConnectX-4, Mellanox | 13.9 | 19.6 |
| PCIe:  2x100GbE (QSFP28) ConnectX-4, Mellanox | 16.1 | 24.8 |
| PCIe:  2x100GbE (QSFP28) ConnectX-5, Mellanox | 16.1 | 25.0 |
| PCIe:  1x8Gb SFP+ (Broadcom LPe12000) | 9.2 | 10.3 |
| PCIe:  2x8Gb SFP+ (Broadcom LPe12002) | 9.2 | 12.3 |
| PCIe:  Intel OPA 100 1-port, x8 HFA | 7.4 | 14.9 |
| PCIe:  CX-5 EDR 1-port adapter for SD 650 | 19.2 | 24.7 |
| PCIe:  Intel QAT8970 Accel Adapter | 20.0 | 40.0 |

**Table 1.7.** *Power summary of different PCIe network cards*

GPUs can also be installed in the PCIe slots and are projected to increase in power. These cards, also known as accelerators, are expected to increase in power by 75% over the next few years. Table 1.8 shows examples of existing accelerators' power consumption available in mid-2018.

Given that these cards are increasing in power while also being rear-mounted within the server with potentially temperature sensitive optical connectors, careful consideration must be given during server configuration. This will limit supported server configurations to support these cards' maximum local inlet air temperature of 55°C (131°F) when these cards are located in the rear of the system.

| GPU PCIe Cards | Idle Power (W) | Max Power (W) |
|---|---|---|
| ThinkSystem NVIDIA Quadro P2000 | 20.0 | 75.0 |
| ThinkSystem NVIDIA Tesla P100 PCIe 16GB | 20.0 | 250.0 |
| ThinkSystem NVIDIA Quadro P6000 PCIe Active GPU | 20.0 | 250.0 |
| ThinkSystem Intel Xeon Phi 7240P | 20.0 | 275.0 |
| NVIDIA Tesla M60 GPU, PCIe (passive) | 20.0 | 300.0 |
| NVIDIA Tesla M10 | 20.0 | 225.0 |
| NVIDIA Tesla P40 24GB | 20.0 | 250.0 |
| NVIDIA Quadro P4000 8GB | 11.1 | 105.0 |
| NVIDIA Tesla P4 8GB PCIe Passive | 20.0 | 75.0 |
| NVIDIA Quadro P600 2GB PCIe Passive | 4.4 | 40.0 |
| NVIDIA Tesla V100 16GB PCIe Passive | 20.0 | 250.0 |
| NVIDIA Tesla V100 16GB FHHL PCIe | 20.0 | 150.0 |
| AMD Radeon Instinct MI25 16GB PCIe Passive | 35.0 | 300.0 |

**Table 1.8.** *Power summary of different PCIe accelerator cards*

## 1.4.9. *Power supplies*

The majority of mainstream IT equipment is designed for connection to an alternating current (AC) source via a power supply. The IT equipment's power supply converts the input AC to lower voltage direct current (DC) for use by the subsystems in the computer. Power supplies are typically designed to handle a wide range of input voltage levels, enabling use around the world with a single supply that can handle input frequencies in the 50–60 Hz range. IT equipment power supplies have come under great scrutiny by IT manufacturers, their customers and regulatory agencies due to the view that the energy consumed by them does not provide any compute capability. The efficiency of a power supply (ratio of output power delivered vs. input power) depends on its load as illustrated in Figure 1.2.

As shown, a PSU can be quite inefficient at low power load. That is why the 80 Plus certification has been created (80 Plus 2011). It states that the PSU will be at least 80% efficient at given power load. Table 1.9 presents the power efficiency required to achieve the different certification levels (80 Plus, Bronze, Silver, Gold, Platinum, Titanium) at different power loads.

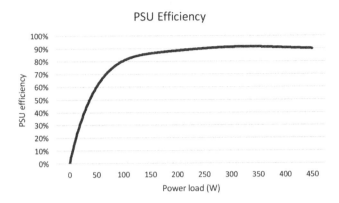

**Figure 1.2.** *Illustrative power efficiency of a 450 W PSU*

| 80 Plus test type | 115 V internal non-redundant | | | | 230 V internal redundant | | | | 230 V EU internal non-redundant | | | |
|---|---|---|---|---|---|---|---|---|---|---|---|---|
| Percentage of rated load | 10% | 20% | 50% | 100% | 10% | 20% | 50% | 100% | 10% | 20% | 50% | 100% |
| 80 Plus test type | | 80% | 80% | 80% | | | | | | 82% | 85% | 82% |
| 80 Plus Bronze | | 82% | 85% | 82% | | 81% | 85% | 81% | | 85% | 88% | 85% |
| 80 Plus Silver | | 85% | 88% | 85% | | 85% | 89% | 85% | | 87% | 90% | 87% |
| 80 Plus Gold | | 87% | 90% | 87% | | 88% | 92% | 88% | | 90% | 92% | 89% |
| 80 Plus Platinium | | 90% | 92% | 89% | | 90% | 94% | 91% | | 92% | 94% | 90% |
| 80 Plus Titanium | 90% | 92% | 94% | 90% | 90% | 94% | 96% | 91% | 90% | 94% | 96% | 94% |

**Table 1.9.** *Efficiency levels required for each 80 Plus certification*

## 1.4.10. *Fans*

Fans are a critical part of IT devices to transport the heat from the internal components of the devices (as described above) to the front or back of the server where it will be captured by the data center. Details on the different cooling techniques are described in Chapter 2.

Table 1.10 presents a power summary of different fans in a server today in mid-2018.

| FANs | Idle Power (W) | Max Power (W) |
|---|---|---|
| System Fan - 2U 60mmx38mm | 0.7 | 17.0 |
| System Fans - 1U 40mmx56mm | 1.2 | 15.0 |
| System Fans - SD530 80mmx80mm | 15.0 | 75.0 |
| System Fans - SD530 60mmx56mm | 7.0 | 50.0 |

**Table 1.10.** *Power summary of different fans*

# Cooling Servers

## 2.1. Evolution of cooling for mainframe, midrange and distributed computers from the 1960s to 1990s

The first general purpose digital computer was built by IBM in 1944. This electromechanical device codeveloped with Harvard was the pioneer in computing. Following in 1948, the electronic calculator SSEC, which contained about 21,400 relays and 12,500 vacuum tubes, was at the origin of power consumption criticality considerations and able to deliver compute performance of thousands of calculations a second. The large mainframe computer from 1944, the ENIAC, consisted of 30 separate units, plus power supply and forced-air cooling, and weighed over 30 tons. Its 19,000 vacuum tubes, 1,500 relays and hundreds of thousands of resistors, capacitors and inductors consumed almost 200 kW of electrical power.

By the mid-1950s, transistors had begun to replace vacuum tubes in computers to improve reliability, performance and power consumption and in 1958, IBM announced the 7070 Data Processing System using transistors that incorporated solid-state technology. A big leap was eventually made in the mid-1960s with the introduction of the IBM S/360 that lead to dominance of mainframe computing for a few decades. The processing unit of the IBM S/360 model 85 (IBM Systems Reference Library 1974) was composed of 13 frames with a total footprint of 15 $m^2$ a power consumption of 9.3 kW and with a clock frequency of 12.5 MHz. In addition to the power consumption, the mainframes needed to operate in a controlled temperature environment where ambient temperatures, relative humidity (RH) and environmental particulate levels had to be tightly controlled. The large airflow and cold air temperature started placing a burden on construction of data centers where the mainframes were housed.

In order to deliver power and high levels of capacity, redundancy and reliability of the mainframe, inlet temperatures of 20–23°C and RH of 40–60% had to be maintained within tight tolerances.

Redundancy of the cooling chilled water loop was also essential. The consequence of the expectation of reliable, resilient operation resulted in infrastructure and operational costs for power and cooling becoming the dominant expenses after the acquisition costs of the computer equipment.

A new paradigm began to emerge in the late 1960s that allowed computing on a smaller scale, namely the minicomputers. The pioneer here was the Digital Equipment Corporation (DEC), whose computer was contained in a single 19″ rack cabinet compared to a mainframe that would fit only in a very large room. The minicomputer provided a large relief to the infrastructure costs. The power consumption of a fully configured PDP-11/70 (PDP-11 1975) was 3.3 kW and could operate in a room with temperature 40°C and 90% RH with a clock frequency of 18 MHz. Computing environments could now be less regulated from a power and cooling perspective.

## 2.2. Emergence of cooling for scale out computers from 1990s to 2010s

In the 1990s, computer evolved further to be located in the hands of the end customer. This was enabled by processors from Intel and Motorola in the form of personal computer, which could be placed on the desk of the user. The footprint shrank to the size of a large book with the power consumption of the units ranging from about 100–300 W.

This dramatic change was enabled by the computing power reduction of the central processing unit (CPU), which had a power consumption of about 5 W for the Intel 486 processor to 15 W for the popular Pentium processor.

The client computers were capable of operating in a wide variety of environments with limited control of temperature or humidity. Special systems could be designed to work in ambient temperatures of 55°C in factory environments. Higher performing processors using the Intel X86 architecture began to be used in servers that housed the client data, analyzed it and store the information for quick retrieval.

From the early 1990s through 2018, the demand for improved performance kept growing at a nonlinear pace. While silicon manufacturing processes kept reducing the transistor sizes on the silicon to deliver improved performance at a higher frequency, the growth of performance expectations resulted in an increasing demand on the power consumption of the server.

An example of the growth of processor power is shown in Table 2.1 from the 1980s to present time.

| Year | Processor | Processor Size | Processor Power (W) | Silicon Junction Temperature | Processor Lid Temperature | Processor Package Type |
|------|-----------|----------------|---------------------|------------------------------|---------------------------|------------------------|
| 1988 | Intel 486 | 160 micron | 5 | 100°C | 70°C | Ceramic PGA |
| 1993 | Pentium | 120 micron | 15 | 90°C | 70°C | Ceramic PGA |
| 1995 | Pentium Pro | 90 micron | 30 | 90°C | 70°C | Ceramic PGA with Cu Spreader |
| 1997 | Pentium II | 65 micron | 45 | 90°C | 70°C | Cartridge with Aluminum Spreader |
| 2000 | Pentium III | 45 micron | 30 | 70°C | 70°C | Organic Carrier with exposed bare silicon |
| 2005 | Xeon | 90 nm | 110 | 65°C | 70°C | Organic Carrier with Cu Lid |
| 2010 | Xeon | 65 nm | 130 | 80°C | 90°C | Organic Carrier with Cu Lid |
| 2012 | Xeon | 45 nm | 145 | 80°C | 90°C | Organic Carrier with Cu Lid |
| 2016 | Xeon SP | 14 nm | 205 | 80°C | 90°C | Organic Carrier with Cu Lid |

**Table 2.1.** *Intel Xeon power and thermal characteristics*

The evolution of systems based on the x86 processor technology allowed for systems to be installed in non-standard data center environments that typically used tightly controlled ambient temperatures, humidity levels and air quality. Systems that had a power consumption of 100–200 W in the extreme could be placed in locations that allowed standard power, even as low as 110 V and could be operated reliably without any recourse to high cooling costs for the installation.

Over time though the steady increase in processor, memory, disk and I/O devices have resulted in servers consuming 1–2 kW and even higher depending on the number of processors in the system. Cooling requirements of servers that consume power in this range require careful planning of the installed environment and special consideration of the design of the cooling to allow for reliable operation and minimal energy consumption attributed to the cooling requirements of the system.

The primary cooling requirement for all systems starts with ensuring that the cooling of the processor is reliably done and the silicon junction temperatures are maintained such that long-term operation of the silicon is ensured at the requisite operating frequency and switching voltage. The heat flux generated at the silicon needs to be transmitted from the junction of the processor to the external environment. The heat flux path from the switching transistor to outside of the silicon is shown in Figure 2.1.

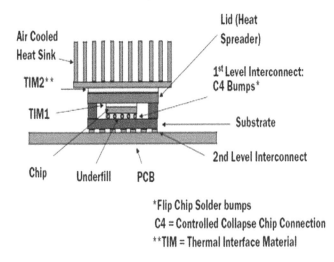

Figure 2.1. *Heat flux on an air-cooled chip. For a color version of this figure, see www.iste.co.uk/brochard/energy.zip*

The illustrative figure above shows an example of a processor or chip package. Although the details of the various processor packages can vary significantly based on the processor technology, the heat flux generated by the processor is extracted from the processor package through the TIM1 interface, which can be a thermal grease, cured gel, soldered indium alloy, etc. The heat spreader allows for a tightly coupled heat flux that allows for, in some instances, efficient transmission of heat flux into a heat sink. The main heat flow path from the chip to air is:

Chip => TIM1 => Lid => TIM2 => Heat sink => Air

The package contribution to this path is determined by the thermal conductivity of TIM1 and of the lid. Advances in the thermal performance of processor packages are ultimately determined by innovations in materials for these components.

There is a synergy in the choice of materials for the TIM and the lid. In order to achieve enhanced thermal conductivities, manufacturers have been substituting metallic particles in thermal greases and gels for the traditional ceramic ones. In order to achieve even higher levels of thermal conductivity, it is necessary to use a TIM1, which is 100% metal, namely a solder. This places further demands on the lid materials. Not only must they have a high thermal conductivity, but also their coefficient of thermal expansion has to be a reasonably close match to silicon in order to maintain the integrity of the solder joint over many thermal cycles.

## 2.3. Chassis and rack cooling methods

An example of a 1U server that consists of processor, memory, disk and I/O is shown in Figure 2.2. This server is based on the Intel Xeon processor that supports 2 CPUs, 24 Memory DIMMs, 3 I/O slots, 10 drives and 2 power supplies.

Cooling of such a unit is enabled by seven-system fans that allow for front to back airflow through the server. In addition, two power supply fans assist in the cooling of the dense power supply. The typical dimensions of such a 1U server are 400 mm (wide) × 800 mm (deep) × 43 mm (high). The airflow into the server is through the front bezel and the exit airflow typically is ventilation from the back of the server through vertical vent regions, which is enhanced by an additional vent area from the top surface of the server.

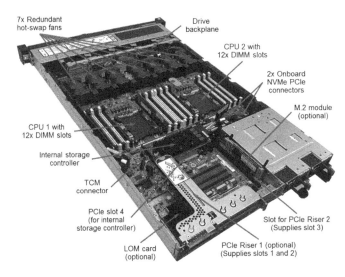

7x Redundant
hot-swap fans

Drive
backplane

CPU 2 with
12x DIMM slots

2x Onboard
NVMe PCIe
connectors

M.2 module
(optional)

CPU 1 with
12x DIMM slots

Internal storage
controller

TCM
connector

PCIe slot 4
(for internal
storage controller)

LOM card
(optional)

Slot for PCIe Riser 2
(Supplies slot 3)

PCIe Riser 1 (optional)
(Supplies slots 1 and 2)

**Figure 2.2.** *Lenovo 1U full width SR630 server. For a color version of this figure, see www.iste.co.uk/brochard/energy.zip*

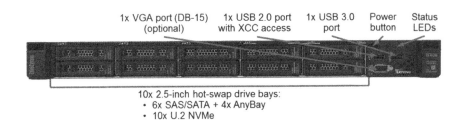

1x VGA port (DB-15)
(optional)

1x USB 2.0 port
with XCC access

1x USB 3.0
port

Power
button

Status
LEDs

10x 2.5-inch hot-swap drive bays:
• 6x SAS/SATA + 4x AnyBay
• 10x U.2 NVMe

**Figure 2.3.** *Front view of an SR630 server. For a color version of this figure, see www.iste.co.uk/brochard/energy.zip*

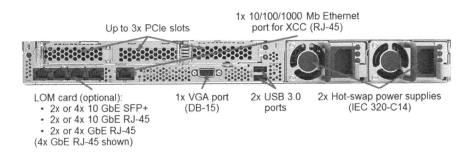

Up to 3x PCIe slots

1x 10/100/1000 Mb Ethernet
port for XCC (RJ-45)

LOM card (optional):
• 2x or 4x 10 GbE SFP+
• 2x or 4x 10 GbE RJ-45
• 2x or 4x GbE RJ-45
(4x GbE RJ-45 shown)

1x VGA port
(DB-15)

2x USB 3.0
ports

2x Hot-swap power supplies
(IEC 320-C14)

**Figure 2.4.** *Rear view of an SR630 server. For a color version of this figure, see www.iste.co.uk/brochard/energy.zip*

When considering the amount of cooled air necessary to provide cooling for about 1 kW of server power, the thermodynamics of the solution very quickly results in the following requirements. It becomes necessary to provide about 120–150 CFM (cubic feet per minute) of airflow through the unit at the extreme power states. In the example shown, each of the seven-system fans would be required to deliver about ~15–20 CFM of airflow. To deliver this airflow, each cooling fan could consume about ~15 W or about 100 W of power. In effect, 10% of the power consumed by the server could be driven by the cooling requirement of the components.

Efficient system operation demands that the 100 W of cooling power is not a steady value; it is modulated based on actual system power consumption and inlet air temperatures. Control algorithms are used to mitigate the cooling power consumed by system fans. Typical system designs target cooling power as low as 2–3% of system power at idle states in benign ambient air environments, increasing to 5% for heavy workloads. However, as the ambient inlet air temperature increases, a system consuming 20 W of cooling power can increase up to 100 W with steady heavy workloads.

Within a server, the cooling air, which has an energy content associated with its delivery, needs to be efficiently managed. Optimal control of the airflow in the server requires modulation of the system fan speeds as well as calibrated flow control to regions and zones within the server that demand it the most.

The magnitude of airflow for a densely populated high-power server that is 1U high is difficult to sustain if deployed in a dense data center environment. Typical racks allow for placement of about 42 units to fill up the rack space. Nonstandard racks of 48U or 60U are also available now. When fully populated, a 42U rack could expect 6000 CFM of airflow in extreme circumstances. The magnitude of this airflow requirement typically would exceed dense data center footprint air delivery capacity for delivered ambient temperature-controlled air to the rack.

The following relationships between fan rotational speed, power and impeller diameter, which are represented by the Fan laws[1], highlight the cooling constraints:

---

1 Available at: https://en.wikipedia.org/wiki/Affinity_laws [Accessed April 29, 2019].

**Law 1: With fan diameter (D) held constant:**

Law 1a: Flow is proportional to fan speed:

$$\frac{V1}{V2} = \frac{N1}{N2} \tag{2.1a}$$

Law 1b: Pressure or head is proportional to the square of fan speed:

$$\frac{H1}{H2} = \left(\frac{N1}{N2}\right)^2 \tag{2.1b}$$

Law 1c: Power is proportional to the cube of fan speed:

$$\frac{P1}{P2} = \left(\frac{N1}{N2}\right)^3 \tag{2.1c}$$

**Law 2: With fan rotational speed (N) held constant:**

Law 2a: Flow is proportional to the fan impeller diameter:

$$\frac{Q1}{Q2} = \frac{D1}{D2} \tag{2.2a}$$

Law 2b: Pressure is proportional to the square of the fan impeller diameter:

$$\frac{H1}{H2} = \left(\frac{D1}{D2}\right)^2 \tag{2.2b}$$

Law 2c: Power is proportional to the cube of fan impeller diameter (assuming constant fan rotational speed):

$$\frac{P1}{P2} = \left(\frac{D1}{D2}\right)^3 \tag{2.2c}$$

where:

– Q is the volumetric flow rate (e.g. CFM or L/s);

– D is the impeller diameter (e.g. in or mm);

– N is the shaft rotational speed (e.g. rpm);

– H is the pressure or head developed by the fan (e.g. psi, Pascal or inA);

– P is the fan shaft power (e.g. W).

## 2.4. Metrics considered for cooling

### 2.4.1. *Efficiency*

The following factors have to be considered in cooling solutions for typical air-cooled servers: the volume occupied by the air-moving device $(cm^3)$; the power consumed in typical operation (W); the power allocated to the cooling elements (W) (which has to be subtracted from the power supply delivery allocation to the compute elements); and the cost of the solution to the supplier as it is passed on through to the purchaser of the system. Efficiency metrics also include the temperature rise of the air across the server, about a 15°C rise would be considered efficient, although 20°C would be ideal. When high-speed air-moving devices are used, the spinning action of the blades can excite aerodynamic noise and impact disk I/O rates or cause vibration that is transmitted through to the spinning drives causing the device to stop functioning.

Typically, the smaller system fans in 1U servers are not as efficient in airflow delivery, that is, the (CFM/W) of cooling airflow to power used is lower than 2U servers that can use larger diameter fans.

Typical efficiency curves (aka "Fan Curve") are shown in Figure 2.5 for an 80 mm fan, where the x-axis is the fan air flow in cubic inch per minute (cfm), the left y-axis is the static air pressure in inches of water (inAq) and the right y-axis is the power in watts (W). The bottom curves represent CFM versus pressure, the top curves represent CFM versus power and the green square dots represent the operating points of the fan which is studied.

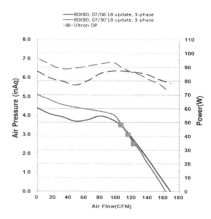

**Figure 2.5.** *Typical efficiency curve for an air moving device. For a color version of this figure, see www.iste.co.uk/brochard/energy.zip*

Systems design for cooling optimization needs to optimize the essential metrics of efficient cooling design. These include the following: allocated cooling energy/power for the system fans, consumed power for cooling at typical operating temperatures for the server in data center operation, normally in recommended range of 18–27°C, optimized temperature rises of the airflow across the server that is typically up to 20°C between the inlet and the exhaust of the server. The amount of power that is normally allocated to efficient server cooling is about 10% of the system power consumption with true power consumption in the range of 3–5% for efficiently designed systems in the recommended range of operating temperatures for servers.

The driving reason to ensure efficient operation of servers is related to the cooling energy requirement of the server in a data center. Excessive allocation of cooling fan power in the server can lead to power constraints for the servers allocated to a rack. Excessive airflow throughput to a server will result in a very low temperature differential for efficient operation of data center cooling infrastructure such as the CRAH/CRAC/in-row cooling units. Since air cooled data centers could allocate between 40% and 60% of the power for the cooling budget, inefficiency in allocating system fan power and airflow can lead to expensive operational costs for a data center.

Systems such as the 1U server can allocate about 100 W of power to the cooling fans and consume about 15–20 W of cooling power during a high-performance workload. Aggregated at a rack level, a dense configuration has about 4 kW of allocated cooling power or about 1 kW of consumed power. Some data centers allocate only 5–10 kW a rack; in effect cooling optimization is essential for dense compute intensive data center deployment.

### 2.4.2. Reliability cost

### 2.4.2.1. Operating temperature and reliability

System design constraints always need to balance the orthogonal vectors of performance, cost of operation and cost of acquisition to the customer, along with reliability of server operation, which is sensitive to operating temperature. There are several studies that describe thermal optimization as it relates to operating system reliability. Standard reliability models use activation energy-based approaches, where the Arrhenius constant can define the relative magnitude of failure rates for systems operating at differing temperatures. Rules of thumb, in the past, have identified a 2× increase in failure rate that is attributable to the operating temperature of the device for every 10°C rise in device operating temperature. In the specific instance of the Intel processor operation, for example, there is a definition of the processor thermal load line that maps the required operating junction temperature to the power state of the processor. There is a requirement from the silicon provider that the system maintains the silicon junction temperature versus power state during its operating life (Intel 2018, Chapter 5).

In addition to the impact of operating temperatures of the devices, the RH of the environment can impose a much higher burden on the failure rates of essential components such as the drives, memory, processors and power supplies. For example, a recent study on system operation in a hyperscale data center documented the stronger impact of changes in RH on failure rates of rotating disks compared to the actual operating temperature of the devices.

### 2.4.2.2. *Gaseous and particulate contamination and reliability*

In many data centers, there is a desire to improve the cooling efficiency by leveraging free-air or air-side economizer-based cooling. These expectations can amplify the failure modes of systems, if suitable monitoring and controls are not placed on the airflow in the data center. Excessive throughput of air for the systems can amplify the consequence of imperfect environmental controls with the data center. ASHRAE standards do require air quality to be maintained as defined for reliable operation with methods such as corrosion coupons and secondary monitoring essential to reliable operation.

### 2.4.3. *Thermal performance*

Each component in the system has the following thermal metrics that must be adhered to ensure functional and reliable operation. In some data sheets, device vendors include an operating temperature of 55°C or 70°C, which is normally defined as an ambient air temperature for the inlet cooling medium for the server. It is essential to determine whether the specified value for the temperature is the air temperature or the device junction/case temperature for an adequate assessment of the cooling requirements.

The values include:

– minimum operating temperature: this is the temperature below which the device signal timings are not validated by the supplier. An example of this value is a typical value of 0°C for the processor;

– maximum operating temperature: this is the temperature above which the device will not function with acceptable signal quality and will start throttling. It is also called maximum junction temperature. An example of this value is 90–100°C for processors or 95°C for memory;

– critical temperature: this is the temperature at which irreparable damage of the hardware will occur. In many instances, the system will power itself off before it gets to this temperature. An example of this value is about 120°C for typical silicon and about 65°C for rotating drives;

– reliable operating temperature: this is the expected normal operating limit where the device can operate 24×7 for its stated operating life. Processors can operate reliably typically in the 70–80°C range, while drives expect a 50°C operating temperature, for example. In reliability predictive models for optimized operating temperatures, there is an expectation that the power consumption of the components is not at this limiting thermal design power state for continuous operation. Utilization rates of the devices are assumed to be in the ~50–70% range to determine the power consumption for the state at which the thermal behavior of the device is to be measured against its predicted reliability. In the example of the Intel Xeon 6148 CPU that has its TDP rated at 150 W and its maximum allowed operating temperature of 96°C, the processor is allowed to operate at 86°C associated with typical power state of 100 W.

Cooling solutions need to recognize the expectations for both maximum and typical operating temperatures for a systems design. If a device were to be allowed to operate close to its maximum operating temperature, continuously the operational life of the system can be impacted significantly and this situation should be avoided. While the advantage of 10°C reduction is critical for improved reliability, and further reductions in temperature would improve the reliability further, the consequence of this change can significantly impact the amount of airflow needed to attain this goal.

Figure 2.6 illustrates the specific example of the improvements in airflow needed to reduce the processor operating temperature.

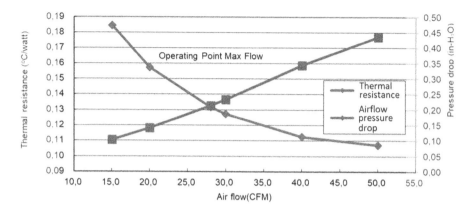

**Figure 2.6.** *Thermal resistance and air flow pressure drop. For a color version of this figure, see www.iste.co.uk/brochard/energy.zip*

To improve the operating temperature of a 150 W processor by 10°C, the thermal resistance of the heat sink that enables the solution has to be reduced by about 25%. According to Figure 2.6, from the operating point, the airflow value through the heat sink has to be increased from 15 CFM through the heat sink to about 28 CFM. The 85% increase in the airflow requirements can only be satisfied by higher fan speeds, which is accompanied with increase in fan, and hence system, power. In the example of the dense system, the reduction of 10°C can result in an increase in fan power of 40 W per server, in effect a 2× increase in the power consumed by the cooling compared to its normally expected value of 35 W per server. Another aspect to be considered would be the almost 80% increase in airflow requirements, which would result in reducing the average exhaust temperature rise through the server by 50%. The lower exhaust temperature then places an added burden in the data center cooling efficiency. The net result is that optimization in systems cooling needs to be balanced with reliability, energy consumption of the server and efficient operation of the data center.

## 2.5. Material used for cooling

Air cooling is traditionally achieved by ensuring the most efficient transport mechanism from the silicon to the external ambient air. Since the heat fluxes involved are high typically 10–100 $W/cm^2$, the surface area of the device itself is not adequate to transport all the heat with a reasonable temperature rise on the device. Enhanced surface area for the heat transport to air is essential. This is accomplished by adding heat sinks to the device.

The heat sink material set that is typically available for system that is both economical and of reasonable performance includes aluminum, which is the most widely used, and copper with thermal conductivity values of 180 W/m-K and 380 W/m-K, respectively.

## 2.6. System layout and cooling air flow optimization

Let us consider now another air-cooled server with a higher density than the 1U SR630 server presented in section 2.3: the Lenovo SD530. The Lenovo SD530 server is a 2U chassis with four air-cooled nodes leading to a ½ U density per node or ½ width nodes. Each node contains two processors from the Intel Xeon processor Scalable family, up to 16 DIMMs, six drive bays, two PCIe slots and two power supplies.

Figure 2.7 shows the 2U chassis, whereas Figure 2.8 shows the node inside.

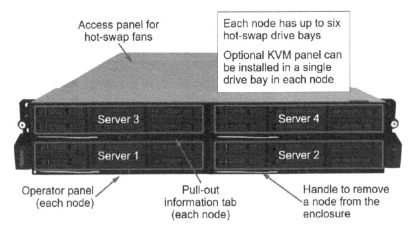

**Figure 2.7.** *Front view of the 2U Lenovo SD530 server with 4½ width nodes. For a color version of this figure, see www.iste.co.uk/brochard/energy.zip*

Comparing the SR630 and SD530 from a processor configuration, we see a different architecture.

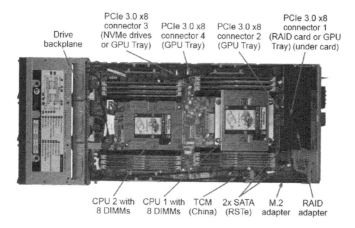

**Figure 2.8.** *Inside view of the ½ width node of a Lenovo SD530. For a color version of this figure, see www.iste.co.uk/brochard/energy.zip*

As shown in Figure 2.9, the SR630 has a spread core configuration while the SD530, due to a reduced board area, has a shadow core configuration. Shadow core configuration is used when the motherboard is too narrow to allow for a spread core configuration. As we will see in Chapter 5, a shadow core configuration has an impact of the processor's thermal behavior.

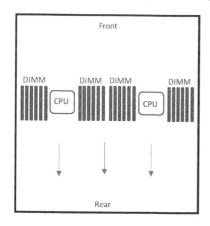 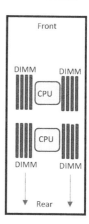

**Figure 2.9.** *Example of a spread core configuration with 12 DIMMs and a shadow core configuration with eight DIMMs*

Due to this higher density, although SD530 supports only eight DIMM slots per CPU versus 12 DIMMM slots for SR630, we can expect some power density challenge. For example, the max DC power per chassis of

SR630 and SD530 with 150 W TDP SKU, full memory and disk configuration is, respectively, 515 W and 1798 W, leading to a 75% higher power density ratio per U of SD530 versus SR630. To support such high-power density configuration with air cooling, some restrictions and innovations are needed. Here, we present some examples for the SD530 (Lenovo n.d.).

With low TDP SKUs, standard 85 mm heat sinks are used for both CPU1 and CPU2 with 16 DIMMs. For medium TDP SKUs, 105 mm heat sink will be used in CPU1, and for its shape, this heat sink limits the number of DIMMs to 12. Standard 85 mm heat sink will be used for CPU2. For high TDP SKUs, thermal transfer module heat sinks will be used for CPU1. As shown in Figure 2.10, the thermal transfer module is two heat sinks connected together via thermal pipes as shown in the following figure. Due to its shape, this heat sink prevents an adapter (RAID or HBA) from being installed in PCIe slot 1 at the rear of the server and limits the number of DIMMs to 12. CPU 2 will use a larger 102 mm heat sink.

This new thermal transfer module (Artman 2018) improves the heat transfer and lowers the average inlet heat sink with the added remote heat displacement area. As shown in Tables 2.2 and 2.3, it results in lower fan speed, power and acoustic levels compared to standard heat sinks.

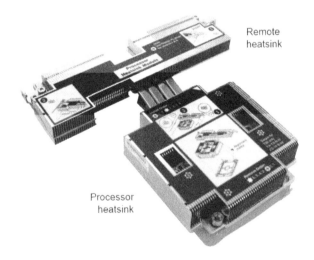

**Figure 2.10.** *Thermal transfer module for SD530. For a color version of this figure, see www.iste.co.uk/brochard/energy.zip*

| Heat Sink comparision with 205W SKU | Fan Power (W) | Fan Speed 60mm (rpm) | Fan Speed 80mm (rpm) | Sound Power (Bel) |
|---|---|---|---|---|
| Standard Heat Sink (205W TDP) | 300 | 19.500 | 15.500 | 9.6 |
| TTM Heat Sink (205W TDP) | 175 | 16.000 | 12.500 | 9.1 |

**Table 2.2.** *Comparison of SD530 fan speed, power and acoustics with 205 W TDP SKU*

| Heat Sink comparision with 150W SKU | Fan Power (W) | Fan Speed 60mm (rpm) | Fan Speed 80mm (rpm) | Sound Power (Bel) |
|---|---|---|---|---|
| Standard Heat Sink (150W TDP) | 135 | 14.500 | 11.000 | 8.8 |
| TTM Heat Sink (150W TDP) | 50 | 9.600 | 7.500 | 8.1 |

**Table 2.3.** *Comparison of SD530 fan speed, power and acoustics with 150 W TDP SKU*

Looking at fan speed and fan power, we note fan power varies as fan speed to the power ~2.5, which is close to the power 3 according to the Fan law [2.1c]. Similarly, we note fan speed varies linearly as ~1.28 times the fan diameter, which is close to the coefficient of 1.33 as given by [2.2b].

At a typical data center ambient temperature (25±2°C) with thermal transfer module, the server fan power can be reduced by 85 W for 150 W TDP SKU and sound pressure can be reduced 8.1 Bels, which is about 70% reduction in loudness. The reduced fan power improves the server ITUE, while the reduced server airflow can improve the data center PUE with reduced CRAH fan power.

This last example and the others we presented in this chapter magnify the challenge of air-cooling regarding power density, and Chapter 3 will present various solutions to this problem at the data center level.

# 3

# Cooling the Data Center

## 3.1. System cooling technologies used

Cooling a "hot" device requires a "cold" fluid to capture its heat and transport it to the data center infrastructure, which will carry it away. In Chapter 2, we discussed how to extract the heat from an air-cooled device. In this Chapter 3, we discuss how the heat is transported and carried away by the data center cooling infrastructure and alternative cooling technologies.

Practically all the electrical power required in a data center is converted into heat, which has to be removed by a proper cooling system. The most suitable cooling solution should be designed, depending on the design criteria, to obtain a high energy efficiency, low cost and reliability. A cooling system should be designed to cover the worst-case scenario, although most servers generally work at much lower capacity than 100%. The control and prediction of temperature rising during a utility power outage is an important aspect for cooling system design. Air-cooled systems represent the backbone of data center cooling systems; they are evolving over the years to cope with the advance in the IT equipment. The evolution of air-cooled system is going toward localized cooling units and physical separation of the airstream within the data center in order to support the rising power densities. On the other hand, liquid-cooled systems are becoming promising and emergent solutions for cooling high power density data centers. Today, the IT equipment is reaching power densities that in some cases justify the liquid-cooled solutions; moreover, if the IT industry grows with the same trend of the recent years, air-cooled systems will not be able to accomplish the cooling process. The bulk cooling capacity is provided by the mechanical equipment: different systems such as chilled water systems, direct expansion air cooled systems and direct expansion glycol cooled systems are used. The heat rejection represents the last step in the heat removal process: cooling towers and dry coolers are the most common heat rejection systems for the data center industry.

## 3.2. Air-cooled data center

### 3.2.1. *Conventional air-cooled data center*

#### 3.2.1.1. *Machine room*

Figure 3.1 represents a conventional air-cooled machine room.

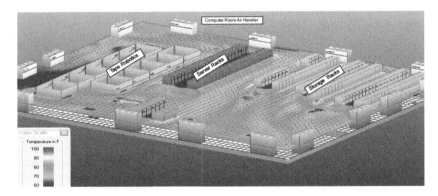

**Figure 3.1.** *Classic air-cooled machine room. For a color version of this figure, see www.iste.co.uk/brochard/energy.zip*

At the periphery of the machine room are the CRAHs (Computer Room Air Handler), which extracts the hot air from the machine room and delivers cold air, as shown in Figure 3.2. In the center of the machine room, we find the IT equipment that are represented here by server racks, storage racks and tape robotics. CRAHs use fans, cooling coils and a water-chiller system to remove heat. This operation can cause some turbulence and hot spots in the machine room depending on the air flow and the heat capacity generated by the racks. The colors represent the temperature and red areas are hot spots (100°F/37.8°C) and dark blue areas are cold spot (60°F/15.5°C). These temperatures have to match the temperature supported by the IT equipment. For example, servers usually can operate at 35°C and under some conditions up to 45°C, while IT manufactures recommend a temperature between 18°C and 27°C.

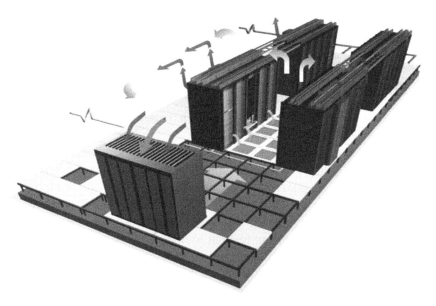

**Figure 3.2.** *Hot and cold air flows in the machine room. For a color version of this figure, see www.iste.co.uk/brochard/energy.zip*

## 3.2.1.2. *Refrigeration equipment*

CRAHs by themselves do not produce cold air. The refrigeration equipment is usually outside the machine room, some on the data center roof, some in the basement or in an adjacent room. Table 3.1 presents a list of the cooling equipment.

| Name | Function | Energy needed |
|---|---|---|
| Chiller | produce cold water by a compressor mecanical action for CRAH or CDU | high |
| Cooling Tower | extract heat to the atmosphere from the hot water coming from data center by evaporative fluid material, cool it to near wet bulb temperature and return the cold water to the data center CRAH or water-side economizer | low |
| Dry-cooler | alternative to cooling tower using a closed circuit with air when outside temperature is too low for Cooling Tower, cool the "hot water" to near dry bulb temperature and return the "cold" water to the data center | medium low |
| Water-side economizer | extract heat from the hot air by a water condenser and reject it to the atmosphere via a dry cooler or cooling tower when enviromental conditions allow it | low |
| CRAH (Computer Room Air Handler) | extract hot air from the machine room with fans and blow cold air produced by the Chillers of Cooling Towers or Dry Coolers | low |
| CDU (Cooling Distribution Unit) | used in conjunction with RDHX to isolate and control the primary water loop from the secondary water loop | low |
| RDHX (Rear Door Heat eXchanger) | extract heat from the rack through a water circuit /coil with cold water produced from Chillers , Cooling Tower or Dry Cooler | low |
| In-Row Cooler | located in between racks to extract hot air from the machine room and return cold air produced by mecanical action | medium high |

**Table 3.1.** *List and function of cooling equipment*

### 3.2.1.3. *Hot and cold aisle containment*

The machine we have described so far with only CRAH in the machine room and chillers/cooling towers on the roof would have, under normal operation, a very bad efficiency, which is characterized by a PUE much larger than 1 and usually around 2. This is mainly due to the poor management of hot air and cold air with fans ingesting/blowing at the periphery of the machine room while the IT equipment is distant in the middle of the machine room. Different techniques are available to minimize the mixing of air flows. A very common and cheap one is the hot or cold aisle containment. It consists of organizing the racks in pairs of rows to isolate hot aisles and cold aisles from each other, and preventing hot and cold air from mixing by having the racks either back to back to blow their hot air in the hot aisle, or front to front to inlet the cold air in the cold aisle and by closing the aisle at each end and at the top to prevent the hot and cold air mixing within the machine room. In Figure 3.1, we see an example of cold aisle containment between the two rows of the servers' racks with a blue-colored area in between the pair of rows.

## 3.3. ASHRAE data center cooling standards

The American Society of Heating, Refrigerating and Air Conditioning Engineers (ASHRAE) publishes 4,000+ standards for the design and maintenance of indoor environments. We are reproducing here some ASHRAE standards published by the Technical Committee 9.9 on Mission Critical Facilities, Data Centers, Technology Spaces and Electronic Equipment.

### 3.3.1. *Operation and temperature classes*

Temperature and operation of the data center is classified by ASHRAE.

Figure 3.3 presents four classes of ASHRAE TC 9.9 for Mission Critical Facilities, Technology Spaces & Electronics Equipment.

Classes are A1 with operating dry bulb room temperatures from 15°C to 32°C, A2 from 10°C to 35°C, A3 from 5°C to 40°C and A4 from 5°C to 45°C. Temperatures represent inlet temperature and humidity limits with altitude de-rating.

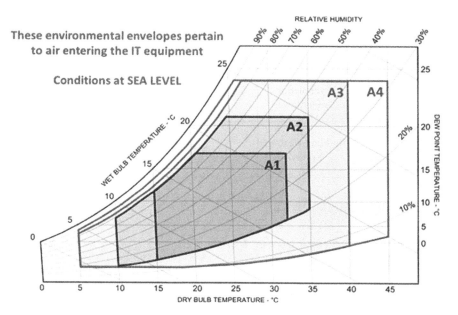

**Figure 3.3.** *ASHRAE classes of data center operation. For a color version of this figure, see www.iste.co.uk/brochard/energy.zip*

### 3.3.2. *Liquid cooling classes*

Table 3.2 presents the ASHRAE classification of liquid cooling classes from the Guide Line for Datacom Equipment Centers, Second Edition. The cooling classes are ranked from lower water temperature (W1) to higher water temperature (W5) and the cooling equipment required for each class. As we will see later, higher water temperature increases free cooling (see section 3.6) and improves TCO (see section 7.3).

| Liquid Cooling Classes | Main Cooling Equipment | Supplemental Cooling Equipment | Facility Water Temperature |
|---|---|---|---|
| W1 | Chiller/Cooling Tower | Water-side Economizer w/drycooler or cooling tower | 2°C–17°C |
| W2 | Chiller/Cooling Tower | Water-side Economizer w/drycooler or cooling tower | 2°C–27°C |

| W3 | Cooling Tower | Chiller | 2°C–32°C |
|---|---|---|---|
| W4 | Water-side Economizer w/ drycooler or cooling tower | N/A | 2°C–45°C |
| W5 | Building Heating System | Cooling Tower | >45°C |

**Table 3.2.** *ASHRAE liquid cooling classes*

### 3.3.3. *Server and rack power trend*

Figure 3.4 presents the heat load trend from 2010 to 2020 per chassis and per racks published by ASHRAE.

**Market Requirements force IT manufacturers to maximize performance/volume creating high heat load/rack**

| Height | No. of Sockets | Heat Load / Chassis (watts) | | | Heat Load / 42U Rack | | | Increase 2010 to 2020 |
|---|---|---|---|---|---|---|---|---|
| | | 2010 | 2015 | 2020 | 2010 | 2015 | 2020 | |
| 1U | 1s | 255 | 290 | 330 | 10,710 | 12,180 | 13,860 | 29% |
| | 2s | 600 | 735 | 870 | 25,200 | 30,870 | 36,540 | 45% |
| | 4s | 1,000 | 1,100 | 1,200 | 42,000 | 46,200 | 50,400 | 20% |
| 2U | 2s | 750 | 1,100 | 1,250 | 15,750 | 23,100 | 26,250 | 67% |
| | 4s | 1,400 | 1,800 | 2,000 | 29,400 | 37,800 | 42,000 | 43% |
| 4U | 2s | 2,300 | 3,100 | 3,300 | 23,000 | 31,000 | 33,000 | 43% |
| 7U (Blade) | 2s | 5,500 | 6,500 | 7,500 | 33,000 | 39,000 | 45,000 | 36% |
| 9U (Blade) | 2s | 6,500 | 8,000 | 9,500 | 26,000 | 32,000 | 38,000 | 6% |
| 10U (Blade) | 2s | 8,000 | 9,000 | 10,500 | 32,000 | 36,000 | 42,000 | 31% |

**These rack heat loads will result in increased focus on improving data center ventilation solutions and localized liquid cooling solutions**

**Figure 3.4.** *ASHRAE 2015–2020 server power and rack heat load trends*

It shows that servers are getting more power hungry and heat load per rack is moving from the 10–20 kW per rack to 40–50 kW per rack with dense power-hungry servers. We will present real examples of this trend in Chapters 4 when we discuss the processor and accelerator power and performance history, and in Chapter 5 when we present power and performance measurement of workload.

Figure 3.5 presents another way, the evolution of the rack heat load and their cooling limits over time.

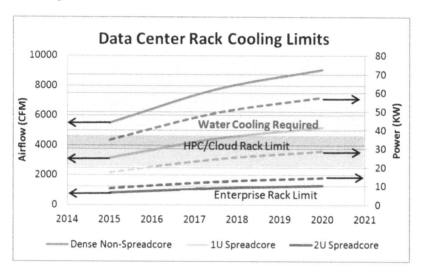

**Figure 3.5.** *Data center rack cooling limits*

The left Y-axis presents the air flow needed (in CFM) to cool the rack, with the corresponding heat load on the right side of the Y-axis. Full lines (red for 2U servers, orange for 1U servers and green for dense servers) represent the heat load of a 42-inch rack full of such servers while the dotted lines represent the air-cooling limit for each type of servers. It shows that air-cooled racks will not be able to cool dense servers with heavy power load.

## 3.4. Liquid-cooled racks

As extracting heat from the periphery of the machine room is not efficient, a more effective solution is to extract heat from the back of the rack where fans are blowing hot air. A simple approach is to replace the rack door with a Rear Door Heat eXchanger (RDHX), as shown in Figure 3.6 and listed in Table 3.1.

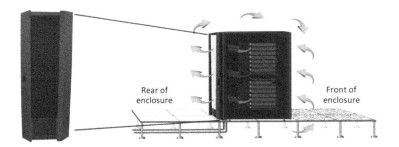

**Figure 3.6.** *Principle of passive RDHX. For a color version of this figure, see www.iste.co.uk/brochard/energy.zip*

Passive RDHX replaces the existing rear doors of the IT enclosures. Chilled water circulates through the tube and fin coils above the dew point (no condensate). The RDHX has chilled water supply and return quick connections. Equipment exhaust air passes through the coil and is cooled before re-entering the room. Heat is removed from the room through the return water connection.

Figure 3.7 shows how RDHXs are connected to CDUs and Chillers through a primary and secondary loop.

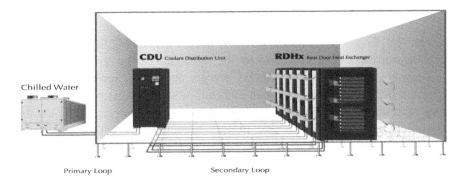

**Figure 3.7.** *RDHX, CDU and chillers. For a color version of this figure, see www.iste.co.uk/brochard/energy.zip*

RDHX extraction capacity is limited since the RDHXs are passive, meaning there is no fan or mechanical action to help the heat extraction through the door. Figure 3.8 presents the passive RDHX capacity depending on the water temperature (in °C), the water flow rate (in gpm, gallon per minute) and the heat load of the rack (in kW). Please note the fan speed is the node fan speed in the server since RDHXs have no fan.

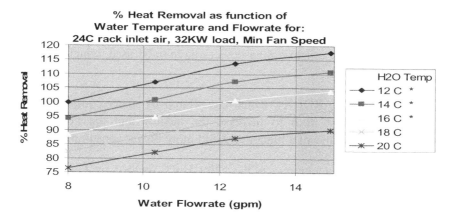

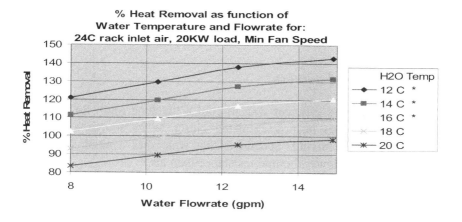

**Figure 3.8.** *RDHX heat removal capacity for a 32 kW and 10 kW rack load. For a color version of this figure, see www.iste.co.uk/brochard/energy.zip*

As we can see, depending on the rack heat capacity, inlet water temperature and water flow rate, a RDHX can absorb 100% of the heat or more meaning the RDHX is cooling the machine room. For the 32 kW heat load, 100% heat removal can be achieved with 10 gpm at 14°C or 12 gpm at 16°C, and 90% heat-to-water removal can be achieved with 8.5 gpm at 16°C or 11 gpm at 18°C. But a colder inlet water means more chiller work and a higher flow rate means more pump work and therefore more energy.

That is the trade-off to be made to optimize the data center cooling and TCO, which is addressed in Chapter 7. When the rack load is very high (for example 40+ kW per rack, which occurs with dense servers using high TDP processors as shown in Chapter 4 and Figure 3.4), passive RDHX will not be able to extract 100% of the heat and either the remaining heat goes into the machine room air or other cooling devices have to be used, which is another trade-off to be made.

Active RDHX (ARDHX), which are offered by many companies, have fans inside the rear door to increase the airflow and the heat-to-water capacity at the expense of a higher cost and more power consumption.

Another similar technique is the "Hot Hut", created by Google (Kava 2012). A "Hot Hut" consists first of a hot aisle containment with fans on top, which pull hot air across water-filed cooling coils and release the cooled air to the data center where servers/IT devices can use it again.

The impact of RDHX versus classic air-cooled center will be addressed on PUE and TCO in Chapter 5.

## 3.5. Liquid-cooled servers

RDHX is a more efficient way to cool a machine room for two major reasons. One is that heat is extracted closer to its source avoiding air turbulence and air mixing. Second is that water has a much higher heat capacity and much lower thermal resistance than air.

### 3.5.1. *Water heat capacity*

Figure 3.9 presents a comparison of the heat capacity and thermal resistance of water versus air.

$c_v$ is the heat capacity and:

$$q'' = Rth * dT \hfill [3.1]$$

is the 1D representation of the heat flux equation from thermodynamics, where q" is the heat flux, $R_{th}$ is the thermal resistance and $dT$ is the temperature gradient.

## Water

1. High heat capacity

$c_v \approx 1$ Wh/(L·K)

2. Low thermal resistance

$\dot{q}'' = R_{th} \cdot \Delta T$

$R_{th} = 0.1$ K cm²/ W

$\dot{q}'' = 50-100$ W/cm²

$\Delta T = 5-10$ C

## Air

1. Low heat capacity

$c_v \approx 0.0003$ Wh/(L·K)

2. High thermal resistance

$\dot{q}'' = R_{th} \cdot \Delta T$

$R_{th} = 1$ K cm²/ W

$\dot{q}'' = 50-100$ W/cm²

$\Delta T = 50-100$ C

**Figure 3.9.** *Water versus air heat capacity and thermal resistance. For a color version of this figure, see www.iste.co.uk/brochard/energy.zip*

The consequence is that water requires a much smaller $\Delta T$ between the processor temperature and the inlet temperature than air. Therefore, to maintain a processor at temperature between 80 and 90°C, the inlet air temperature with air cooling has to be in the 20–30°C range, while the inlet water temperature can be up to 70°C. In practice, the highest inlet water temperature is in the 50–55°C range. Cooling directly the processor (or other active part of a node) with water is called direct water cooling (DWC) versus indirect water cooling as used with RDHX. Depending on the inlet water temperature, we will have cold (around 20°C), warm (around 30°C) or hot direct (40°C or higher) water cooling. We will come back to the influence of inlet water temperatures in Chapter 5.

### 3.5.2. Thermal conduction module

First utilizations of direct water-cooled technology were done with IBM thermal conductor module (TCM) for the IBM mainframes 3080 and 3090 in the 1980s–1990s (Blodgett and Barbour 1982). This expensive technology was needed due to the high-power consumption of these high-end processor (about 300 W per module). These processor and water-cooling technologies were slowly abandoned with the introduction of CMOS technology, which led to powerful microprocessors with a few watts of power consumption like CMOS VAX (Archer *et al.* 1987) and Intel 80x86 (Table 2.1). With the rise of CPU power consumption (205 W on Skylake, 250, 350 and 400 W on Cascade Lake) and GPU (300 W today and more in the future), water-cooling technology reappeared in the early 2010s for high-end commodity servers.

This is well illustrated in Figure 3.10.

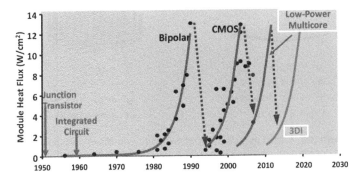

**Figure 3.10.** *Evolution of module heat flux from 1950 to 2020*

More detail on the CPU and GPU power trend is discussed in section 4.1.

### 3.5.3. *Full node heat removal with cold plates*

The first large-scale commercial implementation of a water-cooled x86 server was done with the IBM iDataPlex dx360 m4, originally released as an air-cooled server in 2011 and delivered to LRZ SuperMUC in 2012 (IBM Newsroom 2012). Figure 3.11 presents the water loop assembly of the server.

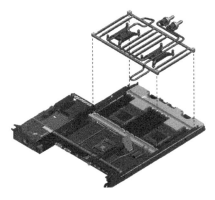

**Figure 3.11.** *Water loop assembly of the IBM iDataPlex dx360 m4.*
*For a color version of this figure, see www.iste.co.uk/brochard/energy.zip*

Besides the CPUs and memory modules, there are additional elements in a system board that require cooling, for example the voltage regulators (VRs) or the Intel platform controller hub (PCB). The water loop assembly covers all these elements and is composed of active and passive elements. For some of the onboard chips, such as the embedded service processor and other low power devices, passive water cooling is sufficient. Passive water cooling means the heat is extracted through a heat spreader connected to the water loop assembly before it goes to water. Active water cooling means the heat is extracted by cold plates, which are directly connected to the water loop. For the IBM iDataPlex dx360 m4, water flow rate is about 0.5 lpm (liters per minute) per node, inlet water temperature is between 20°C and 45°C and the heat-to-water ratio is up to 85% when the temperature delta between inlet water and room temperature is less than 15°C.

The water flow path is illustrated in Figure 3.12. Water enters the cooling loop through the left connector in the back of the chassis, flows to one CPU cold plate and to the second one in sequence and is then distributed in parallel over to the memory modules by the rear cold rail. After collecting heat from the memory modules by the front cold rail, water flows to the Patsburg Intel platform controller and exits the server through the right connector in the back.

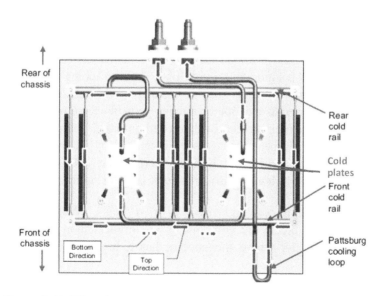

**Figure 3.12.** *Water flow path in the IBM iDataPlex dx360 m4. For a color version of this figure, see www.iste.co.uk/brochard/energy.zip*

### 3.5.4. *Modular heat removal with cold plates*

As the cost to design and manufacture a full water-cooled server can be expensive, some companies are proposing kits of cold plate, tubing and manifolds to adapt on existing air-cooled servers by removing the heat sink and adding a water-cooled circuit. CoolIT[1] and Asetek[2] are offering such solutions for Intel and AMD CPUs, NVIDIA and AMD GPUs, and memory DIMMs. Some vendors are using such cooling devices to enable some of their servers with liquid cooling. The most common use of such modular solutions is to cool only the CPU or GPU of the server. We will study in Chapter 7 the PUE and TCO impacts of such a design, which we will call Hybrid, since only around 60% of the server heat goes to water while the remaining heat goes to air.

### 3.5.5. *Immersion cooling*

Immersion cooling is a different cooling technology based on liquid cooling where instead of using cold plates and heat spreader to cool the most power consuming parts, the server itself is totally immersed in a tank filled with some thermal conductive dielectric liquid coolant.

Immersion cooling has a higher heat-to-liquid ratio than cold-plate cooling as the whole heat of the server is extracted while cold-plate cooling heat-to-liquid ratio is between 60% and 90%. This allows more energy-efficient solutions and the ability to cool higher heat load racks. From a manufacturing perspective, it should be a simpler solution as no cold plate, and no tubing is added to the server. Still some modifications may be needed for immersion cooling. One modification is the need to take out the moving parts like fans. Another potential modification is the replacement of hydrocarbon-based thermal paste used between heat sinks and heat sources (see Figure 2.1) by thermally conductive epoxy-based material or Indium (Indium Corporation 2008) since thermal grease based on hydrocarbon will dissolve in the cooling liquid.

Immersion cooling can be used in two ways. With single-phase immersion cooling electronic components are immersed in a coolant in a sealed accessible tank where the coolant has a higher boiling point and

---

1 Available at: https://www.coolitsystems.com/technology [Accessed April 30, 2019].
2 Available at: https://www.asetek.com/data-center/solutions-for-data-centers [Accessed April 29, 2019].

remains in its liquid phase throughout the process. The heat from the chip is transferred to the coolant and classic pumps are used to flow the heated fluid to a heat exchanger and then cooled using the same techniques we presented previously such as cooling towers or dry coolers. With two-phase immersion electronic components are immerged in a sealed tank where the generated heat boils the coolant into a gaseous state, which rises to the top of the tank. The gas condenses on the lid or a condensation coil and drops back into the tank to repeat the cycle.

Immersion cooling has a great potential and dual-phase immersion can cool higher heat load servers or racks versus single phase. But it has also drawbacks like higher cost, potential safety issues and reliability problems of damaging electronics like power supply and logic boards (Coles and Herrlin 2016). That is why single-phase cooling has been used at some extent so far. It was used by Cray in a commercial product, Cray T90 (CEA 1996), and with commodity x86 servers in production (CGG 2012). But it has also some potential issues like reliability and maintainability, which has impacted its larger adoption. Nevertheless, immersion cooling is explored and tested today by IT companies (Alibaba Group 2018).

### 3.5.6. Recent DWC servers

There have been many other commercial DWC servers since 2012. We will focus on two of them: the IBM Power9 with NVIDIA V100, which was delivered as Summit to Oak Ridge National Lab, USA, and as Sierra to Lawrence Livermore National Lab, USA. These ranked, respectively, numbers 1 and 2 on Top500 in November 2018, and the Lenovo SD650 with Intel Xeon Skylake processor that was delivered as SuperMUC-NG to LRZ, Germany was ranked number 8. We will pay special attention to the SD650 since it is used to measure the power, thermal and performance impact of water cooling presented in Chapter 4 and in the TCO analysis presented in Chapter 5. It should be noted that in this Top10 of November 2018, four systems are water cooled: Summit, Sierra, SuperMUC-NG and Sequoia based on an IBM Blue Gene/Q system (IBM Icons n.d.).

#### 3.5.6.1. IBM Power 9

IBM has been a pioneer of liquid cooling, starting with mainframes like the thermal conduction module (Blodgett and Barbour 1982) and later with Blue Gene (IBM Icons n.d.). For the Summit and Sierra systems that required very powerful and energy-efficient nodes, IBM coupled six NVIDIA V100 chips with two POWER 9 CPUs through NVLink (OLCF n.d.). Each compute node is DWC with eight cold plates (one per Power9 CPUs and one per V100 GPU). Each compute node is about 2.8 kW and each rack about 59 kW. This shows 50 kW per rack is today a reality. Inlet water temperature for the compute rack is 70°F (21.1°C) and the remaining racks are using RDHX.

### 3.5.6.2. Lenovo SD650

The Lenovo ThinkSystem SD650 is the third generation of water-cooled system after the iDataPlex dx360 m4 and the NeXtScale m360 m5.

Figure 3.13 presents one SD650 1 U tray, which hosts two-socket nodes side by side leading to a ½U density per 2S node. The water circuit is cooling in parallel the two nodes on the tray to minimize the water-cooling costs. The water path enters the tray through the blue arrow inlet, is split into two water paths (one for each node) and split again into two water paths, one for the CPUs and one for the 12 DDR4 DIMMs and four Apache Pass (AEP) slots, which are not populated on Skylake but will be on Cascade Lake when Optane DC Persistent Memory (or Optane DIMMs) is supported. The CPU water flow is going first to the CPU slot 1 (highlighted in green), then to CPU slot 2 (highlighted in red) and finally going to the outlet (highlighted in yellow). The impact of such water flow on the processor temperature will be presented in Chapter 5.

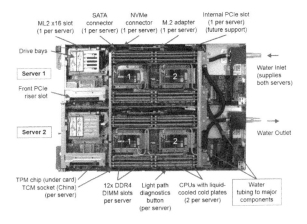

**Figure 3.13.** *Lenovo ThinkSystem SD650 water-cooled node. For a color version of this figure, see www.iste.co.uk/brochard/energy.zip*

The memory water flow is shown in Figure 3.14. Water flows in six parallel different streams to cool the DDR4 DIMMs and AEP slots, and a conductive plate conducts the heat from the disk and network cards to the memory water path.

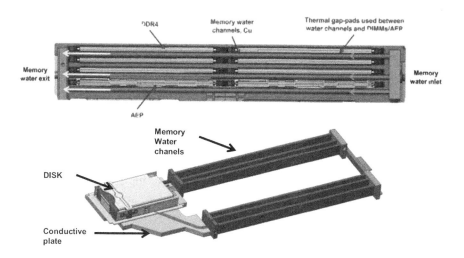

**Figure 3.14.** *Lenovo ThinkSystem SD650 memory water channels. For a color version of this figure, see www.iste.co.uk/brochard/energy.zip*

From a cooling perspective, the major differences between the SD650 and iDataPlex dx360 m4 are:

– higher TDP processors are supported (205 W SKU and even 240 W SKU under some conditions vs. 150 W SKU);

– higher heat-to-water ratio as all devices, except the power supply, are cooled with a better efficiency. For example, 95% of heat is going to water if the room temperature and inlet water temperature are within the following bounds: (air 5–35°C; water 10–50°C);

– higher flow rate of 0.7 lpm per node versus 0.5 lpm per node;

– wider range of inlet water temperature is supported (10–50°C vs. 18–45°C).

It should be noted that SD650 is a ½U 2S server with a shadow processor configuration (Figure 2.9) with water flowing first to CPU0 and then CPU1.

This cooling difference impacts the CPU temperature and will be discussed in Chapter 5.

## 3.6. Free cooling

Free cooling occurs when chillers are not needed to produce cold water and cooling towers or dry coolers can be used instead. Hence, the name "free" cooling since the only power needed is for the pumps and fans when the free-cooling capacity can cover 100% of the need. Therefore, free-cooling usage depends on the environmental conditions, and in particular the outside temperature. Free cooling can start as soon as the temperature difference between the cold-water temperature going to the CRAH, the RDHX or the DWC loop and the outside temperature is between 2°F (1°C) and 4°F (2°C), which is pretty low. Therefore, increasing the room temperature and the water temperature will increase the free cooling of the system and reduces dramatically its PUE and TCO (see section 7.3).

## 3.7. Waste heat reuse

### 3.7.1. *Reusing heat as heat*

The simplest way to reuse waste heat is to use it for heating purposes. A few data centers have been doing it to heat their offices (see Chapter 7 for NREL and LRZ) or heating buildings close by or heating pools (Munroe 2016). The two major drawbacks of reusing waste heat for heating are the difficulty of transporting heat and the temperature of the exhausted heat needed. As the cost of insulated piping to carry and minimize heat loss is expensive, the cheapest way to circumvent the first difficulty is to choose a close "heating target", which explains why this reuse of waste heat is still limited to the data center offices or close by buildings. Regarding the second difficulty related to the temperature of the exhausted heat, the temperature at which the data center operates is crucial. For an air-cooled data center using cold water to feed the CRAH, RDHX or DWC when return temperature is between 28°C (82°F) and 35°C (95°F), heat pumps can be used to increase the heat temperature to 55°C or more, which is the minimum temperature required to reuse efficiently heat, which means inlet water temperature is about 5°C lower. This means that if the inlet water temperature at which the data center operates has to be at least 23°C (73°F). This is well above the temperature at which conventional air-cooled data center operates, which is between 5°C (41°F) and 12°C (72°F). This means the data center needs to operate at higher temperature, like W2 or higher according to ASHRAE operating classes (Figure 3.4). Another potential drawback of such an approach is that the quantity of heat generated by the data center can be larger than the heating quantity needed by the "heating target" and that the need to heat a building is seasonal. In this case, storing the excess energy is a potential solution, which we will discuss in section 7.4. It should be noted that water cooling can minimize the difficulties we just described since a water-cooled system using warm water with inlet water temperatures like 30°C (86°F) will generate outlet water around 35°C (95°F), and possibly higher, up to 45–50°C, inlet water temperature with hot water cooling.

### 3.7.2. *Transforming heat with adsorption chillers*

Transforming heat into cold has been for a long time restricted to high temperature. Adsorption chillers are a new type of machine that is quite different from the previous generation of liquid desiccant absorption chillers. With solid desiccant adsorbers, the desiccant never moves and never changes phase. It is always a solid. There are very few moving parts and no chemicals. In fact, the refrigerant used is regular tap water with no additional additives. The unique property of adsorption machines is their ability to operate at reduced hot water temperatures as low as 130°F (54°C).

#### 3.7.2.1. *Adsorption chillers*

Adsorption chillers generate chilled water using heat as the primary energy source. Contrary to the more common absorption chillers, the heat-pumping effect is generated by a solid instead of a liquid sorption material, which absorbs the refrigerant, typically water. They are being applied, when only low-temperature waste heat is available.

Adsorption chillers are generally designed in two different ways:

– Option 1 design: two-chamber approach using the same heat exchanger for evaporation and condensation of water vapor;

– Option 2 design: four-chamber approach with separated heat exchangers for evaporation and condensation.

As shown in Figure 3.15, an adsorption chiller based on design option 1 consists of two identical vacuum containers, each containing two heat exchangers:

– Adsorber: coated with the adsorbent (silica gel or zeolite);

– Phase changer: evaporation and condensation of water.

– During desorption (module 1), the adsorbent is heated up causing the previously adsorbed water vapor to flow to the condenser (red arrow), where it is condensed to liquid water.

– During adsorption (module 2), the adsorbent is cooled down again causing water vapor to flow back (blue arrow) and evaporate in the evaporator generating cold. Water is evaporated at low temperatures, because the system is evacuated and hermetically sealed from the surroundings.

– Two (or more) identical modules operate phase-shifted to provide continuous cooling.

In the option 2, design evaporation and condensation of the water vapor are carried out in separated vacuum chambers. This approach leads to a system as shown in Figure 3.16.

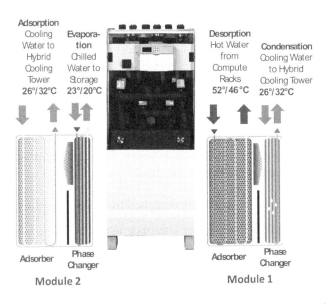

**Figure 3.15.** *Adsorption chiller principle and phases (two chambers design). For a color version of this figure, see www.iste.co.uk/brochard/energy.zip*

While in the option 1 design, the chiller consists of two or more adsorbers, which are alternatively heated and cooled in order to cause desorption and adsorption of water vapor, in the option 2 design (Figure 3.16), the right adsorber is being desorbed, whereas the left adsorber is adsorbing. In the next step, hot water and cooling water are switched and the right adsorber is in adsorption and the left adsorber in desorption state. Evaporation and condensation of the water vapor are carried out in separated vacuum containers where temperature is constant, which was not the case with option 1 design where temperature changed continuously. In order to close the refrigerant loop, the liquid condensate is returned to the evaporator.

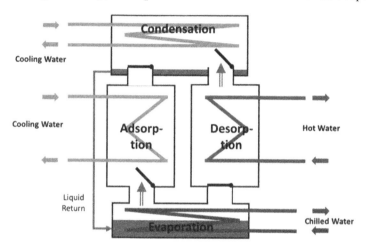

**Figure 3.16.** *Adsorption chiller principle and phases (four containers design). For a color version of this figure, see www.iste.co.uk/brochard/energy.zip*

This design needs four vacuum valves, which also may operate passively by internal pressure differences, controlling the refrigerant flow and which sets higher requirements in designing a vacuum-tight system. On the other hand, due to the constant temperatures of evaporator and condenser, thermal coefficient of performance (COP) and cooling capacity are better. Moreover, because of lower internal temperature losses, higher temperature lifts may be achieved, which is especially important, if the waste heat temperature to the machine is low.

Such new generation adsorption chillers, with inlet hot water coming from the compute racks at about 55°C water temperature can produce cold water at around 20°C.

### 3.7.2.2. Coefficient of performance

In adsorption chillers, two types of energy are used to drive the machine: heat and electricity. Therefore, a distinction has to be made between thermal and electrical efficiency called the coefficient of performance (COP). In a data center, the adsorption chiller is cooling the hot fluid loop (HF) from the compute racks using this heat flow to generate chilled water to be fed into the cold fluid loop (CF) using electricity (EL). Figure 3.17 summarizes this in the Sankey diagram.

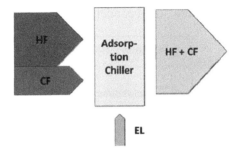

**Figure 3.17.** *Sankey diagram of the energy flows in an adsorption chiller. For a color version of this figure, see www.iste.co.uk/brochard/energy.zip*

For the thermal efficiency, an adsorption chiller can be seen as a heating or cooling system. The thermal coefficient of performance of a heating or cooling system is measured by $COP_{heating}$ and $COP_{cooling}$ as the ratio of heat removed or supplied to the energy required[3].

For $COP_{cooling}$, this means how much cold the chiller produces ($Q_{cf}$) and how much waste heat is needed to produce this amount of cold ($Q_{hf}$).

For $COP_{heating}$, the medium temperature output of the chiller is compared to the high temperature heat input ($Q_{hf}$). Because of energy conservation, this output is the sum of the two inputs ($Q_{cf} + Q_{hf}$), leading to:

$$COP_{cooling} = \frac{Q_{cf}}{Q_{hf}} \qquad\qquad [3.2]$$

$$COP_{heating} = \frac{Q_{cf}+Q_{hf}}{Q_{hf}} \qquad\qquad [3.3]$$

---

3 Available at: https://en.wikipedia.org/wiki/Coefficient_of_performance#Equation [Accessed May 1, 2019].

which leads to:

$$COP_{heating} = COP_{cooling} + 1 \qquad [3.4]$$

and:

$$COP_{heating} > 1 \qquad [3.5]$$

$$COP_{cooling} < 1 \qquad [3.6]$$

For the electrical efficiency, the electrical COP ($COP_{el}$) is the ratio between the total amount of heat removed from the data center to the ambient ($Q_{cf} + Q_{hf}$), divided by the total amount of electricity Pel needed for this task. Adsorption chillers only need electricity for the controller and switching of hydraulic valves, therefore its share of the electricity demand is negligible. Thus, the electricity demand to be included into the calculation of $COP_{el}$ is dominated by the pumps and fans of the hydraulic installation.

Therefore, we have:

$$COP_{el} = \frac{Q_{cf} + Q_{cf}}{P_{el}} \qquad [3.7]$$

Comparing an adsorption chiller with a conventional electrical chiller, the overall electrical COP is of major interest.

The different cooling technologies we have described so far (conventional chillers and adsorption chillers) have very different $COP_{el}$.

Figure 3.18 presents the $COP_{el}$ for adsorption chillers (adsorption cooling total), conventional chillers (compression cooling) and free cooling as measured on the CoolMUC-2 system at LRZ (see section 7.2). A higher $COP_{el}$ value means a more efficient cooling system leading to a lower PUE.

It shows that the energy efficiency of adsorption cooling is much higher than compression cooling and very close to free cooling since the electricity needed to power the adsorption chillers and its pumps is very low: for 1 kW of chilled water produced, adsorption cooling requires 65 W, while compression cooling requires 301 W and mixed compression plus free cooling requires 132 W.

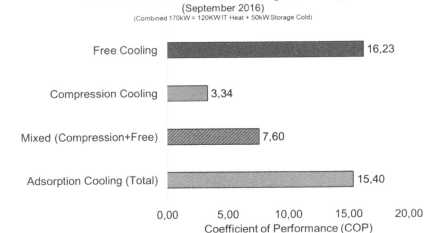

**Figure 3.18.** *Measured COP$_{el}$ values of different cooling technologies. For a color version of this figure, see www.iste.co.uk/brochard/energy.zip*

From now on, we will measure the thermal efficiency of adsorption chillers using COP$_{cooling}$ as defined in [3.2], which we will simply call COP.

### 3.7.2.3. *Coefficient of performance and hot water*

For quite some time, thermal driven cooling was dominated by liquid absorption chillers based on lithium/bromide-water or ammonia-water as sorption pairs, which do not operate at hot water temperatures between 45 and 55°C, which are typical for data centers using hot water cooling.

Adsorption chillers based on the solid adsorption material silica gel and water as refrigerant can generate chilled water at 18–20°C at a hot water temperature around 55°C with a COP of 50% as we will see in section 7.2.3. But with desorption temperatures of 55°C and less, the capacity of the silica gel chiller is considerably below its performance in the usual field of operation at driving temperatures between 70 and 90°C, which leads to the necessity of installing large units compared to the supplied cooling capacity.

In order to overcome this drawback, a series of R&D activities are currently being performed with the aim to develop a more compact adsorption chiller, which is specifically adapted to the conditions in data centers. These activities are mainly concentrated on choosing adsorption materials with adsorption characteristics, which are better adapted to the temperature conditions in data centers, as well as coating heat exchanger surfaces with these materials, in order to enhance heat and mass transfer in the adsorber.

The significance of the properties of the adsorption material and the heat and mass transfer between adsorbent and heat exchanger walls in the adsorber may be easily understood, if the basic terms influencing COP [3.2] and the specific cooling power (SCP) are taken into consideration:

$$COP = \frac{H_{ev} \bullet m \bullet \Delta X - C_{ev} \bullet \Delta T_{ev}}{H_{ad} \bullet m \bullet \Delta X + C_{ad} \bullet \Delta T_{ad}}$$ [3.8]

$$SCP = \frac{H_{ev} \bullet m \bullet \Delta X - Q_{ev} \bullet \Delta T_{ev}}{t_{cyc} \bullet V}$$ [3.9]

where $H_{ev}$ and $H_{ad}$ are the enthalpy of evaporation and adsorption, $m$ is the mass of adsorption material in the adsorber, $\Delta X$ is the specific water uptake of the adsorbent during adsorption, $C_{ev}$ and $C_{ad}$ are the thermal mass of the evaporator and the adsorber, $\Delta T_{ev}$ and $\Delta T_{ad}$ are the temperature swing of evaporator and adsorber, $t_{cyc}$ is the cycle time and $V$ is the volume of the machine.

The design target of adsorption chillers is to keep the thermal masses of adsorber and evaporator as small as possible and avoid a thermal swing in the evaporator as done with option 2 design. Due to the considerably lower thermal conductivity of adsorption materials, a reduction of thermal mass (and consequently the heat exchanger surface of the adsorber) improves COP but also increases the cycle time tcyc and leads to lower SCP [3.9]. Therefore, the dominant term which positively influences COP and SCP is m • $\Delta X$.

Recently, a series of new adsorption materials have been studied as an alternative to silica gel in the field of lower driving temperatures. The most prominent groups of materials are a certain class of zeolites, where silicon is exchanged with phosphor (AlPOs) and metal organic frameworks (MOFs). These materials have the property that a large portion of the overall adsorption capacity is adsorbed in a very narrow range of temperature and vapor pressure conditions. Choosing a material, with its range within the limits of the operation conditions, leads to a considerably higher water uptake than for silica gel.

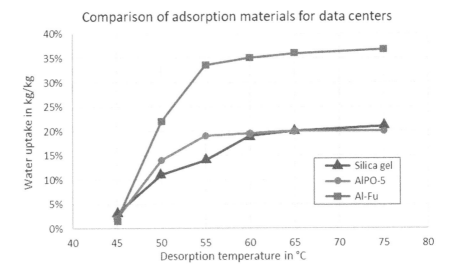

**Figure 3.19.** *Water uptake of new adsorbent material. For a color version of this figure, see www.iste.co.uk/brochard/energy.zip*

Figure 3.19 presents the water uptake of new adsorbents (zeolite AlPO-5 and MOF aluminum fumarate Al-Fu) versus silica gel at temperatures between 45°C and 55°C (outlet water temperature of the water-cooled servers) at an evaporation temperature of 18°C and an adsorption and condensation temperature of 30°C.

These new materials are very promising because for both groups of materials (zeolites and MOFs), coating technologies enable the adsorbents increase in mass in the adsorber while keeping good heat and mass transfer.

For zeolites, SorTech AG (now Fahrenheit GmbH) has developed a coating method that is based on direct crystallization of zeolite on heat exchanger surfaces by partial support transformation of the aluminum surface into zeolite, provided that the aluminum atoms to be incorporated into the lattice of zeolite during synthesis. This process leads to a very dense and stable layer of zeolite on the heat exchangers surface and ensures a good heat and mass transfer for high SCP (Wittstadt *et al.* 2017).

For MOFs, the Fraunhofer-Institute for Solar Energy Systems (ISE) has developed a binder-based coating method, as well a direct crystallization on heat-exchanger surfaces, thus solving the technical task of heat and mass transfer in a similar manner as with zeolite (Fröhlich *et al.* 2016)

Although there is no optimized adsorption chiller for data center applications on the market up to now (January 2019), these new approaches will boost the development of low-temperature chillers and novel products are expected in the near future.

# Power Consumption of Servers and Workloads

This chapter covers the theoretical power and performance characteristics of Intel Xeon processors and NVIDIA GPUs across several generations. It also presents power, thermal and performance measurements of air-cooled platforms equipped with an Intel Xeon processor and NVIDIA GPU running a selection of workloads.

While we take Intel processors and NVIDIA GPUs as examples, CPUs and GPUs developed by other vendors like AMD (Mutjaba 2018; Wikipedia n.d.) or ARM (ARM n.d.) follow the same trends as the law of physics are the same for all.

## 4.1. Trends in power consumption for processors

Table 4.1 presents the Thermal Design Power (TDP), cores/chip, lithography size, core frequency, number of transistors per chip and peak floating-point performance in single and double precision (DP) gigaflops (GFlops) for the Intel Xeon processors from Woodcrest in 2006, which was the first Intel Core microarchitecture[1] up to Skylake in 2017. TDP of a processor is the maximum power it can dissipate without exceeding the maximum junction temperature this CPU can sustain. Single precision (SP) and DP GFlops are the theoretical peak performance of all cores on the socket. This peak performance is obtained by multiplying the number of

---

1 Available at: https://en.wikipedia.org/wiki/Intel_Core_(microarchitecture) [Accessed April 30, 2019].

cores on the socket × the core frequency × the number of SP or DP operations the processor is theoretically capable of executing in one processor cycle. SP and DP are also sometimes called FP32 and FP64 since SP and DP floating point numbers are represented with 32 and 64 bits. The information in this table is extracted from Intel Xeon product specifications[2], with the exception of the number of transistors for Skylake, which we estimated as Intel is not publishing this information anymore. It should be noted that SP and DP peak performance are computed using the nominal frequency not the Turbo frequency, which is addressed in section 4.1.3.

| Release date | Micro-architecture | Processor Model | core / chip | TDP(W) | Lithography (nm) | Transistors (Billions) | Core frequency (GHz) | Peak SP Flops (GFlops) | Peak DP Flops (Gflops) |
|---|---|---|---|---|---|---|---|---|---|
| June 26, 2006 | Woodcrest | Intel Xeon 5160 | 2 | 80 | 65 | 0.291 | 3.0 | 48 | 24 |
| November 12, 2007 | Harpertown | Intel Xeon 5460 | 4 | 120 | 45 | 0.820 | 3.16 | 101 | 51 |
| March 30, 2009 | Nehalem | Intel Xeon 5580 | 4 | 130 | 45 | 0.731 | 3.20 | 102 | 51 |
| March 16, 2010 | Westmere | Intel Xeon 5690 | 6 | 130 | 32 | 1.170 | 3.46 | 166 | 83 |
| May 1, 2012 | SandyBridge | Intel Xeon E5-2690 | 8 | 135 | 32 | 2.270 | 2.90 | 371 | 186 |
| October 1, 2013 | IvyBridge | Intel Xeon E5-2697v2 | 12 | 130 | 22 | 4.310 | 2.70 | 518 | 259 |
| September 9, 2014 | Haswell | Intel Xeon E5-2699v3 | 18 | 145 | 22 | 5.560 | 2.30 | 1325 | 662 |
| March 1, 2016 | Broadwell | Intel Xeon E5-2699v4 | 22 | 145 | 14 | 7.200 | 2.20 | 1549 | 774 |
| July 11, 2017 | Skylake | Intel Xeon 8180 | 28 | 205 | 14 | 13.086 | 2.50 | 4480 | 2240 |

**Table 4.1.** *Intel Xeon processors characteristics from 2006 to 2017*

Figures 4.1 and 4.2 plot how lithography, peak performance measured in SP Gflops, and TDP have evolved over time. Given the ratio of SP to DP Flops is constant and equal to 2 for these processors, the DP GFlops graph will be similar to the SP GFlops graph.

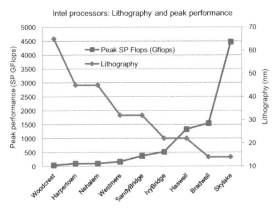

**Figure 4.1.** *Lithography and peak performance (SP GFlops) for Xeon architectures*

---

2    Available    at:    https://ark.intel.com/content/www/us/en/ark.html#@Processors [Accessed May 7, 2019].

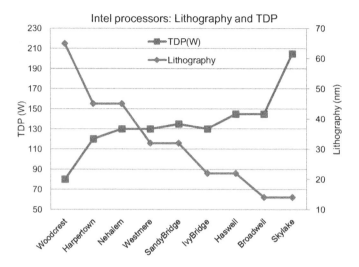

**Figure 4.2.** *Lithography and TDP for Xeon architectures*

In Figure 4.1, the lithography curve in blue shows the well-known Intel "tick-tock" model where a new architecture is introduced at same lithography size ("tock"), while the new finer lithography ("tick") is introduced on the same architecture. This model reduces risks to introduce two innovations at the same time, knowing that a new architecture will improve the chip performance at same lithography size, and a new lithography will improve performance with the same microarchitecture. For example, "ticks" introduce finer lithography from Woodcrest to Harpertown, Nehalem to Westmere, Sandy Bridge to Ivy Bridge, Haswell to Broadwell, while "tocks" introduce new microarchitectures from Harpertown to Nehalem, Westmere to Sandy Bridge, Ivy Bridge to Haswell and Broadwell to Skylake. Figure 4.1 shows the exponential improvement of peak performance over time, which was named as "Moore law" and which we will explain in more detail later in section 4.1.1. Figure 4.1 shows also the major impact of microarchitecture changes, which we will also explain later in sections 4.1.2 and 4.1.3.

Figure 4.2 shows the evolution of lithography size and TDP over the same period.

We note that TDP has been pretty flat from Harpertown to Broadwell, while it increased sharply from Woodcrest to Harpertown, and Broadwell to

Skylake. The increased TDP from Woodcrest to Harpertown comes from the following: the Harpertown chip has many more transistors (about 2.8×, including a much larger cache from 4 to 12 MB) running at about the same frequency as Woodcrest, and the lithography improvement (from 65 to 45 nm) leads to pack these transistors with the same package size. At the same time, the voltage reduction (from 1.0 to 0.85 V) and the increased frequency (from 3.0 to 3.17 GHz) were not able to cope with the increased density transistor leading to an increased TDP (120 W vs. 80 W) and a violation of Dennard scaling law (see next section). The increased TDP from Broadwell to Skylake is due to the new microarchitecture introducing very powerful instruction (AVX-512 instructions are covered in section 4.1.2) with longer registers, leading to a larger chip at the same lithography and frequency. A similar trend for higher TDP will be also reflected for GPUs in section 4.2.

As theoretical peak performance does not reflect the actual performance of a processor, Table 4.2 presents the same information as in Table 4.1 based on the SPEC_fp benchmark instead of theoretical peak performance. SPEC_fp is the floating-point performance of a core measured by the SPEC CPU 2006 benchmark (SPEC 2006), whereas SPEC_fp rate is the floating-point performance measured using all cores on the socket.

| Release date | Micro-architecture | Processor Model | core /chip | TDP(W) | Lithography (nm) | Transistors (Billions) | Core frequency (GHz) | SPEC_fp | SPEC_fp rate |
|---|---|---|---|---|---|---|---|---|---|
| June 26, 2006 | Woodcrest | Intel Xeon 5160 | 2 | 80 | 65 | 0.291 | 3.0 | 17.7 | 45.5 |
| November 12, 2007 | Harpertown | Intel Xeon 5460 | 4 | 120 | 45 | 0.820 | 3.16 | 25.4 | 79.6 |
| March 30, 2009 | Nehalem | Intel Xeon 5580 | 4 | 130 | 45 | 0.731 | 3.20 | 41.1 | 202 |
| March 16, 2010 | Westmere-EP | Intel Xeon 5690 | 6 | 130 | 32 | 1.170 | 3.46 | 63.7 | 273 |
| May 1, 2012 | SandyBridge | Intel Xeon E5-2690 | 8 | 135 | 32 | 2.270 | 2.90 | 94.8 | 507 |
| October 1, 2013 | IvyBridge | Intel Xeon E5-2697v2 | 12 | 130 | 22 | 4.310 | 2.70 | 104 | 696 |
| September 9, 2014 | Haswell | Intel Xeon E5-2699v3 | 18 | 145 | 22 | 5.560 | 2.30 | 116 | 949 |
| March 1, 2016 | Broadwell | Intel Xeon E5-2699v4 | 22 | 145 | 14 | 7.200 | 2.20 | 128 | 1160 |
| July 11, 2017 | Skylake | Intel Xeon 8180 | 28 | 205 | 14 | 13.086 | 2.50 | 155 | 1820 |

**Table 4.2.** *Intel processors characteristics from 2006 to 2017 with SPEC_fp*

### 4.1.1. *Moore's and Dennard's laws*

Moore's law was introduced by Moore (1965). It postulates a reduction in the size of transistors leading to more and more transistors per chip at the cost-effective optimum leading to a doubling of transistors every 2 years. This period was later changed to 18 months.

Dennard's scaling, also known as MOSFET scaling (Dennard *et al.* 1974), was introduced in 1974. It claims that as transistors get smaller, their power density stays constant, so that the power use stays in proportion with area. Therefore, in relation with Moore's law, it claims the performance per watt is growing exponentially at roughly the same rate as Moore's law.

As Moore's and Dennard's scaling laws are empirical, let us check how Intel Xeon processors followed these laws from 2006 to 2017.

Figure 4.3 plots the number of transistors in each chip from 2006 to 2017 as extracted from Table 4.1.

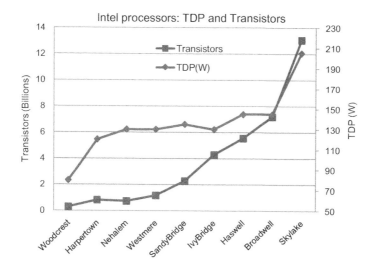

**Figure 4.3.** *Number of transistors and TDP for Xeon architectures*

In Figure 4.3 and Table 4.1, we note that the number of transistors has steadily increased at every chip generation except from Harpertown to Nehalem. Over 11 years, Moore's law predicts that the number of transistors should grow by a factor 45.2 if doubling every 2 years while it should grow by 155 with a doubling every 18 month. As the number of transistors grew by a factor 44.9, we see Moore's law has been followed with a doubling every 2 years. The fact that the number of transistors even decreased from Harpertown to Nehalem is due to a change of microarchitecture with Nehalem introducing memory controller on chip versus front side bus (FSB), which increased greatly the sustained performance of the processor and therefore leading to a reduced cache size from 12 to 8 MB.

Looking ahead, while a new lithography size has been introduced every 30 months from 2006 to 2011 from 65 to 14nm, Intel recently announced (Shenoy 2018) the next Xeon processor Cascade Lake would still be using 14 nm and only Ice Lake in 2020 will use 10 nm, showing a deceleration in Moore's law. Other manufacturer like AMD will introduce smaller lithography sooner like 7 nm (AMD Zen2 2018). While we see deceleration in lithography improvements, there is no deceleration in the increased number of cores.

As Moore's law is also sometimes interpreted as the doubling of performance, let us check how this law has been followed using different performance metrics.

Figure 4.4 plots the SP peak performance and SPEC_fp rate growth of Intel Xeon processors from 2006 to 2017.

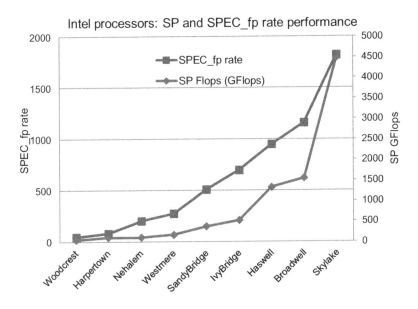

**Figure 4.4.** *SP and SPEC_fp rate performance for Xeon architectures*

Taking SP peak GFlops performance as the performance metric, we note SP peak performance has grown by a factor of 93, showing a doubling of performance every 20 months, leveraging the effect of new microarchitectures and new instructions such AVX2 and AVX-512 (see

Table 4.3). Taking SPEC_fp rate as the performance metric, SPEC_fp rate has grown by a factor of 40, following Moore's law with a doubling of performance every 24 months. This lower performance improvement for SPEC_fp versus peak performance happens since only a few codes, which are part of the SPEC_fp benchmark, make effective use of the new AVX2 or AVX-512 instructions. We will see this again when we look at real applications in section 5.1.6.

Figure 4.5 represents the performance per watt curve over the same period, taking both SP peak performance and SPEC_fp rate performance as metrics.

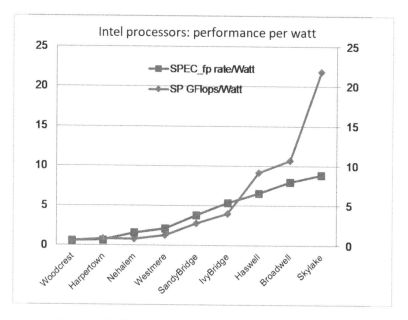

**Figure 4.5.** *Performance per watt for Xeon architectures*

It shows SP peak performance per watt increased by a factor 36.4 over 11 years while SPEC_fp rate per watt increased by a factor 15.6.

From a Dennard's law perspective, SP per watt doubled every 21 months while SPEC_fp rate per watt doubled every 33 months. Therefore, depending on the performance metric used, we see again a different evolution if we look at peak performance or sustained performance measured by SPEC_fp rate. And if we look only at the evolution of SPEC_fp rate per watt from Nehalem to Skylake, we see it has been doubling only every 40 months, showing a deceleration of Dennard's law that is causing serious power and energy issues.

In conclusion, to keep up with Moore's law, Intel Xeon processors are increasing TDP, and this trend will not stop with the next processor generation, leading to a major power problem. From a Dennard's law perspective, taking SPEC_fp as reference, performance per watt growth rate is slower than Moore's law and slowing down significantly.

### 4.1.2. Floating point instructions on Xeon processors

Table 4.3 presents the different instructions set Intel introduced from Woodcrest to Skylake with their floating-point characteristics and the number of SP or DP operations they can theoretically perform.

| Microarchitecture | Instruction Set | register length | FP execution units | SP Flops / cycle | DP Flops / cycle |
|---|---|---|---|---|---|
| Woodcrest | SSE3 | 128 | 2 FP 128 | 8 | 4 |
| Harpertown | SSE4 | 128 | 2 FP 128 | 8 | 4 |
| Nehalem | SSE4 | 128 | 2 FP 128 | 8 | 4 |
| Sandybridge | AVX | 256 | 2 FP 256 | 16 | 8 |
| Haswell/Broadwell | AVX2 & FMA | 256 | 2 FP FMA 256 | 32 | 16 |
| Skylake | AVX-512 & FMA | 512 | 2 FP FMA 512 | 64 | 32 |

**Table 4.3.** *Intel Xeon microarchitecture characteristics*

Over time and the different Xeon microarchitectures, Intel processors have supported more complex and powerful instructions able to produce more Flops per cycle, which is one reason processors have been able to keep up with Moore's law from a performance perspective, but at the expense of increased TDP power as we have discussed in previous section.

Fused multiply-add (FMA) and Advanced Vector Extensions (AVX) instructions are very good examples of such powerful instructions. SSE and AVX instructions are SIMD instructions (single instruction multiple data) introduced to operate on larger number of bits (128 bits for SSE, 256 and 512 bits for AVX) and therefore capable of producing more operations in one cycle as shown in Table 4.3. The FMA instruction set is an extension to the Streaming SIMD Extensions (SSE) and Advanced Vector Extensions (AVX) to perform FMA operations.

FMA is a floating-point multiply-add operation $a+b{\times}c$ performed in one step, with a single rounding. Where a unfused multiply-add would compute the product $b{\times}c$, round it to $N$ significant bits, add the result to $a$ and round back to $N$ significant bits, a fused multiply-add would compute the entire expression $a+b{\times}c$ to its full precision before rounding the final result down to $N$ significant bits in one step. How applications can effectively make use of these complex instructions depends on the type of operations each application uses and what the compiler is able to generate. For example, if a code only uses addition, subtraction or multiplication but no FMA, then the potential of Flops per cycle is divided by two unless the compiler can generate FMA operations by itself based on a succession of additions, subtractions or multiplications.

Examples showing the effective use of these instructions on different workloads will be presented in section 5.1.

### 4.1.3. *CPU frequency of instructions on Intel Xeon processors*

Before Nehalem, Intel processors were operating at a reference frequency called the nominal frequency, meaning all instructions were executed at this base nominal frequency. With Nehalem, Intel introduced Turbo Boost Technology (TBT). TBT is a microprocessor technology developed by Intel that attempts to enable temporary higher performance by opportunistically and automatically changing the P-state (frequency/voltage pair, according to ACPI terminology presented in section 4.5). This feature automatically kicks in on TBT-enabled processors when there is sufficient headroom – subject to power rating, temperature rating and current limits.

With Intel TBT, instructions can be executed at a higher frequency than nominal if those instructions running at nominal frequency were below the TDP of the processor. Therefore, under TBT, instructions can be boosted at a frequency higher than nominal until they reach processor TDP. Later with Sandy Bridge, Intel introduced Intel Turbo Boost Technology 2.0 and then Intel Turbo Boost Max 3.0 in 2016 with Broadwell (WikiChip n.d.), which we will present in section 5.1.

With the introduction of AVX 2.0 instructions (and later with AVX-512 instructions), as these more powerful instructions are using more power than SSE instructions at the same frequency, Intel introduced an AVX 2.0 base frequency and AVX-512 base frequency lower than base non-AVX frequency to take into account these differences of power consumption depending on the type of instructions executed.

Table 4.4 shows the base frequency for non-AVX, AVX 2.0 and AVX-512 instructions for different Xeon Skylake SKUs (Intel Xeon Scalable Specifications 2018). Columns show the maximum core frequency in Turbo mode for each number of active cores.

| SKU | Cores | LLC (MB) | TDP (W) | Base non-AVX Core Frequency (GHz) | 1 | 2 | 3 | 4 | 5 | 6 | 7 | 8 | 9 | 10 | 11 | 12 | 13 | 14 | 15 | 16 | 17 | 18 | 19 | 20 |
|---|---|---|---|---|---|---|---|---|---|---|---|---|---|---|---|---|---|---|---|---|---|---|---|---|
| 6148 | 20 | 27.5 | 150 | 2.4 | 3.7 | 3.7 | 3.5 | 3.5 | 3.4 | 3.4 | 3.4 | 3.4 | 3.4 | 3.4 | 3.4 | 3.4 | 3.4 | 3.4 | 3.4 | 3.4 | 3.1 | 3.1 | 3.1 | 3.1 |
| 6154 | 18 | 24.75 | 200 | 3 | 3.7 | 3.7 | 3.7 | 3.7 | 3.7 | 3.7 | 3.7 | 3.7 | 3.7 | 3.7 | 3.7 | 3.7 | 3.7 | 3.7 | 3.7 | 3.7 | 3.7 | 3.7 | | |
| 6150 | 18 | 24.75 | 165 | 2.7 | 3.7 | 3.7 | 3.5 | 3.5 | 3.4 | 3.4 | 3.4 | 3.4 | 3.4 | 3.4 | 3.4 | 3.4 | 3.4 | 3.4 | 3.4 | 3.4 | 3.4 | 3.4 | | |
| 6142 | 16 | 22 | 150 | 2.6 | 3.7 | 3.7 | 3.5 | 3.5 | 3.4 | 3.4 | 3.4 | 3.4 | 3.4 | 3.4 | 3.4 | 3.4 | 3.3 | 3.3 | 3.3 | 3.3 | | | | |
| 6132 | 14 | 19.25 | 140 | 2.6 | 3.7 | 3.7 | 3.5 | 3.5 | 3.4 | 3.4 | 3.4 | 3.4 | 3.4 | 3.4 | 3.4 | 3.4 | 3.3 | 3.3 | | | | | | |
| 6146 | 12 | 24.75 | 165 | 3.2 | 4.2 | 4.2 | 4 | 4 | 3.9 | 3.9 | 3.9 | 3.9 | 3.9 | 3.9 | 3.9 | 3.9 | | | | | | | | |
| 6136 | 12 | 24.75 | 150 | 3 | 3.7 | 3.7 | 3.6 | 3.6 | 3.6 | 3.6 | 3.6 | 3.6 | 3.6 | 3.6 | 3.6 | 3.6 | | | | | | | | |
| 6126 | 12 | 19.25 | 125 | 2.6 | 3.7 | 3.7 | 3.5 | 3.5 | 3.4 | 3.4 | 3.4 | 3.4 | 3.3 | 3.3 | 3.3 | 3.3 | | | | | | | | |
| 6144 | 8 | 24.75 | 150 | 3.5 | 4.2 | 4.2 | 4.1 | 4.1 | 4.1 | 4.1 | 4.1 | 4.1 | | | | | | | | | | | | |
| 6134 | 8 | 24.75 | 130 | 3.2 | 3.7 | 3.7 | 3.7 | 3.7 | 3.7 | 3.7 | 3.7 | 3.7 | | | | | | | | | | | | |
| 6128 | 6 | 19.25 | 115 | 3.4 | 3.7 | 3.7 | 3.7 | 3.7 | 3.7 | 3.7 | | | | | | | | | | | | | | |

| SKU | Cores | LLC (MB) | TDP (W) | Base AVX 2.0 Core Frequency (GHz) | 1 | 2 | 3 | 4 | 5 | 6 | 7 | 8 | 9 | 10 | 11 | 12 | 13 | 14 | 15 | 16 | 17 | 18 | 19 | 20 |
|---|---|---|---|---|---|---|---|---|---|---|---|---|---|---|---|---|---|---|---|---|---|---|---|---|
| 6148 | 20 | 27.5 | 150 | 1.9 | 3.6 | 3.6 | 3.4 | 3.4 | 3.3 | 3.3 | 3.3 | 3.3 | 3.1 | 3.1 | 3.1 | 3.1 | 2.8 | 2.8 | 2.8 | 2.8 | 2.6 | 2.6 | 2.6 | 2.6 |
| 6154 | 18 | 24.75 | 200 | 2.6 | 3.6 | 3.6 | 3.4 | 3.4 | 3.3 | 3.3 | 3.3 | 3.3 | 3.3 | 3.3 | 3.3 | 3.3 | 3.3 | 3.3 | 3.3 | 3.3 | | | | |
| 6150 | 18 | 24.75 | 165 | 2.3 | 3.6 | 3.6 | 3.4 | 3.4 | 3.3 | 3.3 | 3.3 | 3.3 | 3.3 | 3.3 | 3.3 | 3.3 | 3.1 | 3.1 | 3.1 | 3.1 | 3 | 3 | | |
| 6142 | 16 | 22 | 150 | 2.2 | 3.6 | 3.6 | 3.4 | 3.4 | 3.3 | 3.3 | 3.3 | 3.3 | 3.2 | 3.2 | 3.2 | 3.2 | 2.9 | 2.9 | 2.9 | 2.9 | | | | |
| 6132 | 14 | 19.25 | 140 | 2.2 | 3.6 | 3.6 | 3.4 | 3.4 | 3.3 | 3.3 | 3.3 | 3.3 | 3 | 3 | 3 | 3 | 2.9 | 2.9 | | | | | | |
| 6146 | 12 | 24.75 | 165 | 2.6 | 3.6 | 3.6 | 3.4 | 3.4 | 3.3 | 3.3 | 3.3 | 3.3 | 3.3 | 3.3 | 3.3 | 3.3 | | | | | | | | |
| 6136 | 12 | 24.75 | 150 | 2.6 | 3.6 | 3.6 | 3.4 | 3.4 | 3.3 | 3.3 | 3.3 | 3.3 | 3.3 | 3.3 | 3.3 | 3.3 | | | | | | | | |
| 6126 | 12 | 19.25 | 125 | 2.2 | 3.6 | 3.6 | 3.4 | 3.4 | 3.3 | 3.3 | 3.3 | 3.3 | 2.9 | 2.9 | 2.9 | 2.9 | | | | | | | | |
| 6144 | 8 | 24.75 | 150 | 2.8 | 3.6 | 3.6 | 3.5 | 3.5 | 3.5 | 3.5 | 3.5 | 3.5 | | | | | | | | | | | | |
| 6134 | 8 | 24.75 | 130 | 2.7 | 3.6 | 3.6 | 3.4 | 3.4 | 3.4 | 3.4 | 3.4 | 3.4 | | | | | | | | | | | | |
| 6128 | 6 | 19.25 | 115 | 2.9 | 3.6 | 3.6 | 3.6 | 3.6 | 3.6 | 3.6 | | | | | | | | | | | | | | |

| SKU | Cores | LLC (MB) | TDP (W) | Base AVX-512 Core Frequency (GHz) | 1 | 2 | 3 | 4 | 5 | 6 | 7 | 8 | 9 | 10 | 11 | 12 | 13 | 14 | 15 | 16 | 17 | 18 | 19 | 20 |
|---|---|---|---|---|---|---|---|---|---|---|---|---|---|---|---|---|---|---|---|---|---|---|---|---|
| 6148 | 20 | 27.5 | 150 | 1.6 | 3.5 | 3.5 | 3.3 | 3.3 | 3.1 | 3.1 | 3.1 | 3.1 | 2.6 | 2.6 | 2.6 | 2.6 | 2.3 | 2.3 | 2.3 | 2.3 | 2.2 | 2.2 | 2.2 | 2.2 |
| 6154 | 18 | 24.75 | 200 | 2.1 | 3.5 | 3.5 | 3.3 | 3.3 | 3.2 | 3.2 | 3.2 | 3.2 | 3.1 | 3.1 | 3.1 | 3.1 | 2.8 | 2.8 | 2.8 | 2.8 | 2.7 | 2.7 | | |
| 6150 | 18 | 24.75 | 165 | 1.9 | 3.5 | 3.5 | 3.3 | 3.3 | 3.2 | 3.2 | 3.2 | 3.2 | 2.9 | 2.9 | 2.9 | 2.9 | 2.6 | 2.6 | 2.6 | 2.6 | 2.5 | 2.5 | | |
| 6142 | 16 | 22 | 150 | 1.6 | 3.5 | 3.5 | 3.3 | 3.3 | 2.8 | 2.8 | 2.8 | 2.8 | 2.4 | 2.4 | 2.4 | 2.4 | 2.2 | 2.2 | 2.2 | 2.2 | | | | |
| 6132 | 14 | 19.25 | 140 | 1.7 | 3.5 | 3.5 | 3.3 | 3.3 | 2.8 | 2.8 | 2.8 | 2.8 | 2.4 | 2.4 | 2.4 | 2.4 | 2.3 | 2.3 | | | | | | |
| 6146 | 12 | 24.75 | 165 | 2.1 | 3.5 | 3.5 | 3.3 | 3.3 | 3.1 | 3.1 | 3.1 | 3.1 | 2.7 | 2.7 | 2.7 | 2.7 | | | | | | | | |
| 6136 | 12 | 24.75 | 150 | 2.1 | 3.5 | 3.5 | 3.3 | 3.3 | 3.1 | 3.1 | 3.1 | 3.1 | 2.7 | 2.7 | 2.7 | 2.7 | | | | | | | | |
| 6126 | 12 | 19.25 | 125 | 1.7 | 3.5 | 3.5 | 3.3 | 3.3 | 2.6 | 2.6 | 2.6 | 2.6 | 2.3 | 2.3 | 2.3 | 2.3 | | | | | | | | |
| 6144 | 8 | 24.75 | 150 | 2.2 | 3.5 | 3.5 | 3.3 | 3.3 | 2.8 | 2.8 | 2.8 | 2.8 | | | | | | | | | | | | |
| 6134 | 8 | 24.75 | 130 | 2.1 | 3.5 | 3.5 | 3.3 | 3.3 | 2.7 | 2.7 | 2.7 | 2.7 | | | | | | | | | | | | |
| 6128 | 6 | 19.25 | 115 | 2.3 | 3.5 | 3.5 | 3.3 | 3.3 | 2.9 | 2.9 | | | | | | | | | | | | | | |

**Table 4.4.** *Base and Turbo frequency for non-AVX, AVX 2.0 and AVX-512 instructions on 6xxx Skylake processors*

As we can see, the AVX-512 base frequencies are lower than AVX 2.0 base frequencies, which themselves are lower than non-AVX frequencies.

## 4.2. Trends in power consumption for GPUs

The trend of increasing power consumption and number of transistors and performance per chip we described in section 4.1 is not unique to processors.

Accelerators and GPUs have been following the same evolution. Table 4.5 presents for NVIDIA GPU from 2009 to 2017 the same data as Table 4.1 for Intel Xeon processors. Content is gathered from GPU Database (n.d.) and NVIDIA (2017). This table does not report the Volta Tensor cores, which we will discuss in section 4.4.

| Microarchitecture and GPU model | Chip | # of CUDA Cores | TDP (W) | Lithography (nm) | Transistors (Billions) | CUDA core frequency (GHz) | Peak SP Flops (TFlops) | Peak DP Flops (TFlops) | Ratio SP to DP |
|---|---|---|---|---|---|---|---|---|---|
| Tesla T10 | GT200 | 240 | 188 | 55 | 1.4 | 1.29 | 0.62 | 0.08 | 8 |
| Fermi M20 | GF100 | 448 | 247 | 40 | 3.2 | 1.15 | 1.03 | 0.52 | 2 |
| Kepler K10 | 2 x GK104 | 3072 | 225 | 28 | 7.1 | 0.74 | 4.55 | 0.19 | 24 |
| Kepler K80 | 2 x GK210 | 4992 | 300 | 28 | 14.2 | 0.56 | 5.59 | 1.86 | 3 |
| Pascal P100 SXM2 | GP100 | 3584 | 300 | 16 | 15.3 | 1.48 | 10.61 | 5.30 | 2 |
| Pascal P100 PCIe | GP100 | 3584 | 250 | 16 | 15.3 | 1.30 | 9.32 | 4.66 | 2 |
| Volta V100 SXM2 | GV100 | 5120 | 300 | 12 | 21.1 | 1.45 | 14.89 | 7.44 | 2 |
| Volta V100 PCIe | GV100 | 5120 | 250 | 12 | 21.1 | 1.37 | 14.03 | 7.01 | 2 |

**Table 4.5.** *NVIDIA GPUs characteristics from 2009 to 2017*

The theoretical peak Flops SP is computed based on the base clock frequency of the CUDA cores and not their Max Boost clock frequency to be comparable with the way theoretical peak is reported on Intel Xeon processors in Table 4.1. The theoretical peak Flops DP varies depending on the NVIDA GPU generation with a varying ratio of SP/DP Flops[3] as shown in the last column of Table 4.5, while it was constant and equal to ½ for Intel Xeon processors.

While lithography size has been following the evolution, we note several major differences between Tables 4.1 and 4.10. The first difference is the number of transistors, which is higher for NVIDIA GPUs than for Intel Xeon processors at equivalent lithography size due to the fact that GPU chips are larger and have more transistors than Intel Xeon chips. The second difference is a higher TDP for NVIDIA GPU versus Intel Xeon processors at equivalent lithography size and release date. The third is the performance difference, which if we take SP Flops shows a threefold delta (14 TFlops vs. 4.5 TFlops). This large difference comes from the fact that GPUs are not

---

3 Fermi microarchitecture, available at: https://en.wikipedia.org/wiki/Fermi_(micro architecture)#Performance; Kepler microarchitecture, available at: https://en.wikipedia.org/wiki/ Kepler_(microarchitecture)#Performance; Maxwell microarchitecture, available at: https://en. wikipedia.org/wiki/Maxwell_(microarchitecture)#Performance; Pascal microarchitecture, available at: https://en.wikipedia.org/wiki/Pascal_(microarchitecture)#Performance; Tesla microarchitecture, available at: https://en.wikipedia.org/wiki/Tesla_(microarchitecture)#Performance; Volta microarchitecture, available at: https://en.wikipedia.org/wiki/Volta_ (microarchitecture)# Performance. [All URLs accessed April 30, 2019].

general-purpose processors and therefore use more specialized units which use less die area from a silicon perspective leading to a much higher number of processing cores. This advantage being balanced by the fact GPUs are co-processors requiring specific instructions adding programming complexity and leading to a wide variance of performance depending on the percentage of instructions running on the GPU versus the CPU.

Figures 4.6 and 4.7 plot the lithography size versus SP peak performance and lithography size versus TDP for NVIDIA GPUs similar to Figures 4.1 and 4.2 for Intel Xeon.

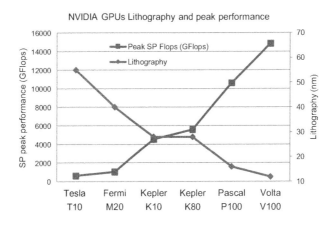

**Figure 4.6.** *Lithography and peak performance (SP GFlops) for NVIDIA GPUs*

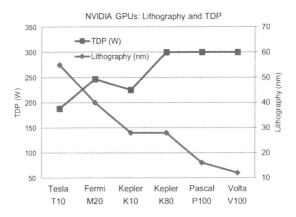

**Figure 4.7.** *Lithography and TDP (Watt) for NVIDIA GPUs*

## 4.2.1. *Moore's and Dennard's laws*

Figure 4.8 plots the number of transistors versus TDP.

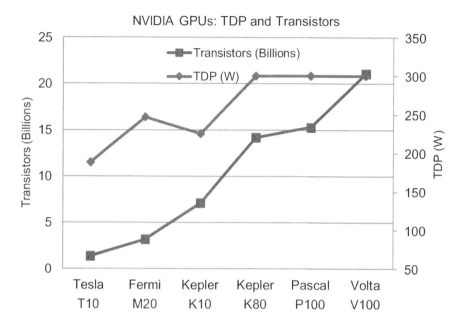

**Figure 4.8.** *TDP and transistors over NVIDIA architectures*

Comparing Figures 4.8 with 4.3 shows that GPUs have about twice as many transistors as CPUs as explained before, while the number of transistors per watt is about the same (70 million transistors per watt for V100 vs. 64 million transistors per watt for Skylake).

From a Moore's law perspective for transistors, the increase has been 15× during 98 months leading to a doubling in size every 25 months, which is quite well aligned with Intel Xeon, as well as for the TDP increase of 1.6× and the lithography progress of 4.6×.

From a Moore's law perspective for peak performance, SP peak Flops increased 24× leading to a doubling every 21.5 months, while DP peak Flops increased 96×, which is due to the microarchitecture improvement for DP instructions. Similar evolution is leading to the introduction of Tensor cores for AI operations, as will be discussed in section 4.5.

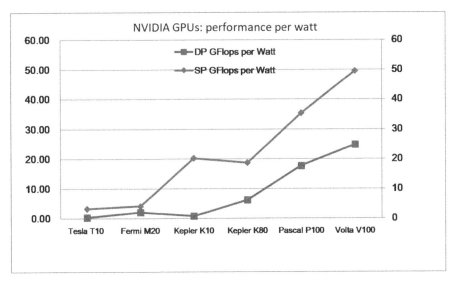

**Figure 4.9.** *SP and DP peak GFlops per watt for NVIDIA GPUs. For a color version of this figure, see www.iste.co.uk/brochard/energy.zip*

As shown in Figure 4.9, from a Dennard's law perspective, SP per watt has increased by 15× doubling every 25 months, which is similar to Intel Xeon doubling every 21 months (Figure 4.5). DP per watt increased 60×, again due to microarchitecture improvements.

## 4.3. ACPI states

Advanced Configuration and Power Interface (ACPI) is an open industry specification co-developed by different vendors. ACPI establishes industry-standard interfaces enabling operating system (OS)-directed configuration, power management and thermal management of mobile, desktop and server platforms. Since 2013, the UEFI Forum has taken over the ACPI mission, but it is still referred as ACPI (ACPI 2014).

Figure 4.10 gives an overall description of the ACPI states.

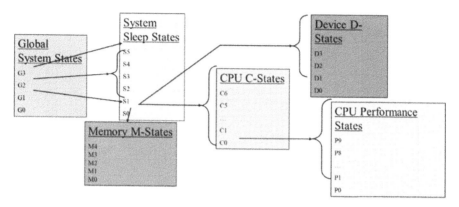

**Figure 4.10.** *ACPI states. For a color version of this figure, see www.iste.co.uk/brochard/energy.zip*

ACPI states define the activity state of all major components in a system: the overall system, the devices, the memory and the CPU. P0 and D0 are, for example, the power consumption and capability states when the processor or device is in active state, until it reaches the state of minimum power consumption Pn and Dn. The number of states for each component is defined by the designer of these components and it has increased a lot since 1999 when ACPI was first published.

G-states, in Figure 4.11, are global system states that define what operational state the entire server is in.

| G-State | Can Applications Run? | Wake up latency | OS Reboot Required | Comments | |
|---------|----------|----------|----------|----------|---|
| G3 | No | Longest | Yes | AC power is removed. Server is only being power by backup battery for RTC and CMOS. | |
| G2 | No | Long | Yes | System is in a soft-off state. For example, the power switch was pressed. System draws power from AUX rail of power delivery circuit. Power supply may or may not be switched off. | HIGHER POWER / HIGHER LATENCY |
| G1 | No | Short to medium | No | Standby or hibernate mode. | |
| G0 | Yes | None | No | System is fully on but some components could be in a power savings state. | |

**Figure 4.11.** *ACPI G-states*

| S-State | G-State | BIOS Reboot | OS Reboot | Comments |
|---------|---------|-------------|-----------|----------|
| S5 | G2 | Yes | Yes | Server is in a soft off state. When turned back on, the server must completely reinitialize with POST and the operating system. |
| S4 | G1 | Yes | No | A.K.A "Hibernate", "Suspend-to-disk". The state of the operating system (all memory contents and chip registers) is saved to a file on the HDD and the server is placed in a soft-off state. |
| S3 | G1 | No | No | A.K.A "Standby", "Suspend-to-RAM". The state of the chipset registers is saved to system memory and memory is placed in a low-power self-refresh state. To preserve the memory contents, power is supplied to the DRAMs in S3 state. |
| S2 | G1 | No | No | CPU caches are powered down. |
| S1 | G1 | No | No | A.K.A "Idle", "Standby" –if S3 not supported. Typically, when the OS is idle, it will halt the CPU and blank the monitor to save power. No power rails are switched off. |
| S0 | G0 | No | No | System is fully on but some components could be in a power savings state. |

**Figure 4.12.** *ACPI S-states*

S-states are system sleep states that define what sleep state the entire server is in.

When servers are idle, S3 state can save large amounts of power while keeping the latency at an acceptable level. This feature was used by IBM LoadLeveler Energy Aware Scheduler (IBM Knowledge Center n.d.) to minimize idle node power consumption.

Figure 4.13 presents the typical power saving and latency associated with the different S-states.

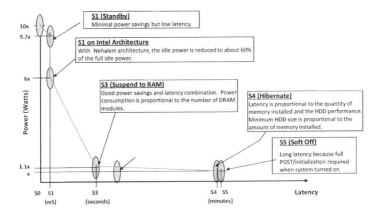

**Figure 4.13.** *Power saving and latency of S-sates*

The most familiar states users are aware of and the one of most interest for us in this section are the CPU P-states and C-states.

The OS places the CPU in different P-states depending on the amount of power needed to complete the current task. That is the difference with the CPU C-states, which are idle power saving states while P-states are execution power saving states.

C-states are CPU power saving states. The CPU transitions to C-states higher than C0 when it is idle after a period of time. All C-states occur when the server is in S0 state and G0 state.

Figure 4.14 presents a summary of each C-state with their implementation for Intel Nehalem architecture.

| C-State | CPU Core Description | CPU Package Description | | |
|---|---|---|---|---|
| C0 | CPU core is fully on | CPU package is fully on | | |
| C1 | CPU core clock is stopped | NA –C1E is the package C1 state. This naming is unique to C1E and is leftover from older CPUs. | | |
| C1E | NA –package only state | At least one CPU core is in C0/C1 state and all others are in higher numbered C-states. VRD switches to minimal voltage state. | HIGHER POWER | HIGHER LATENCY |
| C3 | C1 + CPU core caches are flushed | At least one CPU core is in C3 state and all others are in higher numbered C-states. C1E + Some uncore CLKs stopped and memory placed in fast self-refresh | | |
| C6 | C3 + CPU cores are powered down. CPU core state stored in last level cache | At least one CPU cores is in C6 state and all others are in higher numbered C-states. C3 package + CLKs stopped on most of the uncore and memory placed in slow self-refresh | | |
| C7 | C6 + last thread flushes remaining caches ways | All CPU cores are in C7. CPU package doesn't need to wake up for snoops. | | |

**Figure 4.14.** *Example of C-sates on Intel Nehalem*

CPU package refers to all the hardware contained in a CPU chip. "Uncore" refers to all the hardware except for the CPU cores. C-states can operate on each core separately or the entire CPU package. Core C-state transitions are controlled by the OS. Package C-state transitions are controlled by the hardware. The number of C-states and the savings associated with each is dependent on the specific type and SKU of CPU used.

Figure 4.15 presents a summary of each P-state. P-states are CPU performance states. The OS places the CPU in different P-states depending on the amount of power needed to complete the current task.

| P-State | Comments |
|---------|----------|
| P0 | CPU core running at maximum frequency and voltage |
| P1 | |

. 
. 
. 

| P9 | |
|-----|----|
| P10 | CPU core running at minimum frequency and voltage |

**Figure 4.15.** *Example of P-states*

For example, if a 2-GHz CPU core only needs to run at 1 GHz to complete a task, the OS may place the CPU core into a higher number P-state. P-states operate on each core separately. The OS controls the transitioning among the P-states. The number of P-states and the frequency and voltage associated with each is dependent on the specific type and SKU of CPU used. BIOS can restrict the total number of P-states revealed to the OS and can change this on the fly.

Figure 4.16 shows how frequency and voltage vary across the different P-states. At P0, frequency and voltage are at maximum. Then voltage is reduced down to $V_{min}$ (minimum CPU voltage). From $V_{max}$ to $V_{min}$, voltage and frequency vary linearly. After this point, a lower P-state will be reached by reducing frequency only until it reaches $F_{min}$ and $P_n$.

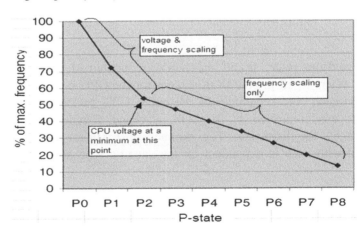

**Figure 4.16.** *P-states, voltage and frequency*

It should be noted that the ranking of P-states we described above with $P_0$ being the nominal frequency is valid when Turbo is not activated. When Turbo is selected (WikiChip n.d.), state $P_0$ is the turbo frequency, state $P_1$ is the nominal frequency and the frequency, which was corresponding to state $P_i$ when Turbo is not activated, is corresponding to state $P_{i+1}$ when Turbo is activated.

## 4.4. The power equation

In Table 4.1, we saw the number of cores on a socket of Intel Xeon processor increased by a factor 14× while its frequency decreased by 20% and TDP increased by 2.5×. On the other hand, for NVIDA GPU, we saw in Table 4.5 the number of cores increased by a factor 14×, while its frequency has been about flat and TDP increased by a factor 1.6×.

Why such an evolution?

TDP of a processor is the maximum power it can dissipate without exceeding the maximum junction temperature the CPU can sustain.

There are two major factors contributing to the CPU power consumption, the dynamic power consumption and the power loss due to transistor leakage currents:

$$P_{cpu} = P_{dyn} + P_{leak} \qquad [4.1]$$

By Ohm's law, the dynamic power $P_{dyn}$ consumed by a processor is given by:

$$P_{dyn} = C \cdot V^2 \cdot f \qquad [4.2]$$

where $C$ is capacitance, $f$ is frequency and $V$ is voltage, which means the dynamic power increases quadratically with the voltage and linearly with the frequency.

While the dynamic power consumption is dependent on the clock frequency, the leakage power $P_{leak}$ is dependent on the CPU supply voltage. We will come back to the power leakage in section 5.3.

If we look at how voltage and frequency vary with ACPI P-states (Figure 4.11), we see that between $P_0$ state and the P-state corresponding to the minimum voltage ($P_m$ with m < n where n is the highest possible P-state), voltage and frequency vary linearly.

Therefore, between $P_0$ and $P_m$, which is the range where a processor is executing workloads, [4.2] can be approximated with:

$$P \cong C.f^3 \qquad\qquad\qquad\qquad [4.3]$$

It shows dynamic power increases as the cube of frequency and how reducing the frequency when an application is running can significantly reduce the power consumption of a server.

Let us take an example. According to [4.3], at the same lithography, decreasing the frequency of a processor by 20% will reduce its dynamic power by $(0.20)^3$ (~50%). Therefore, as power is halved, twice as many transistors would consume the same power and provide a theoretical performance of 1.6 (2 × 0.80) times the theoretical performance of the original processor. On the other hand, if we were increasing the frequency of the original processor to reach the same peak performance, its power consumption would be multiplied by a factor = $1.6^3$ ~ 4.

This power equation is the logic driving the multicores and many cores eras, which all CPU and GPU manufacturers have been following for about 10 years steadily increasing cores at about constant frequency. The number of cores differs significantly between CPUs (in the tens) and GPUs (in the thousands) since a GPU core is much simpler leading to less transistors, die space and power consumption than a more complex CPU core. This is shown in Table 4.1 for the Xeon CPUs where the number of cores has steadily increased from Xeon Woodcrest dual core to Skylake 8180 with 28 cores per socket. For the same reasons, the number of cores will keep increasing as with the second generation Intel Xeon Cascade Lake with up to 56 cores per socket (Cascade Lake 9282 2019) and AMD EPYC Zen2 (Mutjaba 2018) with up to 64 cores per sockets using 7 nm lithography and a core frequency around 2.3 GHz. Similar evolution is shown in Table 4.5 for NVIDIA GPUs, which are playing an increasingly important role with thousands of simple cores running at low frequency like Blue Gene systems (IBM Icons n.d.), leading to greater performance per watt.

It is important to remark that this trend of increasing number of cores has recently taken a new turn with the introduction of more specialized cores, like Tensor cores in NVIDIA Volta GPU[4] and in the Google Tensor Processing Unit (TPU)[5]. Like CUDA cores which were designed by NVIDIA to optimally perform vector SP (FP32) and DP (FP64) operations heavily used by graphics and HPC applications, Tensor cores were designed to optimally perform AI operations. On NVIDIA Volta, Tensor cores implement a mixed precision FMA operation with FP16 multiply and FP32 accumulation to perform 4×4 matrix multiplication and accumulation operations heavily used by AI training and inference. It should be noted that inference sometimes uses only INT8 numbers (integer represented on 8 bits) like on the Google TPU 1.0 while TPU 2.0 and TPU 3.0 have been extended to perform also FP16 operations on top of INT8.

Table 4.6 compares peak SP TFlops (FP32) and Tensor TFlops (mixed FP16 and FP32 precision) performance and performance per Watt (GFlops/W) where only the power of the CPU and GPU is taken in consideration for Xeon Skylake 8180 and NVIDIA V100 to illustrate the trade-off between operation specialization, performance and performance per Watt, as we did for SP Flops in Tables 4.1 and 4.5 and Figures 4.5 and 4.9.

|  | TDP (Watt) | SP Tflops | SP Gflops/W | Tensor Tflops | Tensor Gflops/W |
|---|---|---|---|---|---|
| Intel Skylake 8180 | 205 | 4.5 | 21.9 | NA | NA |
| NVIDIA Volta V100 | 300 | 14.9 | 49.6 | 125 | 416.7 |

**Table 4.6.** *CPU and GPU performance and performance per watt*

While the SP performance ratio of GPU versus CPU is ~3.3× and SP performance per watt is ~2.3×, the Tensor versus FP core comparison is a factor 8.4 both on performance and performance per watt. The performance per Watt comparisons are a bit unfair regarding the CPU since the power used by the GPU does not include the CPU power of the host. We note also that all SP Flops we report in this table and in previous tables do not include Intel Turbo or NVIDIA GPU boost, while NVIDIA publishes Tensor Flops with GPU boost clock only (NVIDA V100 2018). Therefore, Tensor

---

4 Available at: https://www.nvidia.com/en-us/data-center/tensorcore [Accessed April 30, 2019].
5 Available at: https://cloud.google.com/tpu/docs/system-architecture#system_architecture [Accessed April 30, 2019].

performance is a bit optimistic (~5%), although this does not change the comparison much. A similar comparison has been reported by Jouppi *et al.* (2017) when comparing an Intel Haswell CPU, an NIVIDIA K80 GPU and a Google TPU1 tensor processor on real AI workloads. In this chapter, a much higher performance and performance per watt comparing the TPU 1.0 versus CPU or GPU are reported as the measurements are done with inference AI workloads using INT8 operations where TPU 1.0 is best of breed.

# 5

---

# Power and Performance of Workloads

---

## 5.1. Power and performance of workloads

### 5.1.1. *SKU power and performance variations*

The power consumption in a server depends very much on its configuration and the workloads it is executing. As our goal is also to compare the impact of different cooling technologies on power, thermal characteristics and performance, we want to reduce to a minimum the impact of other "variables" such as the power, thermal and performance variations across the same processor chips.

The performance/frequency variations of the same processor SKU have been measured by Aucun *et al.* (2016). It was also measured on the SuperMUC phase 2 system (see section 7.2.3) on nodes with the same configuration based on Intel Xeon Haswell 2697v3, the same "batch" of boards and with the same cooling/thermal conditions since the system was using water-cooled nodes. Figure 5.1 shows the distribution of node AVX2 frequency (x-axis) measured when running single-node HPL across the nodes with the number of nodes on y-axis.

As we can see, while the AVX2 base frequency of the 2697v3 processor is 2.2 GHz, the distribution of AVX2 measured frequency is a "bell" curve varying between 2.2 GHz and 2.4 GHz, which shows all processors are above Intel's 2.2GHz minimum specification but some are 8% faster.

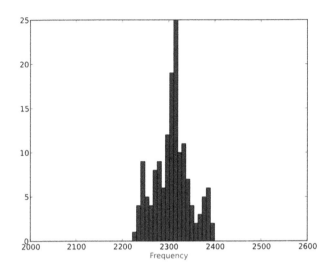

**Figure 5.1.** *AVX2 frequency across different 2697v3 processor SKU*

Therefore, we were careful to use the same system with exactly the same board and the same processors, dual in-line memory modules (DIMMs) and hard disk drive (HDD). In order to do so, we took a Lenovo ThinkSystem SD650, which is a water-cooled server, removed the water-cooling equipment and put the server on an air bench where we set a static volumetric flow rate. Therefore, the node did not handle any of its own cooling and had actually no system fans present during this test. This prototype server will be referred to in the following as "SD650 air-cooled". Then we took the board and the processors, DIMMs and HDD and put them in a water-cooled SD650 server, which we will call "SD650 water-cooled". This detailed work was conducted in the Lenovo Thermal Lab in Morrisville, NC. One side effect of the "SD650 air-cooled" prototype server where the system is not controlling dynamically its fan speed will be seen on the CPU temperature plots, which show an increasing CPU temperature during the workload execution. In section 5.1.7, we will see a different behavior when analyzing the measurements of this prototype air-cooled SD650 and the air-cooled SD530 product where the cooling algorithm is designed to maintain cooling margin on the CPUs and where the system firmware reacts to changes in system behavior to increase the system fans accordingly. The SD530 system fans are initially at their lower idle state before the exerciser is initiated. That is why we will see an initial peek in the CPU temperature, and even a second one for HPL due to the PL2 phase, before the temperature reduces to its steady-state behavior. Our decision to use such an air-cooled prototype has been driven by the desire to measure only the cooling effect between an air-cooled and a water-cooled server.

In section 5.2, we present the power, thermal and performance behavior of this air-cooled server running four different types of workloads. The measurements on the "water-cooled node" will be presented in section 5.3. The server is equipped with 2 Intel Xeon 6148 processors, 12 8GB dual rank DIMMs @ 2666 MHz and one HDD 1TB 2.5" 7.2K. The Intel Xeon 6148 is a 150 W TDP SKU as presented in Table 4.4.

### 5.1.2. *System parameters*

The power consumption of a server when running a workload will depend also on system parameters, which can be defined at boot time or dynamically.

We will discuss here the UEFI, the Turbo mode and the use of governors.

The Unified Extensible Firmware Interface (UEFI) is a specification that defines a software interface between an operating system and platform firmware.

The UEFI operating mode choices that will influence the power consumption and performance of a server are as follows:

1) minimal power mode strives to minimize the absolute power consumption of the system while it is operating. The tradeoff is that performance may be reduced in this mode depending on the application that is running;

2) efficiency-favor power mode maximizes the performance per watt efficiency with a bias toward power savings. It provides the best features for reducing power and increasing performance in applications where maximum bus speeds are not critical;

3) efficiency-favor performance mode optimizes the performance per watt efficiency with a bias toward performance;

4) maximum performance mode will maximize the absolute performance of the system without regard for power. In this mode, power consumption is not taken into consideration. Attributes like fan speed and heat output of the

system may increase in addition to power consumption. Efficiency of the system may go down in this mode, but the absolute performance may increase depending on the workload that is running.

Turbo Technology as explained in section 4.1.3 can also influence the performance and power consumption of a workload.

UEFI settings already configure the utilization of TURBO, setting it to ON or OFF. This attribute limits the maximum frequency to be used by the system. On top of the UEFI configuration, the CPU frequency can be dynamically modified by the CPU frequency driver and the CPU frequency policies supported by the loaded driver. The CPU frequency driver can be automatically compiled with the kernel or loaded as a kernel module. CPU frequency drivers implement CPU power schemes called governors (it can happen that a given driver does not support a specific governor).

CPU frequency is statically or dynamically selected based on the governor and considering the system load, in response to ACPI events, or manually by user programs. More than one governor can be installed but only one can be active at a time (and only one CPU frequency driver can be loaded). All the governors are limited by UEFI settings and policy limits, such as the minimum and maximum frequency, that can be modified by the sysadmin using tools such as cpupower.

The list of governors with main power scheme characteristics is as follows:

1) performance: this governor sets the CPU statically to the highest frequency given the max_freq and min_freq limits;

2) powersave: this governor sets the CPU statically to the lowest frequency given the max_freq and min_freq limits;

3) userspace: this governor allows privileged users to set the CPU to a specific static frequency;

4) Ondemand, conservative and schedutil: these governors set the CPU frequency depending on the current system load but differ on the way to compute the load and the degree of frequency variation, being more or less conservative. The CPUfreq governor "ondemand" sets the CPU frequency depending on the current system load. The system load is computed by the scheduler using the update_util_data->func hook in the kernel. When

executed, the driver checks the current CPU usage statistics for the last period and based on that the governor selects the CPU frequency. The "conservative" governor uses the same approach to compute the system load but it increases and decreases the CPU frequency progressively, rather than going directly to the maximum. This governor is more targeted to battery powered systems. Finally, the "schedutil" governor differs with the previous ones in the way it is integrated with the Linux kernel scheduler. This governor uses the per-entity load tracking mechanism to estimate the system load. Moreover, dynamic voltage and frequency setting (DVFS) is only applied to completely fair scheduler (CFS) tasks, while RealTime (RT) and Deadline (DL) always run at the highest frequency.

When TURBO is set to ON by UEFI settings, the utilization of TURBO frequencies for non-AVX instructions can be avoided by the sysadmin by setting the maximum frequency to the nominal frequency.

With the "userspace" governor, the sysadmin can explicitly set the CPU frequency by selecting one frequency available in the list of P-states. When TURBO is ON in the UEFI settings, the frequency at P-state 0 is a generic value representing the activation of turbo frequencies.

For instance, in a system with a nominal frequency of 2.4 GHz and TURBO set to ON in UEFI settings, the following commands will set CPU frequency to a fixed 2.4 GHz, not allowing the activation of TURBO. The first command selects the userspace governor and the second one sets the frequency to 2.40 GHz.

```
~>cpupower    -r    -frequency-set    -g    userspace
~>cpupower    -r    -frequency-set    -f    2,400,000
```

The following example allows the activation of TURBO frequencies assuming that "userspace" governor is selected and TURBO is set to ON in UEFI settings.

```
~>cpupower    -r    -frequency-set    -f    2,401,000
```

The "cpupower" command provides information about the CPU frequency driver, governor and list of frequencies. The current limits can be obtained with the "-frequency-info" option.

### 5.1.3. *Workloads used*

The four workloads we will be using have been selected to exhibit different power and performance characteristics.

The first, called single instruction, multiple data (SIMD), is a code executing different basic SIMD instructions. We use it to understand the power and performance behavior of different type of SIMD instructions. This test and its results are presented in section 5.2.1.

The second, called High Performance Linpack (HPL), is a well-known benchmark that has been written to exhibit the highest floating-point performance on one or multiples servers (Petitet *et al.* 2018). This test and its results are presented in sections 5.2.2 and 5.3.

The third, called STREAM, is a well-known benchmark that has been written to exhibit the highest memory bandwidth on a server when data is streamed from memory. This test and its results are presented in section 5.2.3.

The fourth, called Berlin Quantum Chromo Dynamics (BQCD), is a user application using hybrid Monte-Carlo methods to solve the lattice Quantum Chromo Dynamics (QCD) theory of quarks and gluons (Haar *et al.* 2017). We selected it because QCD methods are frequently used in high-performance computing and because its power and performance behavior vary when changing its domain decomposition. This test and its results are presented in sections 5.2.4 and 5.3.

But before presenting the power, thermal and performance behavior of these workloads, we introduce first some qualitative and quantitative metrics to classify workloads to better explain their behavior, and then we will present the different measurements for these workloads.

### 5.1.4. *CPU-bound and memory-bound workloads*

We say an application is CPU bound when it makes intensive use of the processor measured by a CPI < 1 (cycle per instruction) value where CPI is defined by:

$$CPI = \frac{number\ of\ instructions\ executed}{number\ of\ cycles} \qquad [5.1]$$

We can also deduce CPI from IPC where IPC is the number of instructions per cycle by:

$$CPI = \frac{1}{IPC}$$    [5.2]

For such a CPU-bound application, the processor being highly utilized means the processor is not waiting for data from memory as they are already in cache or registers.

We say an application is memory bound when CPI > 1, leading to a "more idle" processor waiting for data to be fetched from memory. This memory traffic activity is measured by GBS (gigabytes per second) and defined by:

$$GBS = \frac{number\ of\ memory\ reads\ and\ writes}{Time\ in\ seconds}$$    [5.3]

Section 6.1.2.1 provides the explicit formula to compute CPI, IPC and GBS.

The CPI and GBS values measured for each workload will be presented as part of the performance, power and thermal analysis in sections 5.2 and 5.3.

### 5.1.5. *DC node power versus components power*

For each workload, we will be reporting the following metrics measured by IPMI for node power or ptumon commands for CPU and DIMM power, CPU core frequency and temperature (see section 6.1.1):

– DC_NODE_POWER (or simply node power) is the DC power measured at the node level including all components of the server such the processors, the memory DIMMs, the board, the voltage regulator (VR), PCI slots, PCI adapters, disks and so on;

– CPU0 Power is the DC power consumed by CPU0 (in our case, Intel Xeon 6148);

– CPU1 Power is the DC power consumed by CPU1 (in our case, Intel Xeon 6148);

– PCK_POWER is the sum of CPU0 Power and CPU1 Power;

– MEM0 Power is the power consumed by the DIMMs on channel 0 (in our case, six DIMMs);

– MEM1 Power is the power consumed by the DIMMS on channel 1 (in our case, six DIMMs);

– DRAM_POWER is the sum of MEM0 Power + MEM1 Power;

– CPU0 core frequency is the average frequency of all cores of CPU0;

– CPU1 core frequency is the average frequency of all cores of CPU1;

– node frequency is the average frequency of CPU0 and CPU1;

– CPU0 temperature is the highest temperature of all cores on CPU0;

– CPU1 Temperature is the highest temperature of all cores on CPU1.

For each workload, we will present either the instantaneous metric measured every 1 s or the average value over the execution time of the workloads.

Taking the example of the SD650 air-cooled server with two sockets Xeon 6148, 12 DIMMs of 8GB, one 2.5″ 1TB 7.2K HDD, adding the values measured NODE_POWER, PCK_POWER and DRAM_POWER (Figure 5.3) to the idle power of the HDD (Table 1.5) and the board power (see Table 1.6), we note the sum of all individual components (359 W) is less than the DC node power (390 W) measured in section 5.2.2. This is caused by the efficiency of the DC voltage conversions on the board from 12 V (for DC_POWER) to the specific and lower voltage of each component done by the VRs. In our case, this conversion efficiency is equal to 0.92:

$$DC\ node\ power = 0.92 * (PCK\_POWER + DRAM\_POWER + HDD\_POWER + board\_POWER) \qquad [5.4]$$

Sometimes node power is also reported by the AC node power or more precisely the AC chassis power. As shown in Figure 6.1, AC chassis power is the sum of DC node power [5.4] plus the fan and PSU power, multiplied by the AC to DC conversion efficiency from the PSU (see section 1.4.9).

## 5.2. Power, thermal and performance on air-cooled servers with Intel Xeon

In this section, the UEFI "efficiency-favor performance" was selected.

## 5.2.1. *Frequency, power and performance of simple SIMD instructions*

As we have seen in Table 4.3, Intel Xeon has different type of SIMD instructions that have been introduced over Intel microarchitecture generations to increase performance. SIMD is a simple program that executes a number of times each of the following instructions shown in Table 5.1.

| Instruction name | Instruction type | DP Flops per instruction |
|---|---|---|
| SSE2 DP ADD128 | SSE2 | 4 |
| SSE2 DP MUL128 | SSE2 | 4 |
| FMA DP FMADD128 | SSE2 | 8 |
| AVX DP ADD256 | AVX2 | 8 |
| AVX DP MUL256 | AVX2 | 8 |
| FMA DP FMADD256 | AVX2 | 16 |
| AVX-512F DP ADD512 | AVX512 | 16 |
| AVX-512F DP MUL512 | AVX512 | 16 |
| AVX-512F DP FMADD512 | AVX512 | 32 |

**Table 5.1.** *List and type of instructions executed by the SIMD test*

Table 5.1 presents also the number of DP Flops theoretically produced by each instruction. Figure 5.2 plots the core frequency at which each instruction was executed on the "air-cooled node" with Turbo OFF and ON. As explained in 5.1, Turbo was set to ON in the UEFI settings and the "userspace" governor was selected. Therefore, to run the code with Turbo OFF we used the command "cpupower frequency -set -freq 2,400,000". To run the code with Turbo ON, we used the command "cpupower frequency -set -freq 2,401,000".

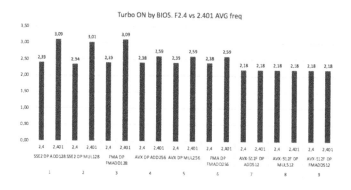

**Figure 5.2.** *Frequency of each instruction type with Turbo OFF and ON*

Figure 5.2 shows the processor frequency at which each instruction of the SIMD test is executing Turbo OFF and ON. SSE2 instructions run at 2.4 GHz, the frequency we set, and 3.1 GHz when we let the processor run at maximum frequency. This is according to Table 4.4 for non-AVX instructions on the 6148 Xeon processor.

AVX2 instructions run at 2.4 GHz, the frequency we set, and 2.6 GHz when we let the processor run at maximum frequency. This is according to Table 4.4 for AVX2 instructions on the 6148 Xeon processor.

AVX-512 instructions run at 2.2 GHz with both settings. Although we set the frequency to 2.4 GHz in the first case and 2.401 GHz in the second case, as 2.4 GHz is higher than the max Turbo frequency for AVX-512 instructions of 2.2 GHz (see Table 4.4), the processors run effectively at 2.2 GHz and not 2.4 GHz or higher.

Tables 5.2 and 5.3 present the performance measured in GFlops and the performance per watt measured in GFlops per watt of these different instructions measured by the SIMD program on the 6148 Intel Xeon processor.

From a performance perspective, we see nearly a doubling of performance from SSE2 to AVX2 and to AVX-512 and we see also nearly a doubling of performance from DP Add to DP FMA, while DP Mult. is a bit lower than DP Add. We note also that Turbo is improving the performance of all instructions except AVX-512 as we have seen already in Figure 5.1.

| Xeon 6148; 2.4 GHz | Instruction set | DP Add | DP Mult. | DP FMA |
|---|---|---|---|---|
| GFlops | SSE2 | 382 | 305 | 763 |
| GFlops | AVX2 | 762 | 763 | 1525 |
| GFlops | AVX-512 | 1396 | 1400 | 2791 |

| Xeon 6148; 2.401 GHz | Instruction set | DP Add | DP Mult. | DP FMA |
|---|---|---|---|---|
| GFlops | SSE2 | 492 | 407 | 984 |
| GFlops | AVX2 | 828 | 828 | 1652 |
| GFlops | AVX-512 | 1399 | 1397 | 2797 |

**Table 5.2.** *DP GFlops at 2.4 GHz and 2.401 GHz*

| Xeon 6148; 2.4 GHz | Instruction Set | DP Add | DP Multiply | DP FMA |
|---|---|---|---|---|
| DP GFlops/W | SSE2 | 1.54 | 1.33 | 3.01 |
| DP GFlops/W | AVX2 | 2.86 | 2.93 | 5.67 |
| DP GFlops/W | AVX-512 | 5.28 | 5.30 | 10.22 |

| Xeon 6148; 2.401 GHz | Instruction Set | DP Add | DP Multiply | DP FMA |
|---|---|---|---|---|
| DP GFlops/W | SSE2 | 1.53 | 1.37 | 3.00 |
| DP GFlops/W | AVX2 | 2.90 | 2.93 | 5.65 |
| DP GFlops/W | AVX-512 | 5.25 | 5.28 | 10.22 |

**Table 5.3.** *DP GFlops per watt at 2.4 GHz and 2.401 GHz*

From a performance per watt perspective, we note that the performance per watt is nearly doubling from DP Add to DP FMA but not from SSE2 to AVX2 and even lower from AVX2 to AVX-512, pointing to the higher power consumption of these more complex AVX2 and AVX-512 instructions. Overall, comparing GFlops per watt of AVX-512 FMA to SSE Add, we note a 6.6× improvement, which is quite significant. We note also that Turbo is not providing a clear benefit versus nominal since the increased frequency is compensated by an increased power consumption. This conclusion is valid for these simple SIMD instructions and will be re-evaluated for the other workloads we will study in the following section.

Figures 5.3 and 5.4 plot the average DC_NODE_POWER, PCK_POWER and DRAM_POWER power consumed by each of the nine instructions when executed on the "air-cooled node" with Turbo OFF and ON.

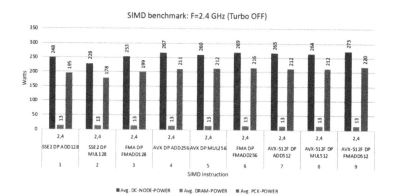

**Figure 5.3.** *Node, CPU and DIMM DC power of SIMD instructions Turbo OFF. For a color version of this figure, see www.iste.co.uk/brochard/energy.zip*

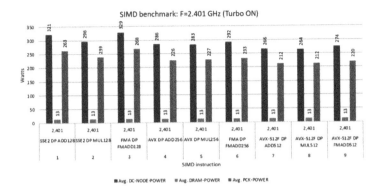

**Figure 5.4.** *Node, CPU and DIMM DC power of SIMD instructions with Turbo ON*

In Figure 5.3, we note the average DC_NODE_POWER varies from 228 W (SSE2 ADD) to 273 W (AVX-512 FMA) and PCK_POWER varies from 178 W (SSE2 ADD) to 220 W (AVX-512 FMA). DRAM_POWER is flat at 13 W across all instructions leading to about 1.1 W per 8GB DIMM (1 DPC). According to Table 1.3, this power per DIMM is pretty close to the idle power (0.9 W), which is because all those instructions have a pretty low memory bandwidth rate (GBS) as data sets are accessed sequentially and mostly from cache. The power consumed by one CPU is also moderate (from 89 to 110 W for a 150 W TDP). We note also the AVX and AVX-512 instructions lead to the highest CPU power consumption (from 106 to 110 W), while in Figure 5.2 we note that AVX-512 instructions run only at 2.2 GHz vs 2.4 GHz for the other instructions. For this reason, we can say that AVX-512 instructions are power hungry instructions.

In Figure 5.4, with Turbo ON, we see the DRAM_POWER is unchanged while the DC_POWER has increased significantly, since all instructions have been executed at a higher frequency except AVX-512. For example, PCK_POWER for SSE ADD instructions increased from 195 to 263 W (35%), while core frequency increased from 2.4 to 3.1 GHz (29%), showing that power increases more than frequency. We note also that for the FMA DP instruction which run at 3.1 GHz, the average power consumed per socket is 134 W, getting close to the 150 W TDP.

### 5.2.2. *Power, thermal and performance behavior of HPL*

HPL is a well-known benchmark based on a dense linear algebra solver called LINPACK, which has been used for many years to rank the world fastest servers and systems and published twice a year by Top500[1]. Because of its simple structure, HPL has been tuned to produce the highest double precision floating point sustained performance. The version we will use is HPL 2.2 (Petitet *et al.* 2018), which on Intel Xeon calls the MKL library (Gennady *et al.* 2018) and where DGEMM operations are using AVX-512 instruction for most of HPL execution time.

### 5.2.2.1. Power consumption

Figures 5.5 and 5.6 show the DC node power, the CPU power of each socket (CPU0 and CPU1) and the DIMM power attached to each memory channel (MEM0 and MEM1) with Turbo OFF and ON when running HPL.

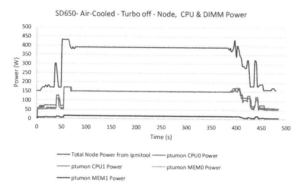

**Figure 5.5.** *Node, CPU and DIMM DC power running HPL Turbo OFF. For a color version of this figure, see www.iste.co.uk/brochard/energy.zip*

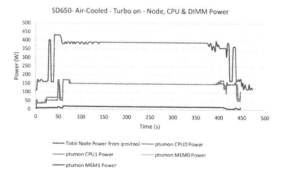

**Figure 5.6.** *Node, CPU and DIMM DC power running HPL Turbo ON. For a color version of this figure, see www.iste.co.uk/brochard/energy.zip*

1 Available at: https://www.top500.org/project/linpack [Accessed April 30, 2019].

## 5.2.2.2. *The different phases of HPL and the Turbo impact*

At first glance, plots in Figures 5.5 and 5.6 are very similar with four different phases in both Turbo OFF or ON runs. The first and fourth phases are the start-up and ending phases, which execute non-AVX instruction. The second and third phases make the plateau phase, which executes AVX-512 instructions that were introduced with the Skylake architecture. This four-phase behavior is due to the fact that HPL spends the major part of its execution running a matrix–matrix multiplication called DGEMM (LAPACK n.d.), which every vendor has carefully tuned, and which Intel has introduced as a highly tuned AVX-512 version in the MKL library for Xeon Skylake (Gennady and Shaojuan 2018).

Therefore, phases 1 and 4 execute non-AVX instructions before and after HPL executes the AVX-512 executions in phases 2 and 3. Phase 2 is a short phase where node and CPU power are higher than during phase 3. DC node power and the PCK_POWER are 390 W and 149 W during phase 3, while they are 440 W and 169 W during phase 2. As phase 3 is executing 100% of AVX-512 instructions, the processor runs very close to TDP, which is 150 W for the 6148 SKU. Phase 2 behavior is due to another feature Intel introduced with SandyBridge processors as part of Intel Turbo Boost Technology 2.0 and the two RAPL (running average power limit) power limits (Rotem *et al.* 2011). PL1 is the long-term power limit and PL2 is the short-term power limit. By default, PL1 is set to TDP and the time constant is infinite (i.e. the CPU can stay there forever). PL1 is what we observe during phase 3. The default for PL2 is 1.2xTDP with a time constant of ~10s, PL2 being typically limited by the thermal conditions of the server. PL2 is what we observe during phase 2 and we note PL2 is only 1.13xTDP due to the thermal conditions of the server.

Since during phases 2 and 3 HPL is executing AVX-512 instructions, which run at maximum possible frequency whether Turbo is OFF or ON (see section 5.1.2), this explains why HPL power curves are identical with Turbo OFF or ON during phases 2 and 3. This is not the case during the first and fourth phases, which execute non-AVX instructions where CPU power is much higher with Turbo ON versus Turbo OFF. This is due to the fact that the frequency of non-AVX instructions gets a significant boost with Turbos as we seen for SIMD and as shown in Table 4.4.

During the PL1 plateau phase, HPL has a much higher node power consumption than the SIMD test. Power per CPU socket is about constant and close to TDP at 150 W for HPL, while varying from 106 to 134 W for SIMD. Similarly, memory power for HPL is more than twice the SIMD memory power (16.5 W for MEM0, 15.5 W for MEM1 leading to a total of 32 W for HPL vs. 13 W for SIMD). This difference will be explained when we analyze CPI and GBS in Figures 5.9 and 5.10.

### 5.2.2.3. Frequency and temperature

Figures 5.7 and 5.8 present the frequency and temperature of each CPU while running HPL with Turbo OFF and ON.

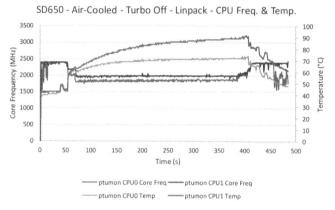

**Figure 5.7.** *CPU frequency and temperature running HPL with Turbo OFF. For a color version of this figure, see www.iste.co.uk/brochard/energy.zip*

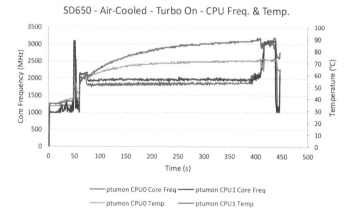

**Figure 5.8.** *CPU frequency and temperature running HPL with Turbo ON. For a color version of this figure, see www.iste.co.uk/brochard/energy.zip*

As we have seen for the power, the only difference between Turbo OFF and ON occurs during the first and fourth phases, which execute non-AVX instructions. The CPU0 and CPU1 frequencies (gray and blue curves) are 2.4 GHz for the first and fourth phases with Turbo OFF and 3.1 GHz with Turbo ON, which match perfectly the non-AVX base and max Turbo frequencies for the 6148 in Table 4.4.

With Turbo OFF, during the PL1 plateau phase, average CPU frequency is 1.91 GHz while CPU 0 frequency is 1.85 GHz and CPU 1 is 1.98 GHz. Average CPU frequency is somewhere between the base and max Turbo frequencies of 6148 (respectively, 1.6 GHz and 2.2 GHz) as expected. The frequency difference between CPU 0 and CPU1 will be discussed in section 5.1.7.

With Turbo OFF, during the PL2 plateau phase, average CPU frequency is 2.1 GHz while CPU 0 frequency is 2.0 GHz and CPU 1 is 2.18 GHz. This higher CPU frequency is normal for the PL2 phase and still within the limit of the max Turbo AVX-512 frequency (2.2 GHz).

The yellow and orange curves represent the CPU0 and CPU1 temperatures. During the PL2 and PL1 plateau phases that execute AVX-512 instruction, CPU0 has a higher temperature (88°C max) than CPU1 (81°C max). Both are well below the max junction temperature of 95°C for the 6148 (Xeon Scalable Thermal Guide, 2018, Table 5.1). The temperature difference between CPU0 and CPU1 will be discussed in section 5.1.7.

### 5.2.2.4. *CPI and GBS*

Figures 5.9 and 5.10 present HPL CPI and GBS during execution time with Turbo OFF and Turbo ON. During PL1 phase, Turbo OFF (and ON) average CPI is 0.4 and average GBS is 68.

It shows clearly that HPL is highly CPU bound, making intensive use of AVX-512 instruction and leading to maximum power consumed by two sockets (around 150 W each), while DIMM power is about 16 W each. We note that memory bandwidth is quite high, while CPI is low. This is due to the BLAS3 dense matrix operations where data are blocked into cache with data being prefetched from memory without stalling the processor. This behavior is quite normal for AVX-512 instructions, which cannot execute well without data in cache and well prefetched data from memory.

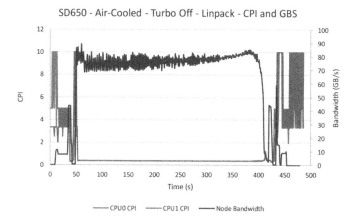

**Figure 5.9.** *CPU0 and CPU1 CPI and node bandwidth running HPL with Turbo OFF. For a color version of this figure, see www.iste.co.uk/brochard/energy.zip*

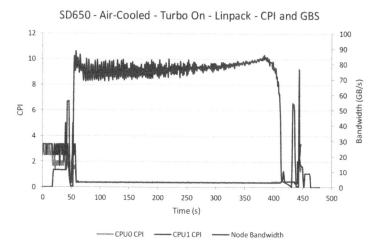

**Figure 5.10.** *CPU0&1 CPI and node bandwidth running HPL with Turbo ON. For a color version of this figure, see www.iste.co.uk/brochard/energy.zip*

## 5.2.3. Power, thermal and performance behavior of STREAM

STREAM (McAlpin 2017) is a highly tuned kernel to measure the highest possible sustained memory bandwidth of a server. To exhibit the highest memory bandwidth on Xeon 6148, the STREAM 5.10 test has been compiled with AVX-512 instructions.

### 5.2.3.1. *Power consumption*

Figures 5.11 and 5.12 present the DC node power, the CPU and memory DC power while running STREAM with Turbo OFF and ON.

Both plots are very similar since STREAM is compiled with AVX-512 instructions. The frequency plots (Figures 5.13 and 5.14) will provide more detail on this topic.

During the plateau phase, node power is 330 W for both Turbo OFF and ON, while CPU0 power is 116 W and CPU1 power is 103 W. Both CPU power values are much less than HPL (150 W) as STREAM is not as CPU intensive, which is confirmed by the higher CPI value of 9.6 (see Figures 5.15 and 5.16).

MEM0 and MEM1 power is 21.5 W leading to 43 W for the whole memory, which is higher than HPL memory power (32 W). This is demonstrated by the highest GBS value of 140 GBS (see Figures 5.15 and 5.16) versus 68 for HPL. This corresponds to 3.6 W per DIMM, which is pretty close to the maximum value of 4.5 W in Table 1.3. The power differences between CPU1 and CPU0 will be discussed in section 2.5.

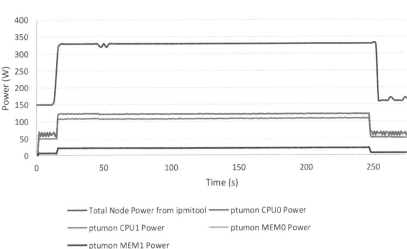

**Figure 5.11.** *Node, CPU and DIMM power running STREAM with Turbo OFF. For a color version of this figure, see www.iste.co.uk/brochard/energy.zip*

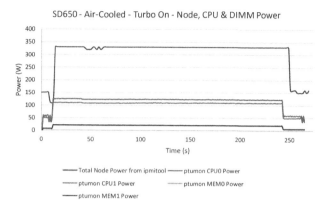

**Figure 5.12.** *Node, CPU and DIMM power running STREAM with Turbo ON. For a color version of this figure, see www.iste.co.uk/brochard/energy.zip*

## 5.2.3.2. *Frequency and temperature*

Figures 5.13 and 5.14 present the frequency and temperature of both CPUs while running STREAM with Turbo OFF and ON. During the plateau phase, both CPUs have a frequency of ~2.4 GHz Turbo OFF and ON. A constant frequency Turbo OFF and ON indicates the code is not running non-AVX instructions, which is expected as STREAM is complied with AVX-512 option. But this frequency is not in the range of AVX-512 frequencies for the 6148 as shown in Table 4.4. This could indicate that STREAM is executing AVX-2 instructions and not AVX-512. A detailed analysis of the code showed that instructions have 0% of AVX-512 instructions and 67% of AVX-2 instructions.

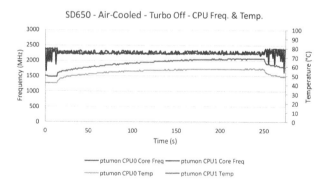

**Figure 5.13.** *CPU temperatures and frequencies running STREAM with Turbo OFF. For a color version of this figure, see www.iste.co.uk/brochard/energy.zip*

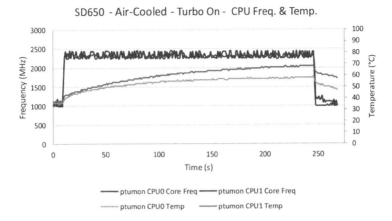

**Figure 5.14.** *CPU temperatures and frequencies running STREAM with Turbo ON. For a color version of this figure, see www.iste.co.uk/brochard/energy.zip*

### 5.2.3.3. *CPI and GBS*

Figures 5.15 and 5.16 present CPI of both CPUs and node bandwidth (GBS) when running STREAM with Turbo OFF and ON.

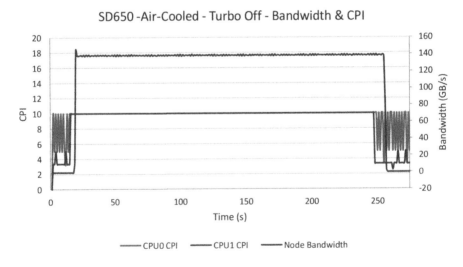

**Figure 5.15.** *CPU CPIs and node bandwidth running STREAM with Turbo OFF. For a color version of this figure, see www.iste.co.uk/brochard/energy.zip*

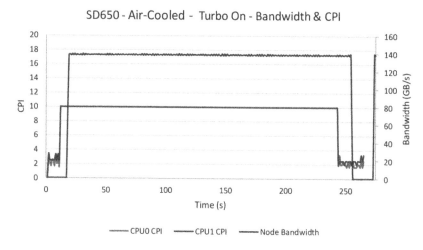

**Figure 5.16.** *CPU CPIs and node bandwidth running STREAM with Turbo ON. For a color version of this figure, see www.iste.co.uk/brochard/energy.zip*

During the plateau phase, GBS is around 140 GBS while CPI for CPU0 is 9.8 and 9.4 for CPU 1. As discussed earlier, the high GBS value causes the high memory power of 43 W compared to 32 W for HPL.

### 5.2.4. Power, thermal and performance behavior of real workloads

HPL is a highly tuned kernel to demonstrate the highest possible sustained performance with an extremely low CPI of 0.4, since most of its execution time is spent in the DGEMM routine from Intel MKL library, which makes intensive use of AVX-512 instructions (Gennady *et al.* 2018). STREAM is another extreme benchmark, which has been created to measure the highest possible memory bandwidth on a server with an extremely high GBS value of 140.

Workloads used by scientists and engineers in their daily job have different characteristics. They have neither extremely low CPI (with some not even using AVX-512 instructions) like HPL nor a very high GBS like STREAM.

To highlight how real workloads behave, we chose an application that is well used by the HPC community and can exhibit a CPU-bound and memory-bound behavior with the same code pattern. BQCD (Haar *et al.* 2017) is a hybrid Monte-Carlo program for simulating lattice QCD with dynamical Wilson fermions. It has a distributed memory version, implemented with MPI and the same code running on a single server with different processor grid decompositions exhibiting either a CPU-bound behavior, when the data set computed per core is small and fits reasonably into the processor's cache, or a memory bound behavior when the data set computed per core is large enough such that it does not fit into the processor's cache. BQCD has been compiled with no AVX option so that it executes only SSE instructions. In the following, we present the same measurements as for HPL and STREAM except that we will use two BQCD use cases: BQCD128, the memory bound test case, has been compiled with the following parameters LATTICE = 48 6 24 48 - PROC = 1 1 2 2. BQCD1K, the CPU-bound test case, has been compiled with parameters LATTICE = 48 6 12 12 - PROC = 1 1 2 2.

### 5.2.4.1. *Power consumption*

Figures 5.17 and 5.18 show the DC node, CPU0/1 and MEM0/1 power of the air-cooled SD650 prototype while running the two BQCD test cases with Turbo OFF.

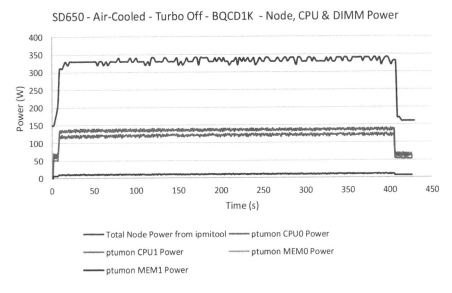

**Figure 5.17.** *Node, CPU and DIMM power running BQCD1K with Turbo OFF. For a color version of this figure, see www.iste.co.uk/brochard/energy.zip*

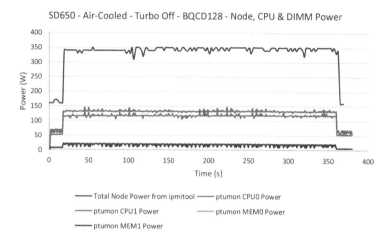

SD650 - Air-Cooled - Turbo Off - BQCD128 - Node, CPU & DIMM Power

**Figure 5.18.** *Node, CPU and DIMM power running BQCD128 with Turbo OFF. For a color version of this figure, see www.iste.co.uk/brochard/energy.zip*

During the plateau phase of BQCD1K and BQCD128 with Turbo OFF, average DC node power is, respectively, 320 W and 344 W, CPU0 and CPU1 node power is 136 W and 121 W, and 133 W and 118 W. MEM0 and MEM1 power is, respectively, 11 W and 10 W, and 18 W and 18 W. The power difference between CPU 0 and CPU 1 will be addressed in section 5.1.7. The slightly higher CPU power of BQCD1K versus BQCD128 can be explained by its lower CPI (0.64 vs. 1.24), and its lower memory power by a lower GBS (27 vs. 73), as presented in section 5.1.6.3.

Figures 5.19 and 5.20 show the DC node, CPU0/CPU1 and MEM0/MEM1 power of the air-cooled SD650 prototype while running the two BQCD test cases with Turbo ON.

With Turbo ON, we note average CPU0 power for both test cases is 149 W very close to the TDP limit of 150 W with peaks slightly over 150 W. This is according to Turbo ON definition, which run instructions at maximum frequency until it reach TDP or the thermal limit of the processors. In this case, the limiting factor is CPU power since CPU0 temperature is still below the max junction temperature of the 6148, which is 95 °C as we will see in the next section on frequency and temperature. Average CPU1 power for the two test cases is 133 W leading to a difference of about 16 W between CPU0 and CPU1 as already noted. This will be addressed in section 5.2.5.

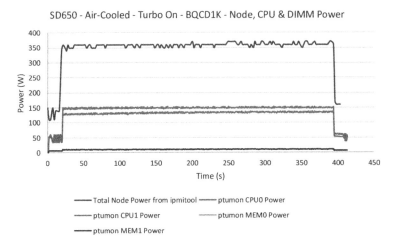

**Figure 5.19.** *Node, CPU and DIMM power running BQCD1K with Turbo ON. For a color version of this figure, see www.iste.co.uk/brochard/energy.zip*

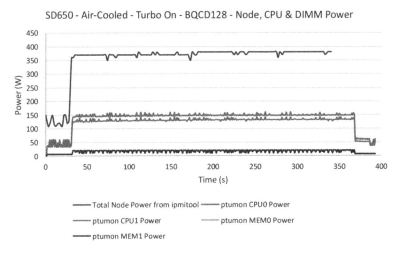

**Figure 5.20.** *Node, CPU and DIMM power running BQCD128 with Turbo ON. For a color version of this figure, see www.iste.co.uk/brochard/energy.zip*

### 5.2.4.2. *Frequency and temperature*

Figures 5.21 and 5.22 present the frequency and temperature for BQCD1K and BQCD128 with Turbo OFF and Figures 5.23 and 5.24 present the frequency and temperature for BQCD1K and BQCD128 with Turbo ON.

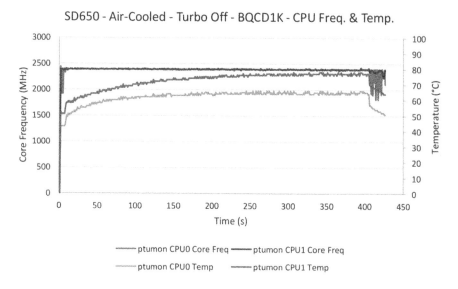

**Figure 5.21.** *CPU temperatures and frequencies running BQCD1K with Turbo OFF. For a color version of this figure, see www.iste.co.uk/brochard/energy.zip*

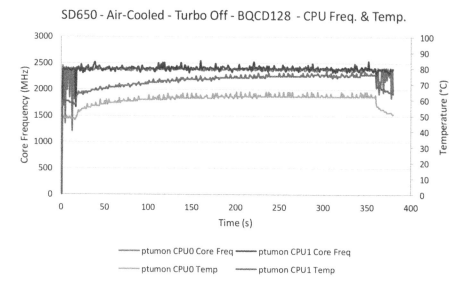

**Figure 5.22.** *CPU temperatures and frequencies running BQCD128 with Turbo OFF. For a color version of this figure, see www.iste.co.uk/brochard/energy.zip*

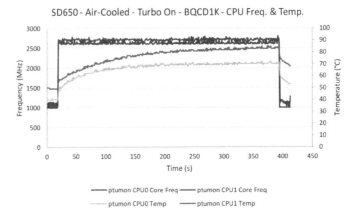

**Figure 5.23.** *CPU temperatures and frequencies running BQCD1K with Turbo ON. For a color version of this figure, see www.iste.co.uk/brochard/energy.zip*

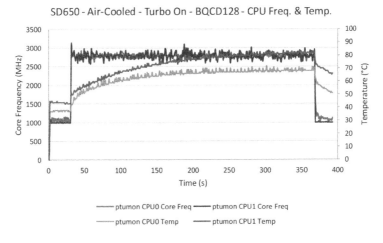

**Figure 5.24.** *CPU temperatures and frequencies running BQCD128 with Turbo ON. For a color version of this figure, see www.iste.co.uk/brochard/energy.zip*

In Figures 5.21 and 5.22 for BQCD1K and BQCD128 with Turbo OFF, core frequency of both CPUs is 2.4 GHz for both test cases, which is, according to Table 4.4, the 6148 base non-AVX frequency, since the code has been compiled with no AVX. In Figures 5.23 and 5.24 with Turbo ON, core frequency of both CPUs is around 2.7 GHz, which is a significant boost but still below the max possible frequency of 3.1 GHz. This is due to the fact that CPU0 is reaching the TDP limit of 150 W.

We note also that with BQCD 1K CPU0 core frequency is slightly higher than CPU1 frequency (2.7 GHz vs. 2.6 GHz) while with BQCD 128 both CPUs have the same frequency (2.8 GHz). These differences will be addressed in section 5.2.5.

### 5.2.4.3. *CPI and GBS*

Figures 5.25 and 5.26 present CPI and GBS for the two BQCD test cases with Turbo OFF.

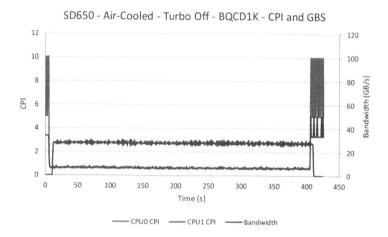

**Figure 5.25.** *CPU CPIs and node bandwidth running BQCD1K with Turbo OFF. For a color version of this figure, see www.iste.co.uk/brochard/energy.zip*

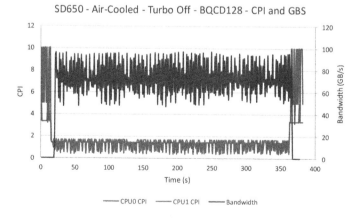

**Figure 5.26.** *CPU CPIs and node bandwidth running BQCD128 with Turbo OFF. For a color version of this figure, see www.iste.co.uk/brochard/energy.zip*

During the plateau phase, BQCD1K and BQCD128 Turbo OFF have, respectively, an average node bandwidth of 27 and 73 GBS, while CPU0/CPU1 CPI are, respectively, 0.63 and 0.64, and 1.19 and 1.29. BQCD1K shows stable values around 0.6 for CPI and 27 for GBS, while BQCD128 shows high oscillations with CPI and GBS values, respectively, between 0.4–2.0 and 47–97. This behavior is due to the fact that BQCD is using a conjugate-gradient iterative solver with some routines working on local data, which are not impacted by the domain decomposition and have always low CPI and GBS value, and other routines working on data in memory that are impacted by the domain decomposition and which will have high CPI and GBS values for BQCD128 and low CPI value/medium GBS value for BQCD1K. This explains the BQCD128 CPI and GBS oscillations and BQCD1K stability. This can be also expressed by saying that BQCD1K has a stable CPU-bound behavior with low CPI (0.6) and medium node bandwidth (27 GBS), while BQCD128 oscillates between CPU-bound and memory-bound routines leading to average CPI value of 1.2 and an average high node bandwidth of 73 GBS, which is why we can say that BQCD128 is a memory bound use case.

Figures 5.27 and 5.28 present CPI and GBS for the two BQCD test cases with Turbo ON.

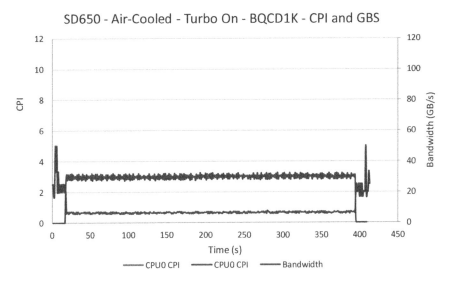

**Figure 5.27.** *CPU CPIs and node bandwidth running BQCD1K with Turbo ON. For a color version of this figure, see www.iste.co.uk/brochard/energy.zip*

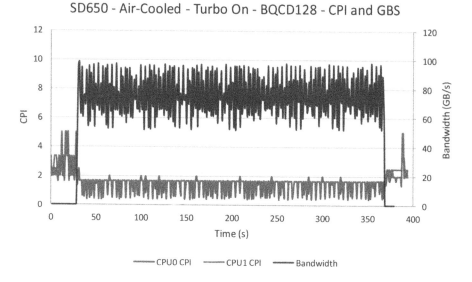

**Figure 5.28.** *CPU CPIs and node bandwidth running BQCD128 with Turbo ON. For a color version of this figure, see www.iste.co.uk/brochard/energy.zip*

We note CPI and GBS have similar behavior and values with Turbo ON or OFF.

## 5.2.5. *Power, thermal and frequency differences between CPUs*

In the measurements we reported above, CPU0 and CPU1 displayed different temperatures, frequencies or powers.

Although we were careful to make these measurements under the same conditions, there are two differences we could not eliminate, which are the cooling and SKU differences.

By cooling differences, we mean the impact of the air flow on a shadow processor configuration (Figure 2.9), like on the air-cooled SD650 (Figure 3.14), where when air is flowing first to CPU1 and then to CPU0 such the inlet air temperature on CPU0 is about 5 to 7°C hotter than on CPU1. In our case that could explain why CPU1 temperature is higher than CPU0. To verify this assumption, we made the same set of measurements as shown above with the same configuration (SKU, DIMM, HDD) but with another air-cooled shadow configuration server, the Lenovo SD530 (Figure 2.8) where the air is flowing first to CPU0 and then CPU1. We labeled these measurements as "SD530".

By SKU differences, we mean the performance variations from SKU to SKU as shown in section 5.1, and Figures 5.1 and 7.11. In our case, it could explain why one CPU power is higher than the other CPU. To verify this assumption, we made the same set of measurements as shown above but swapping the CPUs on the SD650 air-cooled system. We labeled these measurements as "SD650 swapped".

Figures 5.29–5.31 present six plots for BQCD1K Turbo OFF (Figure 5.29), BQCD1K Turbo ON (Figure 5.30) and HPL Turbo ON (Figure 5.31), where the first three plots present the CPU temperature and frequency and the last three plots present the node, CPU and DIMM power consumptions on the three platforms "SD530", "SD650 air-cooled" and "SD650 swapped" to highlight the cooling and SKU differences across these three platforms.

For running BQCD1K Turbo OFF in Figure 5.29, core frequency is set at nominal fixed 2.4 GHz for all three servers. On "SD530", we note that CPU0 temp > CPU1 temp and CPU0 power > CPU1 power while on 'SD650 air-cooled" we have CPU1 temp > CPU0 temp and CPU0 power > CPU1 power and on "SD650 swapped" we have CPU1 temp > CPU0 temp and CPU1 power > CPU0 power. Knowing the only difference between "SD650 air-cooled" and "SD650 swapped" is the swapping of CPUs, we can conclude that the power consumption difference is caused by a CPU performance variation, as described in section 5.1.1, such that the best CPU consumes less power at the same core frequency. Regarding the CPU temperature difference, knowing that the only difference between "SD530" and "SD650 air-cooled" is the air flowing in opposite direction, we can conclude that the CPU temperature difference is due to the air flow, which is cooling the first processor at a cooler temperature than the second one in a shadow processor design (Figure 2.9).

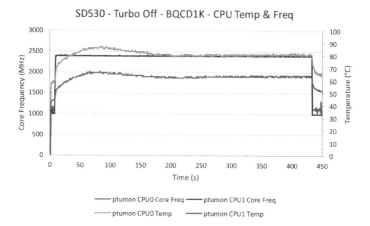

SD530 - Turbo Off - BQCD1K - CPU Temp & Freq

SD650 - Air-Cooled - Turbo Off - BQCD1K - CPU Freq. & Temp.

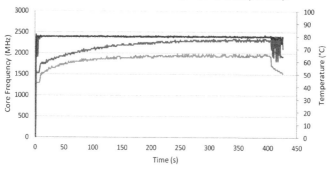

SD650 - Air-Cooled - Turbo Off - BQCD1K - CPU Temp & Freq - Swapped

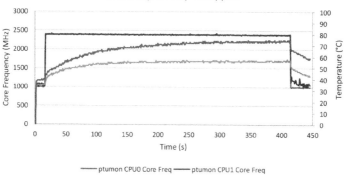

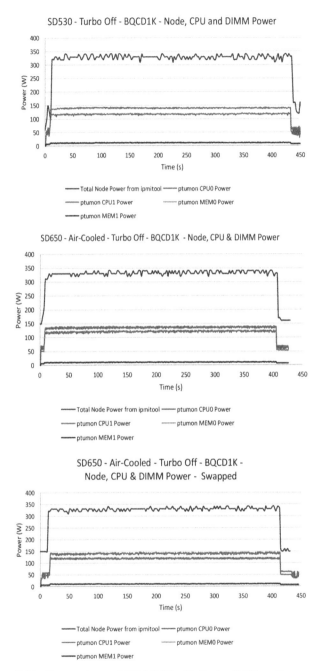

**Figure 5.29.** *Comparison of BQCD1K with Turbo OFF on three servers. For a color version of this figure, see www.iste.co.uk/brochard/energy.zip*

### SD530 - Turbo On - BQCD1K - CPU Temp & Freq

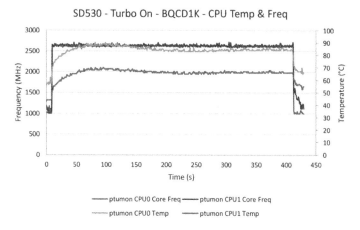

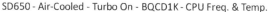

### SD650 - Air-Cooled - Turbo On - BQCD1K - CPU Freq. & Temp.

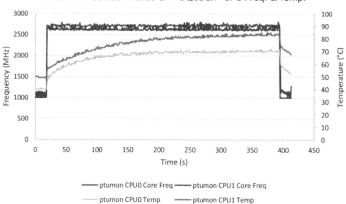

### SD650 - Air-Cooled - Turbo On - BQCD1K - Temp & Freq Swapped

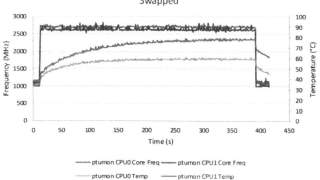

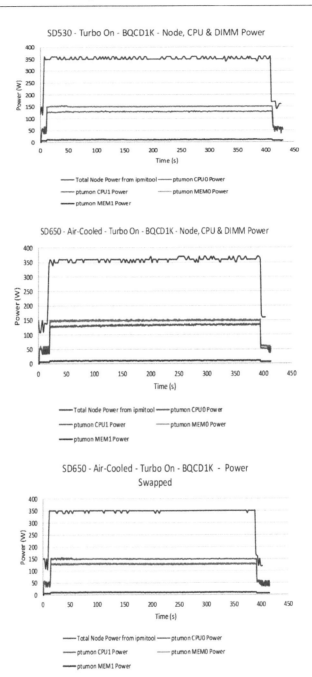

**Figure 5.30.** *Comparison of BQCD1K with Turbo ON on three servers. For a color version of this figure, see www.iste.co.uk/brochard/energy.zip*

Figure 5.30 presents BQCD1K with Turbo ON where core frequency is not locked at nominal frequency and will increase up to thermal or power limits are hit. From Figure 5.29, we understood the best CPU for SD530 and SD650 is in slot 1, whereas the best CPU for "SD650 swapped" is in slot 0. For BQCD1K with Turbo ON, we note that only one CPU is reaching TDP (CPU0 for SD530 and SD650 and CPU1 for "SD650 swapped"), which happens as the CPU in slot 0 is the "worst" SKU on SD650 while the "worst" SKU is in slot 1 for "SD650 swapped". We note that the CPU temperatures are still below the junction temperature (95°C). Regarding the CPU frequencies and temperature difference, we note that on "SD650 swapped", CPU0 temperature is about 10°C lower than on SD650 due to the fact the best CPU is in slot 0. Finally, we note that for SD650 and "SD650 swapped", CPU0 frequency is slightly higher than CPU1, which can be explained by the fact CPU0 has always a lower temperature as it is cooled first on both servers.

Figure 5.31 presents HPL with Turbo ON. In this case, we see that both CPUs are able to reach the TDP limit. Therefore, the best SKU is reaching the highest frequency on all three servers (CPU1 for SD530 and SD650 and CPU0 for "SD650 swapped"). The cooling difference has the same effect as in Figure 5.30 where the SKU, which is cooled first, has a lower temperature than the other SKU.

As explained in section 5.1.1, we note that for all three workloads, the CPU temperature rise curves on "SD650 air-cooled" and "SD650 swapped" are logarithmic because the CPU is initially being over-cooled during the start of the run, and the temperature gradually rises to its steady-state temperature with the given airflow. The temperature curve has a very different shape on SD530, which is a server designed for air-cooling where system firmware is dynamically controlling the fan speed.

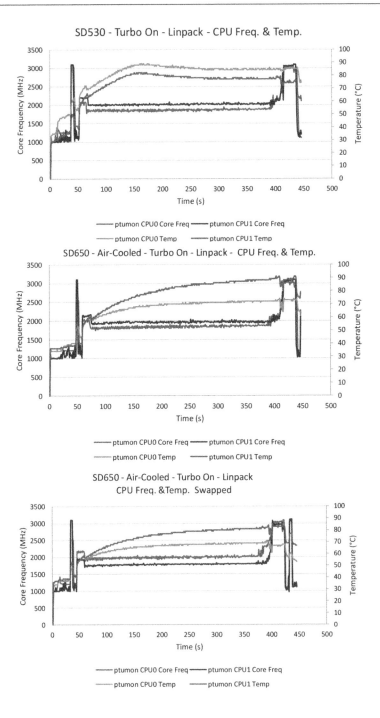

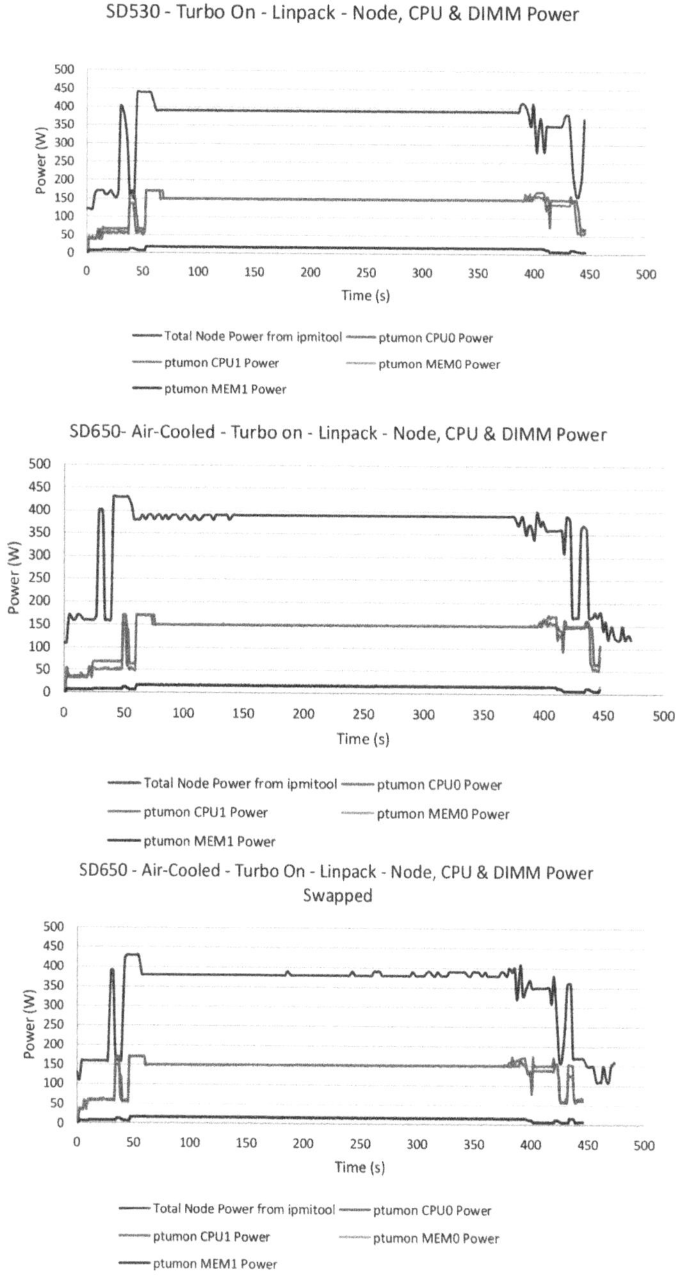
SD530 - Turbo On - Linpack - Node, CPU & DIMM Power
Power (W)
Time (s)
Total Node Power from ipmitool
ptumon CPU0 Power
ptumon CPU1 Power
ptumon MEM0 Power
ptumon MEM1 Power
SD650- Air-Cooled - Turbo on - Linpack - Node, CPU & DIMM Power
Power (W)
Time (s)
Total Node Power from ipmitool
ptumon CPU0 Power
ptumon CPU1 Power
ptumon MEM0 Power
ptumon MEM1 Power
SD650 - Air-Cooled - Turbo On - Linpack - Node, CPU & DIMM Power Swapped
Power (W)
Time (s)
Total Node Power from ipmitool
ptumon CPU0 Power
ptumon CPU1 Power
ptumon MEM0 Power
ptumon MEM1 Power

**Figure 5.31.** *Comparison of HPL with Turbo ON on three servers.*
*For a color version of this figure, see www.iste.co.uk/brochard/energy.zip*

## 5.3. Power, thermal and performance on water-cooled servers with Intel Xeon

In section 5.2, we presented the power, thermal and performance behavior of the prototype version of the air-cooled prototype server ThinkSystem SD650, which we referred as "SD650 air-cooled" when running specific workloads. This section is presenting the impact of cooling on the same SD650 server, which is either air cooled or water cooled while running HPL and BQCD. We will refer to these servers as "SD650 air-cooled" and "SD650 water-cooled". The inlet water temperature of the "SD650 water-cooled" will be set at 30°C, 45°C and 55°C while the room temperature is constant at 21°C.

We will also present measurements for the "SD650 water-cooled" with two UEFI settings ("efficiency-favor performance" and "maximum performance"), while the "SD650 air-cooled" runs are performed with the "maximum performance" UEFI setting only. Goal of these runs with two UEFI is to determine how water cooling can improve frequency and potentially performance even at the expense of power consumption.

The following sections will present how the CPU temperature, voltage and frequency, power and performance vary depending on the cooling and the inlet water temperature when running HPL and BQCD on "SD650 air-cooled" and "SD650 water-cooled" servers.

### 5.3.1. Impact on CPU temperature

Tables 5.4–5.6 present the average CPU temperature measured during the PL1 phase when running HPL and the plateau phase when running BQCD1K and BQCD128 with Turbo OFF and ON on the "SD650 air-cooled" and "SD650 water-cooled" servers with inlet water temperature of 30°C, 45°C and 55°C with UEFI "efficiency-favor performance" referred as "eff." and UEFI "maximum performance" referred as "perf.". The water flow rate is 0.25 L/min (lpm) per node.

| HPL | | | | | | | | | | | | | | |
|---|---|---|---|---|---|---|---|---|---|---|---|---|---|---|
| cooling/inlet temperature | air 21°C | | water 55°C | | | | water 45°C | | | | water 30°C | | | |
| Turbo | OFF | ON | OFF | | ON | | OFF | | ON | | OFF | | ON | |
| UEFI Setting | eff. | eff. | eff. | perf. | eff. | perf. | eff. | perf. | eff. | perf. | eff. | perf. | eff. | perf. |
| avg. processor PL1 temperature °C | 76 | 75 | 72 | 76 | 72 | 76 | 62 | 65 | 62 | 65 | 46 | 50 | 46 | 50 |

**Table 5.4.** *CPU temperature running HPL*

| BQCD1K | | | | | | | | | | | | | |
|---|---|---|---|---|---|---|---|---|---|---|---|---|---|
| cooling/inlet temperature | air 21°C | | water 55°C | | | | water 45°C | | | | water 30°C | | |
| Turbo | OFF | ON | OFF | | ON | | OFF | | ON | | OFF | | ON | |
| UEFI Setting | eff. | eff. | eff. | perf. | eff. | perf. | eff. | perf. | eff. | perf. | eff. | perf. | eff. | perf. |
| avg. Plateau processor temperature °C | 68 | 72 | 68 | 66 | 70 | 70 | 57 | 57 | 59 | 59 | 42 | 42 | 43 | 43 |

**Table 5.5.** *CPU temperature running BQCD1K*

| BQCD128 | | | | | | | | | | | | | |
|---|---|---|---|---|---|---|---|---|---|---|---|---|---|
| cooling/inlet temperature | air 20°C | | water 55°C | | | | water 45°C | | | | water 30°C | | |
| Turbo | OFF | ON | OFF | | ON | | OFF | | ON | | OFF | | ON | |
| UEFI Setting | eff. | eff. | eff. | perf. | eff. | perf. | eff. | perf. | eff. | perf. | eff. | perf. | eff. | perf. |
| avg. Plateau processor temperature °C | 67 | 70 | 67 | 64 | 69 | 69 | 56 | 56 | 58 | 58 | 41 | 41 | 43 | 43 |

**Table 5.6.** *CPU temperature running BQCD128*

We observe that on all measurements the CPU temperatures with BQCD128 and BQCD1K are always lower than with HPL, which is due to the lower CPI of BQCD versus HPL. We also observe that the CPU temperatures are always lower with QBCD with Turbo OFF versus Turbo ON since as BQCD execute non-AVX instructions, which get a significant frequency boost with Turbo ON as we have seen in the previous section.

We note also the CPU temperatures measured with an inlet water temperature of 30°C and 45°C is always lower than the CPU temperatures measured on the air-cooled server. The difference between the inlet water and the CPU temperature is about 12°C for BQCD and 15°C for HPL on the water-cooled server, while the difference between the room temperature and the CPU temperature is about 47°C for BQCD and 55°C for HPL on the air-cooled server.

With an inlet water temperature of 55°C, the CPU temperatures of the air-cooled server and the water-cooled serve are about the same.

### 5.3.2. Impact on voltage and frequency

Tables 5.7–5.9 present the impact of a lower CPU temperature on the core voltage and frequency of the CPU.

| HPL | | | | | | | | | | | | | |
|---|---|---|---|---|---|---|---|---|---|---|---|---|---|
| cooling/inlet temperature | air 21°C | | water 55°C | | | | water 45°C | | | | water 30°C | | |
| Turbo | OFF | ON | OFF | | ON | | OFF | | ON | | OFF | | ON | |
| UEFI Setting | eff. | eff. | eff. | perf. | eff. | perf. | eff. | perf. | eff. | perf. | eff. | perf. | eff. | perf. |
| avg. processor PL1 temperature °C | 76 | 75 | 72 | 76 | 72 | 76 | 62 | 65 | 62 | 65 | 46 | 50 | 46 | 50 |
| avg. PL1 processor frequency MHz | 1913 | 1910 | 1938 | 2131 | 1952 | 2129 | 1906 | 2126 | 1908 | 2125 | 1870 | 2107 | 1866 | 2104 |
| avg. PL1 processor voltage V | 0.728 | 0.729 | 0.730 | 0.756 | 0.730 | 0.756 | 0.741 | 0.766 | 0.741 | 0.774 | 0.752 | 0.778 | 0.764 | 0.778 |

**Table 5.7.** *CPU temperature, voltage and frequency running HPL*

| BQCD1K | | | | | | | | | | | | | | |
|---|---|---|---|---|---|---|---|---|---|---|---|---|---|---|
| cooling/inlet temperature | air 21°C | | water 55°C | | | | water 45°C | | | | water 30°C | | | |
| Turbo | OFF | ON | OFF | | ON | | OFF | | ON | | OFF | | ON | |
| UEFI Setting | eff. | eff. | eff. | perf. | eff. | perf. | eff. | perf. | eff. | perf. | eff. | perf. | eff. | perf. |
| avg. Plateau processor temperature °C | 68 | 72 | 68 | 66 | 70 | 70 | 57 | 57 | 59 | 59 | 42 | 42 | 43 | 43 |
| avg. Plateau processor frequency MHz | 2393 | 2670 | 2393 | 2396 | 2671 | 2681 | 2393 | 2394 | 2672 | 2669 | 2393 | 2394 | 2681 | 2666 |
| avg. Plateau processor voltage V | 0.799 | 0.832 | 0.799 | 0.803 | 0.836 | 0.850 | 0.808 | 0.808 | 0.845 | 0.843 | 0.822 | 0.822 | 0.856 | 0.855 |

**Table 5.8.** *CPU temperature, voltage and frequency running BQCD1K*

| BQCD128 | | | | | | | | | | | | | | |
|---|---|---|---|---|---|---|---|---|---|---|---|---|---|---|
| cooling/inlet temperature | air 20°C | | water 55°C | | | | water 45°C | | | | water 30°C | | | |
| Turbo | OFF | ON | OFF | | ON | | OFF | | ON | | OFF | | ON | |
| UEFI Setting | eff. | eff. | eff. | perf. | eff. | perf. | eff. | perf. | eff. | perf. | eff. | perf. | eff. | perf. |
| avg. Plateau processor temperature °C | 67 | 70 | 67 | 64 | 69 | 69 | 56 | 56 | 58 | 58 | 41 | 41 | 43 | 43 |
| avg. Plateau processor frequency MHz | 2389 | 2783 | 2388 | 2383 | 2786 | 2786 | 2396 | 2388 | 2785 | 2778 | 2388 | 2386 | 2779 | 2781 |
| avg. Plateau processor voltage V | 0.800 | 0.861 | 0.799 | 0.803 | 0.865 | 0.875 | 0.809 | 0.809 | 0.869 | 0.869 | 0.822 | 0.822 | 0.882 | 0.880 |

**Table 5.9.** *CPU temperature, voltage and frequency running BQCD128*

In the three tables, we observe the processor voltage is increasing as the processor temperature is decreasing. The processor voltage is set by the VR. VRs are programmed to work in the 70–80°C range. The CPU temperature is in this range with the air-cooled node and with the water-cooled node when the inlet water temperature is 55°C. But as the water temperature gets lower (45°C and 30°C), the CPU temperature gets lower, and the VR increases the voltage to keep the processor stable. As voltage is increasing, in order to keep the dynamic power stability the CPU frequency is not increasing as much as it would be if voltage was constant as we will see below.

In Table 5.7 for all temperatures, we note the frequency is about constant at about 1,900 MHz with the UEFI "efficiency-favor performance", while it increases to ~2,100 MHz with the UEFI "maximum performance", just one bin less than the max Turbo frequency for AVX-512 instructions according to Table 4.4, leading to a 10% frequency increase. We also note that the highest frequency is reached with a 55°C inlet water temperature, which corresponds to the processor temperature of the air-cooled node. Similarly, as the inlet water temperature is getting colder (45°C and 30°C), the processor voltage is increasing and the processor frequency is decreasing compared to 55°C.

In Tables 5.8 and 5.9, we note the impact of Turbo on the voltage and frequency due to the non-AVX instructions of BQCD. We note also the same impact of a colder CPU on the processor voltage as we have seen with HPL in Table 5.7. But the frequencies with Turbo ON and UEFI "maximum performance" are constant on the air-cooled and water-cooled servers at

2,670 MHz for BQCD1K and 2,770 MHz for BQCD128. This shows water cooling does not enable frequencies above 2,770 MHz, although, according to Table 4.4, the maximum Turbo frequency with all cores loaded is 3.1 GHz for non-AVX instructions, while it was enabling a frequency increase from 1,900 to 2,100 MHz for HPL and AVX-512 instructions. Could a different VR programming versus the CPU temperature be able to enable frequencies higher than 2,700 MHz and closer to the maximum Turbo frequency for non-AVX instructions is something we were not able to determine.

We also note that Turbo ON BQCD1K is running at a lower frequency than BQCD 128 (~2,670 MHz vs. ~2,780 MHz on the air-cooled node). This is due to the fact that BQCD1K CPI is 0.65 while BQCD12 CPI is 1.37 and therefore BQCD1K will have CPU0 which reach the TDP limit at a lower frequency with BQCD1K than with BQCD128.

### 5.3.3. Impact on power consumption and performance

Table 5.10 presents the CPU temperature, frequency, voltage and the node power and performance of HPL on the SD650 air-cooled node and water-cooled node at different inlet water temperature, Turbo OFF and ON and with the two different UEFI settings.

| HPL | | | | | | | | | | | | | | |
|---|---|---|---|---|---|---|---|---|---|---|---|---|---|---|
| cooling/inlet temperature | air 21°C | | water 55°C | | | | water 45°C | | | | water 30°C | | | |
| Turbo | OFF | ON | OFF | | ON | | OFF | | ON | | OFF | | ON | |
| UEFI Setting | eff. | eff. | eff. | perf. | eff. | perf. | eff. | perf. | eff. | perf. | eff. | perf. | eff. | perf. |
| avg. processor PL1 temperature °C | 76 | 75 | 72 | 76 | 72 | 76 | 62 | 65 | 62 | 65 | 46 | 50 | 46 | 50 |
| avg. PL1 processor frequency MHz | 1913 | 1910 | 1938 | 2131 | 1952 | 2129 | 1906 | 2126 | 1908 | 2125 | 1870 | 2107 | 1866 | 2104 |
| avg. PL1 processor voltage V | 0.728 | 0.729 | 0.730 | 0.756 | 0.730 | 0.756 | 0.741 | 0.766 | 0.741 | 0.774 | 0.752 | 0.778 | 0.764 | 0.778 |
| avg PL1 node power consumption W | 390 | 389 | 390 | 445 | 390 | 440 | 390 | 430 | 390 | 440 | 386 | 441 | 385 | 440 |
| GFLOPS reported | 1981 | 1940 | 1938 | 2125 | 1952 | 2178 | 1983 | 2166 | 1980 | 2142 | 1909 | 2109 | 1922 | 2104 |

Table 5.10. *CPU temperature, voltage, frequency, node power and performance running HPL*

We note the node power is increasing significantly with UEFI "maximum performance" (about 13% comparing the air-cooled node Turbo OFF), which is the price to get higher frequency (about 11%) and performance (about 10%). This confirms that HPL is a CPU-bound application since performance is increasing with frequency. Power is increasing more than performance since $P_{dyn}$ is varying with the square of voltage × frequency [4.2], while performance is only varying with frequency. We can also verify the impact of $P_{leak}$ on the node power by comparing the power of the SD650 water-cooled node at inlet water with temperature 45°C and 55°C. At 45°C, the node power is the same as at 55°C (440 W), while the voltage is higher (0.774 V vs. 0.756 V) and the frequency is approximately the same (2,125 MHz vs. 2,129 MHz). As $P_{dyn}$ varies with the square of voltage, $P_{dyn}$ at 45°C is higher than at 55°C leading to the conclusion $P_{leak}$ is lower at 45°C that at 55°C, which confirms that $P_{leak}$ decreases with the CPU temperature.

Tables 5.11 and 5.12 present the CPU temperature, frequency, voltage and the node power and performance of BQCD1K and BQCD128 on the SD650 air-cooled node and SD650 water-cooled node at different inlet water temperature, with Turbo OFF and ON and with the two different UEFI settings.

| BQCD1K | | | | | | | | | | | | | | |
|---|---|---|---|---|---|---|---|---|---|---|---|---|---|---|
| cooling/inlet temperature | air 21°C | | water 55°C | | | | water 45°C | | | | water 30°C | | | |
| Turbo | OFF | ON | OFF | | ON | | OFF | | ON | | OFF | | ON | |
| UEFI Setting | eff. | eff. | eff. | perf. | eff. | perf. | eff. | perf. | eff. | perf. | eff. | perf. | eff. | perf. |
| avg. Plateau processor temperature °C | 68 | 72 | 68 | 66 | 70 | 70 | 57 | 57 | 59 | 59 | 42 | 42 | 43 | 43 |
| avg. Plateau processor frequency MHz | 2393 | 2670 | 2393 | 2396 | 2671 | 2681 | 2393 | 2394 | 2672 | 2669 | 2393 | 2394 | 2681 | 2666 |
| avg. Plateau processor voltage V | 0.799 | 0.832 | 0.799 | 0.803 | 0.836 | 0.850 | 0.808 | 0.808 | 0.845 | 0.843 | 0.822 | 0.822 | 0.856 | 0.855 |
| avg PL1 node power consumption W | 333 | 359 | 334 | 340 | 358 | 365 | 328 | 329 | 357 | 357 | 325 | 325 | 350 | 347 |
| GFLOPS reported | 112 | 117 | 111 | 113 | 115 | 119 | 112 | 112 | 117 | 118 | 112 | 112 | 116 | 117 |

**Table 5.11.** *CPU temperature, voltage, frequency, node power and performance running BQCD1K*

| BQCD128 | | | | | | | | | | | | | | |
|---|---|---|---|---|---|---|---|---|---|---|---|---|---|---|
| cooling/inlet temperature | air 20°C | | water 55°C | | | | water 45°C | | | | water 30°C | | | |
| Turbo | OFF | ON | OFF | | ON | | OFF | | ON | | OFF | | ON | |
| UEFI Setting | eff. | eff. | eff. | perf. | eff. | perf. | eff. | perf. | eff. | perf. | eff. | perf. | eff. | perf. |
| avg. Plateau processor temperature °C | 67 | 70 | 67 | 64 | 69 | 69 | 56 | 56 | 58 | 58 | 41 | 41 | 43 | 43 |
| avg. Plateau processor frequency MHz | 2389 | 2783 | 2388 | 2383 | 2786 | 2786 | 2396 | 2388 | 2785 | 2778 | 2388 | 2386 | 2779 | 2781 |
| avg. Plateau processor voltage V | 0.800 | 0.861 | 0.799 | 0.803 | 0.865 | 0.875 | 0.809 | 0.809 | 0.869 | 0.869 | 0.822 | 0.822 | 0.882 | 0.880 |
| avg Plateau node power consumption W | 344 | 360 | 345 | 345 | 377 | 380 | 340 | 339 | 370 | 370 | 336 | 337 | 365 | 364 |
| GFLOPS reported | 60 | 60 | 59 | 60 | 60 | 60 | 60 | 60 | 60 | 60 | 59 | 60 | 60 | 60 |

**Table 5.12.** *CPU temperature, voltage, frequency, node power and performance running BQCD128*

As noted earlier, we see that BQCD128 performance is constant at 60 GFlops, while BQCD1K performance is increasing from 112 to 119 GFlops depending on the UEFI setting, Turbo mode and inlet water temperature. This confirms BQCD128 is memory bound and BQCD1K is CPU bound. Therefore, for memory-bound applications using non-AVX instructions, the optimal energy corresponds to the power minimization. Due to the impact of inlet water temperature on the VRs, the minimum power is reached at 35°C water temperature for both BQCD128 and BQCD1K. Although BQCD1K best performance is reached at 55°C water temperature with Turbo ON and

UEFI "maximum performance", the optimal energy is still reached at 35°C water temperature with Turbo OFF and UEFI "efficiency-favor performance" since the performance improvement is quite small for the reasons we explained earlier.

Let us present now measurements done on the air-cooled and water-cooled NeXtScale node equipped with Xeon Haswell processors 2697v3 running HPL at different inlet water temperature with UEFI "efficiency-favor performance".

These measurements are done while running single node HPL on 12 different nodes at different inlet water temperature. All 12 nodes have the configuration, Lenovo NeXtScale with 2697v3, 14C, 2.6GHz, 145W processor and the same memory configuration. The base frequency of 2697v3 is 2.6 GHz and its AVX2 base frequency is 2.2 GHz with a possible max Turbo AVX2 frequency of 2.9 GHz when all cores are loaded.

Figure 5.32 presents the effect of various cooling technologies on the 2697v3 processor (Haswell architecture) temperature and the corresponding HPL performance.

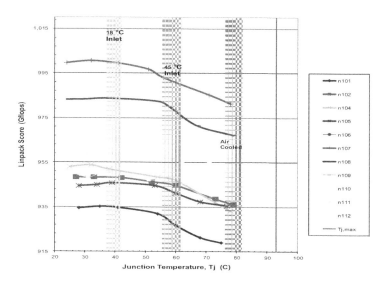

**Figure 5.32.** *Cooling impact on 2697v3 temperature and performance. For a color version of this figure, see www.iste.co.uk/brochard/energy.zip*

Y-axis of the graph presents the HPL performance measured on each node. HPL performance varies from 920 GFlops to 1,005 GFlops. Using an HPL efficiency of 92% and the theoretical 16 DP Flops per cycle provided by AVX2 on Xeon (Table 4.3), the sustained AVX2 frequency when running HPL can be estimated at 2.23 GHz (for 920 GFlops) and 2.44 GHz (for 1,005 GFlops). These frequency variations are due to processor temperature variations, which come from several factors: processor quality and cooling as explained below.

Each of the 12 curves represents the HPL performance on one node (n101 ,..., n112) for different junction processor temperature. The blue (left), green (middle) and orange (right) areas represent the processor junction temperature for a server equiped with DWC with 18°C inlet water, DWC with 45°C inlet water and air cooling, respectively.

The performance difference between the 12 curves is due to the performance variations of processors with the same SKU when running with Turbo ON or running HPL as discussed in section 5.1, Figure 5.1 and Aucun et al. (2016).

Looking at a single curve across different cooling zones, for DWC with cold water (blue area, 18°C inlet) and hot water (green area, 45°C inlet) performance (and frequency) remains mostly flat, while HPL performance (and frequency) drops when junction temperature increases due to air cooling leading to an increased processor power leakage.

Table 5.13 presents detailed data about nodes n101 and n102.

| | n101 | | n102 | |
|---|---|---|---|---|
| | | Linpack | | Linpack |
| T_water_inlet | T_j | Score | T_j | Score |
| (°C) | (°C) | (Gflops) | (°C) | (Gflops) |
| 8 | 28 | 934.5 | 27 | 948.4 |
| 18 | 35 | 935.2 | 33 | 948.3 |
| 24 | 41 | 934.7 | 42 | 948.1 |
| 35 | 54 | 931.9 | 52 | 946.3 |
| 45 | 60 | 926.7 | 60 | 944.7 |
| 55 | 68 | 921.3 | 73 | 938.5 |
| 55[1] | 75 | 918.9 | 79 | 936.1 |

**Table 5.13.** *Inlet water temperature impact on processor temperature and HPL*

Typical flow rate per node is 0.5 L/min (lpm) and is 0.25 lpm/node for the data reported as "55*". At these low flow rates, the processor temperature is about 20°C higher than inlet water temperature, while with air cooling it would be about 60°C due to the lower thermal resistance of water versus air (see section 3.5.1). DWC with inlet water close to 50°C still leads to a lower junction temperature than air at 20°C and therefore the lower processor leakage power either reduces the processor power consumption at fixed frequency or improves the performance with Turbo ON or AVX instructions like HPL. We also note that water cooling with 18°C inlet temperature improves performance by about 2% compared to the same node with air cooling. This differs from the Skylake measurements where performance of the water-cooled node was about 3% lower. We suspect this performance difference is due to the different VR programing on Haswell and Skylake.

## 5.4. Conclusions on the impact of cooling on power and performance

We have seen that the impact of cooling on voltage, frequency, power and performance depends mainly on four parameters: the type of instructions executed by the workload, the UEFI setting, the processor temperature and the processor type.

For AVX-512 intensive applications (like HPL), we see the UEFI "maximum performance" and water cooling deliver an increased performance (about 10%) at the expense of a higher power consumption (about 13%) versus air cooling. In this case, the 55°C inlet water temperature delivers the best performance due to the VRs, which increase the processor voltage as the inlet water temperature and the CPU temperature decrease. With the UEFI "efficiency-favor performance", we note a performance/ power difference on Haswell and Skylake. With Haswell, water cooling can provide up to 2% of power saving at equal performance while on Skylake water-cooling delivers 1% less power but with 3% less performance. We explain this difference by the Haswell and Skylake VRs different reactions to a colder CPU temperature.

For non-AVX applications (like BQCD), the UEFI "efficiency-favor performance" is best for performance and power consumption. Water cooling delivers a power saving of about 2% with no performance degradation versus air cooling. With the UEFI "maximum performance", water cooling is not enabling higher frequency than with the UEFI "efficiency-favor performance" due to an increased processor voltage in reaction to CPU temperatures below its normal operating range of 70–80°C.

For all instruction types with the UEFI "efficiency-favor performance", the lowest inlet water temperature delivers the lowest power consumption due to the reduction in processor power leakage.

Regarding Turbo, Turbo ON delivers the best performance with AVX-512 instructions and the UEFI "maximum performance", while Turbo OFF delivers the best for performance and power consumption with the UEFI "efficiency-favor performance". With non-AVX instructions, Turbo ON delivers the best frequency performance whatever is the UEFI setting and delivers the best performance with CPU-bound applications only.

# Monitoring and Controlling Power and Performance of Servers and Data Centers

This chapter will present some techniques to monitor and control the power and performance of IT devices (we will focus on servers), and the data center infrastructure itself with its pumps, chillers and so on.

When changes have to be made on a system, it is important to understand what is the potential impact of the changes on the system's behavior and therefore to have models or tools to predict their impact. These tools can predict the impact of a frequency change on a server's performance or energy or the impact of a cooling change on the data center PUE. We will present first the low-level components and application programming interface (API) to measure power and performance of servers equipped with Xeon processors and NVIDIA accelerators, then some modeling techniques to predict the power and performance of servers and finally high-level software to manage and control the power and performance of servers in the data centers.

## 6.1. Monitoring power and performance of servers

Measuring and monitoring accurately is mandatory step before controlling the behavior. We will discuss first the sensors and related APIs to measure power and temperature and next how to monitor the performance.

### 6.1.1. *Sensors and APIs for power and thermal monitoring on servers*

Power and thermal measurement is error prone since the accuracy of measurements can vary a lot depending on the granularity and the accuracy of the sensor and API used. By granularity, we mean the sampling rate at which the sensor is reading the data, and the reporting rate at which the readings are reported to the user through the API or high-level software. That is why we will describe in detail the power accuracy and granularity of power measurements.

#### 6.1.1.1. *Power and thermal monitoring on Intel platforms*

On Intel platforms, node manager (NM) and running average power limit (RAPL) are the fundamental interface reporting power. Figure 6.1 presents the different components for reporting AC and DC node power on a Lenovo dense ThinkSystem server.

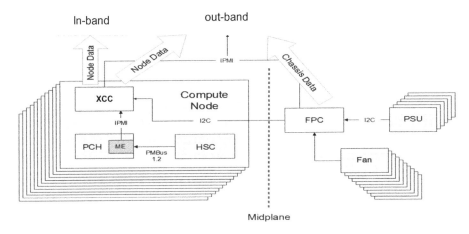

**Figure 6.1.** *Node power management on Lenovo ThinkSystem.*
*For a color version of this figure, see www.iste.co.uk/brochard/energy.zip*

PCH is the platform controller hub (i.e. south bridge), ME is the management engine (embedded in PCH) that runs Intel NM firmware and HSC is the hot swap controller that provides power readings.

On Lenovo ThinkSystem servers, XCC (xClarity Controller) runs the node-level system management. XCC is based on a baseboard management controller (BMC) using a dual-core ARM Cortex A9 service processor. It monitors DC power consumed by the node (as a whole and by the CPU and memory subsystems), it monitors inlet air temperature for the node and it caps DC power consumed by the node as a whole. It also monitors the CPU and memory subsystem throttling caused by node-level throttling and enables or disables power savings for node.

FPC is the fan/power controller for the chassis-level systems management. It monitors AC and DC power consumed by individual power supplies and aggregates to chassis level. It also monitors DC power consumed by individual fans and again aggregates to chassis level.

As shown in Figure 6.1, the information reported by the node-level system management can be reported in-band where the measurement is done on the node itself, or out-band where the measurement is requested by another node such as the cluster manager.

Figure 6.2 presents the reporting frequencies at the different levels from sensors to the application for NM and RAPL power management flows.

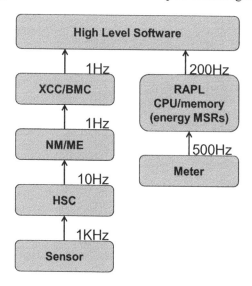

**Figure 6.2.** *Node manager and RAPL reporting frequencies*

For NM, the sensor level sampling rate is 1 KHz and the node power reported at the application level has a 1Hz frequency. For RAPL, the sampling from the energy Model Specific Registers (MSRs) for CPU and memory is 500 Hz and the reporting frequency is 200 Hz.

Therefore, as RAPL only reports CPU and memory power, the DC node power sampling frequency is only 1 Hz. This limits the scope of DC node power measurements to large granularity, such as job level, and is clearly not enough fine grain to measure DC node power at the subroutine or loop level. To achieve such fine grain measurements, other solutions have been implemented on top of NM (Hackenberg *et al.* 2014; Benini 2018; Libri *et al.* 2018).

An example of such a solution has been developed by Lenovo for the ThinkSystem SD650 with a new circuit and data flow. Figure 6.3 presents the new data flow and the reported frequency at each level, leading to a 100Hz DC node power frequency.

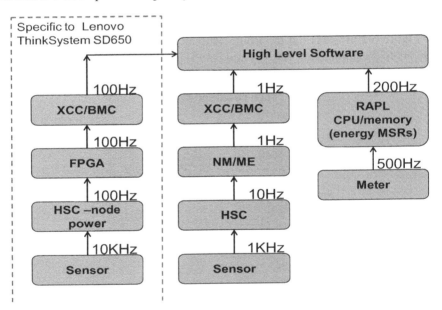

**Figure 6.3.** *New circuit to get higher resolution DC node power on SD650*

Figure 6.4 shows the circuits that provide both the usual NM interface and this new high accuracy DC node power measurement through an Intelligent Platform Management Interface (IPMI) raw command (see section 6.1.1.3).

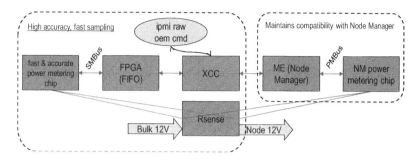

**Figure 6.4.** *New circuit to get higher resolution DC node power on SD650. For a color version of this figure, see www.iste.co.uk/brochard/energy.zip*

Figure 6.5 presents the percentage of error of the power readings of the different circuits we have presented, depending on the power load in the node. In the light-yellow rectangle on the left side of Figure 6.5, the server is idle or very little used, while on the light-yellow rectangle at the right side of the Figure 6.5 the server is highly loaded. When the node is idle or little used, the error is dominated by the offset error, while when the node is highly loaded the error is dominated by the gain error. The green, blue and orange curves present the error with three different circuits: green and blue curves represent the error for NM readings on an industry standard solution based on circuits such as TI LM25066, Analog Devices ADM1278 or Maxim VT505 (green) and on Lenovo NeXtScale nx360 m5 (blue). The orange curve represents the error on Lenovo SD650 with the high accuracy circuits presented in Table 4.15. This shows that these new circuits report not only higher frequency, but also much better accuracy.

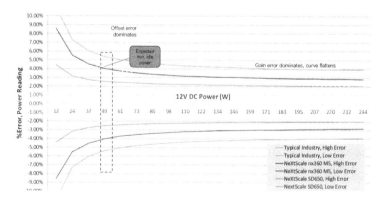

**Figure 6.5.** *Power accuracy of different circuits. For a color version of this figure, see www.iste.co.uk/brochard/energy.zip*

RAPL stands for running average power limit. It is the low-level interface used by Intel to collect energy information from the CPU and memory subsystems. NM consolidates the raw energy data and converts it to power by subtracting two energy readings and dividing by the time between the two readings.

### 6.1.1.2. *Circuits and interface for monitoring power and thermal on NVIDIA GPUs*

The basic tool for power and thermal monitoring on NVIDIA graphics processing units (GPUs) is the NVIDIA Management Library (NVML 2019). This is an API, based on C language, for monitoring and managing states of NVIDIA GPU devices, such as GPU utilization rate, running process, clock and performance, state, temperature and fan speed, power consumption and power management. Its sampling rate is ~500 Hz and the power accuracy for the entire board is ±5 W. NVIDIA System Management Interface (NVSMI) is a command line utility based on NVML to aid in the management and monitoring of NVIDIA GPU devices (NVSMI n.d.). NVSMI is a high-level command line interface and has a low sampling rate (~1 Hz) (Ferro *et al.* 2017).

NVML has query commands to query the state of the different GPU devices such as:

– ECC error counts: both correctable single bit and detectable double bit errors are reported. Error counts are provided for both the current boot cycle and for the lifetime of the GPU;

– GPU utilization: current utilization rates are reported for both the compute resources of the GPU and the memory interface;

– active compute process: the list of active processes running on the GPU is reported, along with the corresponding process name/id and allocated GPU memory;

– clocks and P-State: max and current clock rates are reported for several important clock domains, as well as the current GPU performance state.

– temperature and fan speed: the current core GPU temperature is reported, along with fan speeds for non-passive products;

– power management: for supported products, the current board power draw and power limits are reported.

NVML also has devices commands, like setting the power management limit (nvmlDeviceSetPowerManagementLimit), also called power cap elsewhere in this book, or setting the clock frequencies of the memory of graphics devices (nvmlDeviceSetApplicationsClocks) at which the compute and graphics applications will be running.

### 6.1.1.3. *IPMI*

IPMI is the major standard to request and collect information from IT devices (IPMI 2009). IPMI commands are a convenient low-level method to get sensor readings from monitored devices.

Out-of-band commands collect information through an access server or card (such as a BMC), which is connected to a management port of the monitored devices. In-band commands collects information on the device itself. IPMI raw commands are specified in hexadecimal value and are specific to the vendor.

Examples of IPMI commands like "IPMI-DCMI power set limit" to set a power limit in watts or "IPMI-sensors" to get CPU temperature, voltage and fan speed are provided by freeIPMI (2018)[1].

The following IPMI raw command reads the energy from the NM on SD650: "ipmitool raw 0x2e 0x81 0x66 0x4a 0x00 0x20 0x01 0x82 0x0 0x08".

Such a command has a reporting rate of ~1 Hz with NM on Intel platforms. A similar reporting rate is achieved with NVSMI on NVIDIA GPUs.

The following IPMI raw command will retrieve energy from the high sampling rate sensors on SD650 with a reporting rate of ~100 Hz: "ipmitool raw 0x3a 0x32 4 2 0 0 0".

For higher sampling and reporting rates (300–500 MHz), RAPL for Intel platforms and NVML for NVIDIA GPU should be used.

### 6.1.1.4. *Power API*

IPMI is a low-level interface to get information but it does not abstract the system and the relation between all its components, which is the goal of power API.

---

1. Available at: https://www.gnu.org/software/freeipmi/.

Power API (Grant *et al.* 2016) is the result of collaboration among national laboratories, universities and major HPC vendors to provide a range of standardized power management functions, from application-level control and measurement to facility-level accounting, including real-time and historical statistics gathering.

Power API describes a system by a hierarchical representation of objects (cabinet, chassis, node, board, power plane, core). It defines roles that interact with the system. Each object has certain attributes (e.g. power cap, voltage) that can be accessed depending on the role of the requester. Get/set functions enable basic measurement and control for the exposed object attribute.

Support is already available for Intel and AMD CPUs with the support of different hardware vendors like Cray, HPE, IBM and software vendors like Adaptive Computing.

### 6.1.1.5. Redfish

Redfish is a standard led by the Distributed Management Task Force (DMTF n.d.). The goal of Redfish is to replace and extend IPMI to deliver simple and secure management for converged, hybrid IT and the Software Defined Data Center, both human readable and machine capable. The main advantage over IPMI is its RESTful API. Redfish v1.0 is supported by all the major IT vendors.

It allows the user to retrieve basic server information and sensor data (like temperatures, fans, power supply) and facilitates remote management tasks such as reset, power cycle and remote console. Until now, the Redfish specification has covered only IT equipment. However, work is in progress to extend its scope to cover power with the Data Center Equipment Schema Bundle[2].

## 6.1.2. *Monitoring performance on servers*

### 6.1.2.1. Performance monitoring on Intel platforms

Hardware performance counters are specific registers built in the processor to store the count of hardware events like number of instructions executed, number of floating point/integer instructions executed, number of cycles, number of L1/L2 cache misses and so on. As the number of hardware counters is limited, prior to using the counters, each counter has to be programmed with the index of the event type to be monitored (Intel 2017).

---

2 Available at: https://www.dmtf.org/dsp/DSP-IS0005 [Accessed April 30, 2019].

The Performance Application Programming Interface (PAPI, see Terpstra *et al.* 2010) is an open source machine independent set of callable routines that provides access to the hardware performance counters on most modern processors like x86, ARM, Power and GPUs. It also provides access to RAPL functions for Intel x86.

In Chapter 5, we used cycles per instructions (CPI) [5.1] and gigabytes of memory read or written per second (GBS) [5.2] to characterize application performance. CPI was computed with the PAPI core events as:

$$CPI = \frac{PAPI\_TOT\_CYC}{PAPI\_TOT\_INS} \qquad [6.1]$$

GBS was computed with the uncore events (Intel 2012) of the Integrated Memory Controller (IMC) as:

$$GBS = \frac{CAS\_COUNT.RD + CAS\_COUNT.WR}{time \ x \ 1,000,000,000} \qquad [6.2]$$

On Intel platforms, the Intel Performance Tuning Utility (ptu or ptumon) is an easy way to collect performance temperature and power metrics reported in Chapter 5, although it is not officially supported by Intel anymore.

High-level tools are also available to visualize and help the developer to analyze the performance of workload running on a system. Some are proprietary like Intel Vtune[3] and Intel Advisor[4] who run on Intel processors and like ARM Forge and ARM Performance Reports[5] who run on Intel, AMD, ARM, OpenPower processors and NVIDIA GPU accelerators. There are also many open source tools such as gprof, TAU, Vampir, Paraver, Scalasca, Periscope and so on.

## 6.1.2.2. *Performance monitoring on NVIDIA platforms*

NVIDIA GPUs also have hardware performance counters to monitor the activity of the multiple functional units (NVIDIA 2015).

The NVIDIA CUDA Profiling Tools Interface (CUPTI) provides performance analysis tools with detailed information about GPU usage in a

---

3 Available at: https://software.intel.com/en-us/vtune [Accessed April 29, 2019].
4 Available at: https://software.intel.com/en-us/advisor [Accessed April 29, 2019].
5 ARM Cross-platform tools. Available at: https://developer.arm.com/tools-and-software/server-and-hpc/cross-platform-tools [Accessed April 29, 2019].

system. CUPTI is used by performance analysis tools such as nvprof, NVIDIA Visual Profiler, NVIDIA NSight, TAU and Vampir Trace.

PAPI CUDA is a PAPI version available on NVIDIA CUDA platform, which provides access to the hardware counters inside the GPU. PAPI CUDA is based on CUPTI and provides detailed performance counter information regarding the execution of GPU kernels.

NVIDIA Nsight Systems is a system-wide performance analysis tool designed to visualize an application's algorithms. It helps to identify the largest opportunities to optimize, and tune to scale efficiently across any number of CPUs and GPUs.

Open source high-level tools such as TAU, Vampir and Scalasca are also available on NVIDIA GPUs.

## 6.2. Modeling power and performance of servers

Through the measurements we presented in Chapter 5, we saw that power consumption depends on the workload and the system on which it is executing. In this section, we present a few models to quantity this relation.

### 6.2.1. *Cycle-accurate performance models*

Cycle-accurate simulators have been use for years by microprocessor designers to help them in their work (Hu *et al.* 2003). These tools are supposed to be the most accurate since they simulate the execution of every instruction at each cycle based on a register-transfer level (RTL) description of the circuit they want to simulate. RTL abstraction is used in hardware description languages to create high-level representations of a circuit, from which lower level representations and ultimately actual wiring can be derived.

Unfortunately, these tools take a huge amount of time to simulate a small piece of codes and that is why they cannot be used to make near real time decision to control the power or performance of a code while it is executing.

### 6.2.2. *Descriptive models*

Descriptive models are used when the events to simulate can be described quantitatively in an analytical way. A large drawback is that the descriptive model approach will not work for complex system problems, because the system is too complex to model completely or accurately. That is why these models are more educational or useful as a first-level analysis than production oriented. A descriptive model is clearly at the opposite spectrum end to a cycle-accurate simulator, a macroscopic model versus a microscopic one.

### 6.2.2.1. Application-specific models

Predicting the performance of a given algorithm on a specific system has been done for many years where the application execution time is split into computation, communication and I/O time. Each of these is then described by a simple equation related to its algorithmic complexity (number of operation to be performed) and some hardware characteristics of the system (time to compute a DP operation, to send a DP or SP word or to read/write one byte or one record to storage, etc.). Many examples of such techniques for specific numerical algorithms exist from early examples (Keyes and Gropp 1986; Brochard 1989) up to more recent examples (Bonfa *et al.* 2018).

For example, the elapsed time is split as:

$$T_{total} = T_{comp} + T_{comm} + T_{io}$$

where $T_{total}$ is the total elapsed time, $T_{comp}$ is the computation time, $T_{comm}$ the communication time and $T_{io}$ the I/O time, with no overlapping assumed between the different tasks.

For a matrix multiplication of rank n, computation time in ms would be:

$$T_{comp} = n^3/GFlops/1,000$$

where GFlops is evaluated as in Table 5.2 for the Intel Xeon 6148 taking into account the type of instructions executed. For a matrix multiplication when using a tuned BLAS library (NVIDIA Developer n.d.; Gennady and Shaojuan 2018), it should be GFlops for AVX-512 FMA, while if the code is written by hand with no compiler, optimization GFlops should be taken as SSE2 ADD or MULT. This simple example shows clearly how difficult it is to select the right parameters since they highly depend on the type of instructions executed.

Similar work has been done regarding power consumption by splitting the total power of the device across its different components (CPU, memory, storage, etc.) and eventually splitting each component power into static and dynamic power. But the coefficients cannot be expressed by simple arithmetic formulas. This drawback is corrected by the predictive methods as described in section 6.2.3.

### 6.2.2.2. *Application signature/surrogate-based performance models*

Other performance prediction methods have introduced some level of abstraction to characterize the applications (application signature) and the system hardware (system signature) at a higher level than using the application and system characteristics. Examples of such approach are Todi *et al.* (2007) and Snavely *et al.* (2013). Another approach is to decompose an application behavior as a linear equation of surrogates, which are small enough such that they have been projected by cycle-accurate simulators and which represent the workloads to be projected (Sameh *et al.* 2012).

### 6.2.3. *Predictive models*

A predictive model refers to a mathematical model that can accurately predict future outcomes based on historical data using statistical or neural network (NN) methods.

### 6.2.3.1. *Statistical power models*

Several authors have worked to build linear power models where coefficients are calculated by best fit (or linear multiregression) statistical methods. With such models, accuracy is limited between 5% and 10%, but given their simplicity they can be used to make real time decisions.

An example of such a model is presented below. Economou *et al.* (2006) is another example.

As in every statistical method, the events and data used are critical. Looking at the measurements presented in Chapter 5, we saw that CPU power is varying with CPI, the core frequency and the processor temperature of the processors while DIMM power is varying with GBS.

The impact of CPI (CPI = 1/IPC) on CPU power and GBS on DIMM power is visible when we compare the CPU power of the various workloads Turbo OFF. HPL in Figures 5.3–5.6 has a very low CPI (0.45) and the highest possible CPU power of 150 W and a DIMM power of 32 W with a

GBS of 70 for the plateau PL1 phase. For STREAM in Figures 5.11–5.16 we note an average CPU power of 125 W with a CPI ~10 and a DIMM power of 43 W with a GBS of 140. We see the same behavior on BQCD where BQCD128 has an average CPU power of 118 W with a CPI of 1.10 and BQCD1K has an average CPU power of 121 W with a CPI of 0.70. Similarly, BQCD128 has a DIMM power of 33 W and BQCD1K of 21 W with a respective average GBS value of 74 and 27.

This correlation of CPU power with 1/CPI and DIMM power with GBS leads to a simple CPI/GBS model, which was first introduced by Brochard *et al.* (2010) to predict the power and the performance of a workload at any possible frequency $f_n$ on a given system when this workload has run already once at nominal frequency $f_0$ on the same system with no temperature variation.

Such a simple model enables real time decisions on which frequency to set while the workload is running to minimize power or energy (see section 6.3).

In this model, DC power at frequency $f_n$ is given by:

$$Power(f_n) = A(f_n) * GIPS(f_0) + B(f_n) * GBS(f_0) + C(f_n) \quad [6.3]$$

where GIPS is the number of giga instructions per second and GBS is the number of giga bytes of memory read or written per second with:

$$GIPS(f_0) = f_0 * IPC(f_0) \quad [6.4]$$

The elapsed time of a code at frequency $f_n$ is given by:

$$Time(f_n) = Number\ of\ instructions * \frac{CPI(f_n)}{f_n} \quad [6.5]$$

As the number of instructions in a code is independent of the frequency at which it is executed, we can write [6.5] at frequency $f_0$ and from it derive:

$$Time(f_n) = Time(f_0) * \frac{CPI(f_n)}{CPI(f_0)} * \frac{f_n}{f_0} \quad [6.6]$$

where the CPI at frequency fn is given by:

$$CPI(f_n) = D(f_n) * CPI(f_0) + E(f_n) * TPI(f_0) + F(f_n) \quad [6.7]$$

The $A(f_n)$, $B(f_n)$, $C(f_n)$, $D(f_n)$, $E(f_n)$ and $F(f_n)$ are the hardware coefficients of the server computed through the least squares fitting of [6.3] and [6.5] measuring power and elapsed time of a suite of small kernels run at all possible frequency $f_0$ to $f_n$ (Brochard *et al.* 2010).

Therefore, with [6.3], [6.6] and [6.7], the elapsed time and power of a code can be computed at frequency fn given its power, time, CPI and GBS at frequency $f_0$ and the hardware coefficients that have been computed and stored once and for all unless the hardware configuration changes.

This model was later modified to better predict the DC power since [6.3] has no information on the actual power measured at $f_0$ and [6.3] was replaced by

$$Power(f_n) = A(f_n) * Power\ (f_0) + B(f_n) * TPI(f_0) + C(f_n) \qquad [6.8]$$

where TPI is the number of memory transactions per instruction.

This latter model based on [5.12] and [4.12] was used by IBM LoadLeveler Energy Aware Scheduling (Brochard *et al.* 2011; IBM Knowledge Center n.d.), which will be described in section 6.3.1. The LRZ data center, which we will present in section 7.2, has been using LoadLeveler Energy Aware Scheduler (EAS) from 2012 until 2018 and measured the accuracy of this model on a large selection of real workloads, demonstrating an average error less than 5% (Auweter *et al.* 2014).

An extension of this model where power and elapsed time can be predicted from any frequency fi instead of only $f_0$ was introduced and used by Energy Aware Runtime (BSC n.d.).

These models have been developed such that the predicted performance and power can be computed near real time while the application is executing such decisions can be made to change their performance, power and energy either at the job level or at the iteration level (see section 6.3).

## 6.2.3.2. *NN-based models for power prediction*

Neural network (NN) methods are a new class of predictive methods that are not using classic statistical methods, but rather NNs that have been trained by ingesting real data gathered from the data center sensors to predict some behavior.

Figure 6.6 presents an example of an NN with $x_i$ inputs, hidden layers and one output P.

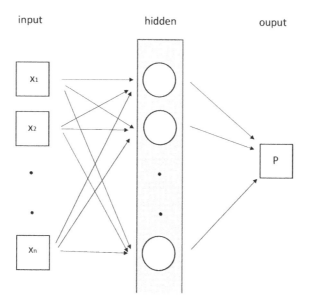

**Figure 6.6.** *Neural network example*

Puzovic *et al.* (2018) use an NN model to predict the power consumption of workloads on three different servers equipped with Intel Xeon E5 v4, IBM Power8 System S822LC and Cavium ThunderX ARMv8 processors and compare it to the linear regression model based on CPI and GBS as described above. For statistical methods, the selection of the data is critical, but also now their raw number as we will see. In this study, they use the following hardware performance counters as the input of the NN:

1) total number of instructions (INST) – the number of instructed retired;

2) cycles (CYC) – number of cycles during the execution time. It should be denoted as INST/CYC = IPC, which we saw has a major impact on the processor power;

3) dispatched/fetched instructions (IFETCH) – the previous metric (IPC) only accounts for instructions that have been retired, but it does not take into account instructions that have been speculatively executed. These instructions still consume power;

4) stalls (STALL) – due to multiple issues and out-of-order execution, contemporary processors stall due to dependencies such as data and resource conflicts. The conflicts draw power and are not accounted for by any of the previous counters.

5) branch hit ratio (BR) – in order to find contribution to power consumed by speculatively executed instructions due to branch misprediction, the percentage of correctly predicted branches during the application execution is measured;

6) floating point instructions (FLOPS) – for HPC applications, the largest contributor toward power consumption are instructions that are utilizing the floating-point unit as they represent the majority of executed instructions;

7) L1 cache hit – due to the fact that the previous counters measure only power that is consumed within the processor, the number of hits in local cache (L1) is measured;

8) last level cache miss – the number of misses in the shared last level cache (LLCM) is also measured to record power from memory.

The above hardware performance counters were extracted from 43 benchmarks to train the model, which comes from the MATLAB Neural Network Toolbox.

The accuracy of the NN model increases with the number of hardware performance counters, the different benchmarks in the training set as well as running multiples copies of the same benchmark. The accuracy of the NN model is also shown to be less than 3% across the three servers, better than the statistical linear regression model based on CPI and GBS.

Another example of an NN model (Gao 2014) predicts the PUE of a data center. This NN utilizes five hidden layers and 50 nodes per hidden layer. The training dataset contains 19 normalized input variables (listed below) and one normalized output variable, the data center PUE:

1) total server IT load [kW];

2) total Campus Core Network Room (CCNR) IT load [kW];

3) total number of process water pumps (PWP) running;

4) mean PWP variable frequency drive (VFD) speed [%];

5) total number of condenser water pumps (CWP) running;

6) mean CWP variable frequency drive (VFD) speed [%];

7) total number of cooling towers running;

8) mean cooling tower leaving water temperature (LWT) set point [F];

9) total number of chillers running;

10) total number of dry coolers running;

11) total number of chilled water injection pumps running;

12) mean chilled water injection pump set point temperature [F];

13) mean heat exchanger approach temperature [F];

14) outside air wet bulb (WB) temperature [F];

15) outside air-dry bulb (DB) temperature [F];

16) outside air enthalpy [kJ/kg];

17) outside air relative humidity (RH) [%];

18) outdoor wind speed [mph];

19) outdoor wind direction [deg].

Between predicted and actual PUE measured on a major data center, the model achieved a mean absolute error of 0.004 and standard deviation of 0.005 on the test dataset or 0.4% error for a PUE of 1.1, which is quite amazing and better than what was achieved by descriptive models. Note that the model error generally increases for PUE values greater than 1.14 due to the scarcity of training data corresponding to those values. The model accuracy for those PUE ranges is expected to increase over time as Google collects additional data on its DC operations. After this calibration phase, the model was used for identifying optimization opportunities.

## 6.3. Software to optimize power and energy of servers

One way to manage and optimize the power and energy of servers is at the job scheduler level when jobs are submitted. A more dynamic approach is to do it at run time when workloads are executing and doing changes on the fly. The system power is obtained by aggregating bottom up the information of all jobs running on the system. Another approach is to start from the system power or energy budget and proceed by splitting this total power budget to each node in a top down approach. This section will give examples of these different approaches.

### 6.3.1. *LoadLeveler job scheduler with energy aware feature*

The EAS feature of the LoadLeveler job scheduler and resource manager (IBM Knowledge Center n.d.) was introduced in 2012.

The goal of LL EAS is to determine and apply at the job level the optimal frequency to all cores and nodes running the job to match an energy policy selected. This frequency is set by setting the appropriate P-state using dynamic voltage and frequency setting (DVFS).

This frequency is determined and applied before the job is submitted through the use of an Energy Tag, which is added to the LL submit command. If this Energy Tag is new, meaning this job is submitted for the first time, LL EAS collects all the metrics (CPI, TPI and GBS) described in section 6.3.1 and compute the power and elapsed time of the job if it was run at any possible frequency based on the hardware coefficients computed in the learning phase as described above. When the job is submitted another time with the same energy tag and a selected energy policy, EAS determine the optimal frequency to match the policy. The energy policies proposed are *minimize time to solution* and *minimize energy to solution.*

With minimize time to solution, the goal is to accelerate the jobs that make efficient use of a higher frequency. For this policy, a default frequency fd, lower than nominal frequency f0, has to be defined by the system administrator such that all jobs by default run at the frequency fd if unless their predicted performance variation is higher than a threshold, also defined by the system administrator. With such a policy, memory bound jobs will run at default frequency and their performance will not be hurt, while only application whose performance will benefit from a higher frequency will run at a higher frequency. It is this minimize time to solution policy, which has been used on SuperMUC in production and whose efficiency is reported in Auweter *et al.* (2014).

Minimize energy to solution is the opposite of minimize time to solution. With minimize energy to solution, jobs by default run at a nominal frequency and their frequency is decreased from $f_0$ to $f_n$ if it would reduce the energy of the job without hurting its performance more than a given threshold, defined by the system administrator.

On top of optimizing the power of active nodes, LoadLeveler was also minimizing the power of idle nodes by implementing the S3 state (Figure 4.11) on the nodes, which were idle and had no work waiting to be executed in the batch queue.

LL EAS was first released at LRZ in 2012 with the SuperMUC Phase 1 system (see section 7.2).

### 6.3.2. Energy Aware Runtime (EAR)

EAR (2018) is an energy management run time framework with different components. We describe here the EAR library and EAR Global Manager (EARGM). The EAR library uses similar power and performance models and energy policies as LL EAS, which we described above. However, they differ widely since EAR is open source and dynamic. To achieve dynamicity and transparency, EAR detects automatically at run time the iterative structures of a code and controls its frequency at the outer loop level. With such an approach, no code modification or energy tag is required and the frequency applied can change during the execution of the code if the performance and powers profiles (called the application signature) have changed over the iteration space. The EAR library targets applications written with the Message Passing Interface (MPI) or hybrid MPI + OpenMP applications. To detect the iterative structures of a code without modifying them, EAR relies on the Profiling MPI (PMPI) interface plus the LD_PRELOAD mechanism to be automatically loaded with MPI jobs. Figure 6.7 shows EAR library software stack.

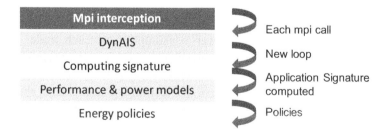

**Figure 6.7.** *EAR software stack*

Once MPI calls are intercepted, EAR passes the sequence of MPI calls together with their arguments to Dynamic Application Iterative Structure detection (DynAIS) to identify repetitive regions in parallel applications (outer loops). DynAIS is an innovative multilevel algorithm with very low overhead. DynAIS receives as input a sequence of events and reports different values that represents the role of the event in the outer repetitive sequence detected. By using DynAIS, EAR can detect MPI calls corresponding to the beginning of a new loop or MPI calls corresponding with a new iteration of an already detected loop.

Since EAR is aware of application loop iterations, it is able to self-evaluate policy decisions, one of the key differences between EAR and other solutions. Because of DynAIS, EAR computes the Application Signature at runtime corresponding to one loop iteration. The Application Signature is a very reduced set of metrics that characterize application behavior. The Application Signature together with the hardware characterization (called the System Signature) is the input for the power and performance models used by EAR.

Given the iterative behavior of many scientific applications, the Application Signature of one iteration in the main loop is representative of the application behavior, allowing EAR to do a frequency selection at runtime, avoiding the necessity of using historic information guided by user hints. EAR proposes a totally distributed frequency selection design avoiding interferences and additional noise in the network or the file system.

The Application Signature is a set of metrics that uniquely identifies and characterizes the application for a given architecture and one particular execution (that could differ depending on many factors such as input data and node list). The Application Signature includes CPI, TPI, time and average DC node power.

The System Signature is a set of coefficients that characterize the hardware with performance and power consumption of each node in the system. It is computed during a learning phase at EAR installation time or every time a configuration change is happening to the nodes. The EAR learning phase is similar to the LL EAS learning phase except that the hardware coefficients of each node are kept and used in a distributed way as explained above for the frequency selection.

Regarding the energy policies, EAR uses other criteria to EAS. For minimize time to solution, EAR uses a performance gain threshold called EAR threshold such that a new frequency is set from $f_i$ to $f_{i+1}$ if:

$$PerfGain \geq FreqGain * EAR\_threshold \qquad [6.9]$$

with:

$$PerfGain = \frac{Time(f_i) - Time(f_{i+1}))}{Time(f_i)} \qquad [6.10]$$

$$FreqGain = \frac{f_{i+1} - f_i}{f_i} \qquad [6.11]$$

As well as controlling the frequency of the outer loop level in an MPI application, EAR uses EARGM to control the total power consumption and energy of the system such that if a power or energy capping value has been defined and is exceeded, EARGM will ask the EAR library to be more restrictive on the energy policies. For example, with minimize time to solution, it will decrease the default and/or maximum frequency by 1 bin or increase the performance gain threshold.

EAR overhead, predictions and decisions accuracy have been analyzed by nine application tests running on a cluster of up to 1040 cores (Corbalan and Brochard 2019) and installed on SuperMUC-NG at LRZ (see section 7.2) to optimize its energy.

### 6.3.3. *Other run time systems to manage power*

Many other tools have been developed for power management using DVFS.

The main goal of Adagio (Rountree *et al.* 2009) is the power balancing across nodes in order to stay within a given power capping. Adagio is a runtime library targeted to save as much energy as possible while minimizing the performance penalty. Adagio makes its frequency decisions at runtime and does not need user intervention. *Conductor* (Marathe *et al.* 2015) is a run-time system that intelligently distributes available power to nodes and cores to improve performance. It is also based on detecting critical paths and using more power in these parts, however, *Conductor* requires the user to mark the end of the iterative time step. *Conductor* targets MPI and OpenMP applications and it can be envisioned as an extension of Adagio since it exploits similar concepts in a different context. *Conductor* exploits the thread level by doing a reconfiguration of the concurrency level and later redistributing the power per job to speed up the critical path. After this power reallocation, *Conductor* checks its impact by doing global synchronization for a few time steps. While global synchronizations can have a major overhead on the system performance, as applications are expected to run many time step, this overhead is negligible.

GEOPM (Eastep *et al.* 2017) is an open source framework for power management. GEOPM implements a hierarchical design to support Exascale systems. GEOPM is an extensible framework where new policies can be added at the node level or application (MPI) level. Some of the policies require application modifications but some others do not have this requirement. Energy control in GEOPM is not included as part of the GEOPM framework. Rather it offers an API to be used by the resource manager.

DVFS has been also used in other works to reduce the power consumed by applications. In the context of MPI applications, DVFS has been used inside the MPI library to reduce the power consumed during communication periods (Lim *et al.* 2006; Etinski *et al.* 2009; Venkatesh *et al.* 2015). The goal of these proposals is to reduce the power consumed inside the MPI library without introducing a significant performance degradation in the application execution.

Power capping has been also targeted at the scheduler and resource manager level, for instance, in SLURM (2018) and PBS (PBS Works n.d.) to control the total power consumption. Although effective, such power capping implementation applies the same policy to all applications without taking into account their performance or energy characteristics.

## 6.4. Monitoring, controlling and optimizing the data center

### 6.4.1. *Monitoring the data center*

Data Center Integrated Monitoring (DCIM) is a wide topic with much software readily available. Meyer *et al.* (2016) gives a good overview of the different DCIM used in different high-performance computing data centers in Europe.

The following major functions of a DCIM are extracted from this report:

– Asset management

Most popular DCIM solutions have the ability to catalogue IT assets such as network equipment and servers, which are installed in rack cabinets in the data center. Also, there are some packages that map all connections between devices and from where a particular device is supplied with electricity. In addition, a DCIM solution provides tools to generate QR codes or barcode labels. Labels can then be scanned by an administrator using a smartphone or tablet.

– Capacity management

Most DCIM software available on the market are able to inform the user if there is enough space, available network ports or electric sockets in rack cabinets for new equipment. Furthermore, some DCIM software can detect that equipment is too heavy for a particular rack cabinet, or that the power supply or the cooling system has reached its limits and new equipment cannot be added.

– Real-time monitoring and alerting

Complex DCIM applications gather data and can inform the administrators if equipment parameters exceed thresholds so that they can react to the situation immediately.

– Trends and reporting

DCIM systems that monitor equipment parameters in real time are often able to save that data to visualize changes of parameters in the form of graphs or reports.

– Data center floor visualization

In most cases, DCIM systems provide 2D or 3D visualization of server rooms. Some solutions are even able to calculate heat dissipation and display it as a thermal-vision view of the server room.

– Simulations

Most complex DCIM solutions have functions to calculate "what if" scenarios, such as a power failure, a cooling system malfunction or the deployment of new equipment, to better understand consequences of such events and take appropriate actions.

– Workflow

Some DCIM software implements ticket systems to help automate and document change requests for assets in a data center. Thus, only qualified personnel are responsible for performing changes to IT assets.

– Remote control

Parts of DCIM solutions allow storing login credentials in an encrypted database to help administrators cope with a huge number of IT assets that require remote control.

– Application programming interface

Some DCIM applications are able to communicate with third party software by providing an API.

– Mobile and web-based interface

More and more often developers add a possibility to manage a data center through mobile or web-based applications for ease-of-use from anywhere.

## 6.4.2. *Integration of the data center infrastructure with the IT devices*

Dynamic optimization of the data center operations based on the data gathered by the DCIM and the data gathered from the IT devices (power and energy consumption of servers, storage and network switches) is the challenge ahead.

Google's PUE Neural Network model (section 6.2.3.2) is a good example of a tool to optimize the data center energy efficiency based on data collected by the infrastructure and building sensors. However, it still lacks the integration of the data collected from the IT devices (servers, storage and network switches).

LRZ started such an attempt with a toolset called Power Data Aggregation Monitor (PowerDAM) (Shoukourian *et al.* 2013), which collects and evaluates data from all aspects of the HPC data center (e.g. environmental information, site infrastructure, information technology systems, resource management systems and applications). The aim of PowerDAM was not to improve the HPC data center's energy efficiency, but to collect energy relevant data in a single place for analysis, typically by cloning them from already existing databases. Without this, energy efficiency improvements are non-trivial as data have typically to be pulled from multiple databases with different access restrictions, protocols, formats and sampling intervals. As such, PowerDAM was a first step toward a truly unified energy efficiency evaluation toolset needed for improving the overall energy efficiency of HPC data centers.

Recently, LRZ started development of a fully integrated and scalable monitoring solution called Data Center Data Base (DCDB n.d.). The goal of DCDB is to collect all sensor data that are relevant for HPC operations in a single database from the beginning instead of cloning it from other databases. For this purpose, DCDB provides a rich set of data collection plugins to talk to a multitude of devices via their native protocol (such as IPMI and SNMP for IT devices, Bacnet and Modbus for building infrastructure, or JSON/XML for Internet of Things (IoT) devices like smart meters, sensors, thermostats). Further stressing the comprehensiveness of DCDB's approach, it can also collect information relevant for application performance such as CPU performance counters, parallel file system performance metrics and interconnect transfer rates and error counters. The main philosophy of DCDB is to collect as much data as possible at the highest sampling rate possible, without aggregating data during collection. To facilitate such extensive data collection, DCDB employs Apache Cassandra as a distributed non relational (NoSQL) database backend that provides the necessary scalability to ingest hundreds of thousands of sensors with subsecond sampling periods. The collected data can then easily be analyzed in a Grafana-based dashboard that is accessible from any web browser.

# PUE, ERE and TCO of
# Various Cooling Solutions

## 7.1. Power usage effectiveness, energy reuse effectiveness and total cost of ownership

### 7.1.1. *Power usage effectiveness and energy reuse effectiveness*

When we introduced energy reuse effectiveness (ERE) in [I.3], we used the definition given by Patterson *et al.* (2010) where ERE measures the benefit from waste heat produced by the data center without taking into account the potential benefit to the data center. In other words, the energy reuse from [I.3] is the waste heat energy dissipated by the IT equipment and reused outside the data center as we will see with National Renewable Energy Laboratory (NREL) Research Support Facility (RSF) in section 7.2.1. With such an approach, ERE is defined by:

$$ERE = \frac{Total\ energy - enery\_reuse}{IT\ equipment\ energy} \qquad [I.3]$$

with:

$$ERE = (1 - ERF) * PUE \qquad [7.1]$$

where ERF is the energy recovery factor:

$$ERF = \frac{Enery\_reuse}{Total\ energy} \qquad [7.2]$$

If we want to measure the impact when waste heat is reused by the data center itself as with adsorption chillers producing cold water (see section 3.7) as done with CoolMUC at Leibnitz Supercomputing Center (LRZ) (see section 7.2.2), we have to introduce a new definition of ERE, which we will call ERE_DC given by:

$$ERE_{DC} = \frac{Total\ energy - energy_{\_DCreused}}{IT\ equipment\ energy} = \frac{Total\ energy_{\_reused}}{IT\ equipment\ energy} \quad [7.3]$$

Where $energy_{\_DCreused}$ is the waste heat energy effectively reused by the data center and $total\ energy_{\_reused}$ is the net total energy consumed by the data center.

It should be noted that in such a situation:

$$ERE_{DC} = PUE_{ERE\_DC} \quad [7.4]$$

where $PUE_{ERE\_DC}$ is the power usage effectiveness (PUE) computed as defined in [I.1] where the total energy is the net total energy consumed by the data center, which is equal to the total energy without reuse minus the energy reused by the data center.

In such a case, as we will see with CoolMUC-2, $PUE_{ERE\_DC}$ is lower than 1 (see section 7.2.2.3) while Patterson *et al.* (2010) and Sheppy *et al.* (2011) thought it cannot be the case.

Total cost of ownership represents the system cost over the life time of the system. Total cost of ownership (TCO) is the sum of CAPEX and OPEX, where CAPEX includes all capital expenditure to install the system (acquisition and installation) and OPEX includes all operating expenditure to run the system (maintenance, electricity, etc.). In the situation where waste heat is not reused, we have:

$$TCO = CAPEX + OPEX \quad [7.5]$$

$$CAPEX = System\ acquisition\ and\ installation\ cost + \\ data\ center\ installation\ cost \quad [7.6]$$

where *data center installation cost* includes the price to install or upgrade cooling equipment, which have some importance in TCO.

$$OPEX = Operational\ cost + energy\ cost \quad [7.7]$$

where *operational cost* includes maintenance costs and floor space cost per square meter or square feet, which have an impact in TCO when density of servers is taken into consideration to maximize the capacity of the data center.

$$Energy\ cost_{noreuse} = Total\ energy * Electricity\ price \qquad [7.8]$$

Where *energy cost$_{noreuse}$* is the energy cost when waste heat is not reused, total energy is the amount of energy consumed by the computer facility over its life time and electricity price is the price of 1 kW/h.

Substituting PUE definition from [I.1] into [7.8], this becomes:

$$Energy\ cost_{noreuse} = IT\ equipment\ energy * PUE * energy\ price \qquad [7.9]$$

In the case of a hybrid cooling, the overall PUE is computed by:

$$PUE = e_{air} * PUE_{air} + e_{rdhx} * PUE_{rdhx} + e_{dwc} * PUE_{dwc} \qquad [7.10]$$

where $PUE_{air}$, $PUE_{rdhx}$ and $PUE_{dwc}$ are, respectively, the PUE of systems cooled by air like computer air handling units (CRAH) or in-row coolers by chilled water like RDHX and chilled or hot water like direct water cooled (DWC) and where:

$$e_{air} = \frac{Energy\ of\ IT\ equipment\ cooled\ by\ air}{IT\ Equipment\ Energy} \qquad [7.11]$$

$$e_{rdhx} = \frac{Energy\ of\ IT\ equipment\ cooled\ by\ RDHX}{IT\ Equipment\ Energy} \qquad [7.12]$$

$$e_{dwc} = \frac{Energy\ of\ IT\ equipment\ cooled\ by\ DWC}{IT\ Equipment\ Energy} \qquad [7.13]$$

As we will see later, these different PUE have different values and have a great impact on TCO.

As TCO has become a critical element in the selection of IT equipment, some organizations introduced it in procurements to select the right solution. Therefore, there is a need to provide a proper way to evaluate TCO before the end of the system life time. To do that, a workload has to be defined that will be used to measure its energy during a short period of time at system delivery, and this energy will have to be scaled up to the life of the system to be introduced in the OPEX part of the TCO.

The easiest way is to use High Performance Linpack (HPL) (Petitet *et al.* 2018) or another classic benchmark like SPEC Power (SPEC 2008) as the reference workload. But as we have seen, HPL is not representative of real applications since it consumes more power than real workloads. Therefore, some organizations (Boyer 2017) have introduced their own TCO model using a benchmark to measure the energy of the system (including compute nodes, networks and disks) when running this workload, multiplied by the number of times this benchmark can be executed over the life time of the system. In principle, this benchmark should be composed of a suite of workloads, which represent as closely as possible what the system will be executing in production whether it is HPC or AI oriented or a mix of both.

This approach is rather thorough but still does not consider the possible waste heat reuse or the impact of free cooling. This will be discussed in the following sections.

### 7.1.2. *PUE and free cooling*

As discussed in section 3.6, free cooling occurs when chillers or mechanical compressors do not need to run since the temperature difference between the outside temperature and the cold water temperature is at least 1°C or 2°C (2–4°F).

To take this effect into consideration in the PUE calculation, we introduce $f_{air}, f_{cold}$ and $f_{warm}$ as:

$$f_{air} = \frac{Number\ of\ hours\ of\ free\ cooling\ by\ air}{Total\ number\ of\ hours} \qquad [7.14]$$

$$f_{rdhx} = \frac{Number\ of\ hours\ of\ free\ cooling\ by\ RDHX}{Total\ number\ of\ hours} \qquad [7.15]$$

$$f_{dwc} = \frac{Number\ of\ hours\ of\ free\ cooling\ by\ DWC}{Total\ number\ of\ hours} \qquad [7.16]$$

And in such case PUE is computed by:

$$PUE = (1 - f_{air}) * e_{air} * PUE_{air} + (1 - f_{rdhx}) * e_{rdhx} * PUE_{rdhx} + (1 - f_{dwc}) e_{dwc} *$$
$$PUE_{dwv} + (f_{air} * e_{air} + f_{rdhx} * e_{rdhx} + f_{dwv} * e_{dwc}) * PUE_{free} \qquad [7.17]$$

where $PUE_{free}$ is the PUE of free cooling, which is very close to 1 since free cooling uses only the energy of the pumps. We will see the impact of free cooling on TCO in section 7.5.

### 7.1.3. ERE and waste heat reuse

When waste heat is reused, we have to introduce a variant of [7.8] where we deduce the energy produced from the waste heat and delivered back to the data center:

$$Energy\ cost_{reuse} = (Total\ energy - energy_{-DCreused}) * \\ electricity\ price \qquad\qquad [7.18]$$

where $energy\ cost_{reuse}$ is the energy cost when waste heat is reused by the data center and $energy\ cost_{DCreused}$ is the amount of reused energy delivered to the data center. A typical example of waste heat reused by the data center is the adsorption chillers described in section 3.7.2 to produce cold water from the wasted heat captured by warm water cooling. Such an example will be presented in section 7.2.3.

Substituting in [7.18] "Total energy – energy_DCreused" by "ERE_DC * IT equipment energy" from [7.1], and "IT equipment energy" by "Total energy/PUE" from [I.1], and by the definition of "Energy cost_noreuse" [7.8], we have:

$$Energy\ cost_{reuse} = Energy\ cost_{noreuse} * \frac{ERE\_DC}{PUE} \qquad\qquad [7.19]$$

where PUE is the system PUE with no heat reuse.

Therefore, when waste heat is not reused according to [7.9], a low PUE is important to reduce the energy cost, while when waste heat is reused according to [7.19], a low ERE_DC/PUE is critical. In the latter case, it is important to note that a low PUE is not as critical as it is when waste heat is no reused as long as ERE_DC is low. For example, in a data center where waste heat is reused, it is more important to get the lowest ERE_DC value than to get a lower PUE value.

We will now present a few examples of data centers and their PUE, ERE and ERE_DC.

## 7.2. Examples of data centers PUE and EREs

We present two data centers examples, one air-cooled built by NREL in Golden, CO and one water-cooled built by the LRZ in Garching close to Munich in Germany.

### 7.2.1. *NREL Research Support Facility, CO*

#### 7.2.1.1. *RSF data center*

From breakthroughs in fundamental science to new clean technologies to integrated energy systems that power people lives, the mission of the NREL is to work on technologies that will transform the way the United States and the world use energy. In June 2010, the NREL completed construction of the new 22,000 $m^2$/220,000ft$^2$ RSF, which included a 190 $m^2$/1,900 ft$^2$ data center. The RSF was then expanded to 3,600 $m^2$/360,000 ft$^2$ with the RSF expansion wing in December 2011. The original "legacy" data center had annual energy consumption as high as 2,394,000 kWh, which would have exceeded the total building energy goal. As part of meeting the building energy goal, the RSF data center annual energy use had to be approximately 50% less than the legacy data center's annual energy use.

#### 7.2.1.2. *RSF PUE and ERE*

Sheppy *et al.* (2011) present the comparison of a Legacy Data Center and the RSF both managed by NREL where electricity price was $0.057/kWh. RSF was designed to reduce the energy cost of an air-cooled data center. Sheppy *et al.* (2011) present all the techniques they used to get the best of breed air-cooled data center including neat rack wiring cabling, hot aisle/cold aisle rack arrangements with hot aisle containment and maximum use of free air cooling, since outside air, due to the climate in Golden, allows for much of the data center cooling needs.

The figures in this section are reprinted with permission of the NREL from Sheppy *et al.* (2011).

Figure 7.1 presents RSF data center power consumption and its different components for the first 11 months of production from October 2010 to August 2011. Figure 7.2 presents RSF hourly PUE for the same period.

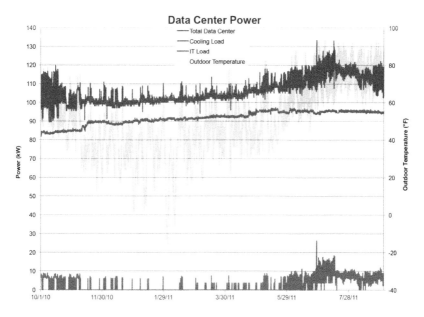

**Figure 7.1.** *RSF load profile for the first 11 months of operations.*
*For a color version of this figure, see www.iste.co.uk/brochard/energy.zip*

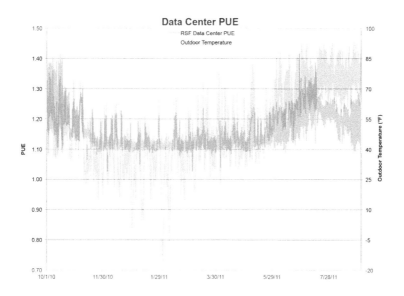

**Figure 7.2.** *RSF hourly PUE over the first 11 months.*
*For a color version of this figure, see www.iste.co.uk/brochard/energy.zip*

With such a limited use of cooling energy, RSF annual average PUE of 1.16 was measured for the first 11 months of operations versus a PUE of 2.28 for the Legacy Data Center. Free-air cooling was key to achieving such a low cooling energy and PUE as we can see in Figures 7.1 and 7.2, where low cooling loads correspond to the lowest outside temperature periods and to the lowest PUE of 1.10. We will come back to this aspect in section 7.4 on TCO.

Waste heat was also reused in other parts of the building outside the data center during the working office hours and days and under specific temperature conditions. As RSF had not the appropriate metering equipment to measure ERE, Sheppy *et al.* (2011) approximated the average ERE to be 0.91 by a detailed energy balance discussion. Figure 7.3 shows the calculated ERE for the RSF data center for the 11-month period where ERE is shown as a function of outdoor air temperature ($T_{OA}$).

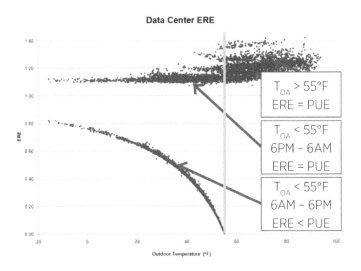

**Figure 7.3.** *RSF ERE as a function of outdoor temperature. For a color version of this figure, see www.iste.co.uk/brochard/energy.zip*

## 7.2.2. Leibnitz Supercomputing data center in Germany

### 7.2.2.1. LRZ mission

LRZ is located in Garching, near Munich, in Germany. It is the IT service provider for the Munich universities and colleges as well as a growing number of research organizations in Munich and throughout Bavaria. In addition, LRZ is a National Supercomputing Centre for Germany (along with Juelich and Stuttgart) and a European Supercomputing Center (PRACE n.d.).

As LRZ paid the electricity €0.15/kWh in 2012, €0.178/kWh in 2014 and €0.185/kWh in 2018, this was a major reason for LRZ energy-efficient strategy.

### 7.2.2.2. LRZ data center

The LRZ data center has 3,160 m² of floor space for IT equipment, 6,393 m² of floor space for infrastructure, 2 × 10 MW of power supply provided by renewable energy and an average power consumption of 5.5 MW.

The LRZ data center is composed of two cubes housing the two supercomputers we will describe below.

Figure 7.4 presents LRZ data center sections with cooling towers on the roof, supercomputers on the third floor, Linux clusters and general-purpose servers on the second floor, storage and archive/backup on the first floor, cooling and water processing on ground level and power and UPS below.

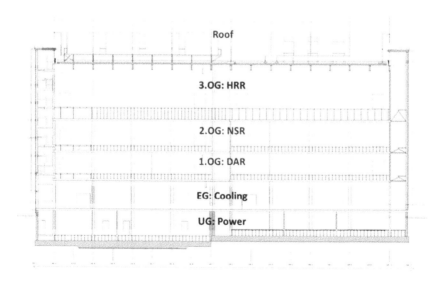

**Figure 7.4.** *Sectional view of LRZ data center. For a color version of this figure, see www.iste.co.uk/brochard/energy.zip*

Figure 7.5 presents the cooling infrastructure overview for the different floors and systems.

For cooling, LRZ has cold water and hot water distribution circuits. Figure 7.5 presents the cooling infrastructure overview for the different floors and systems.

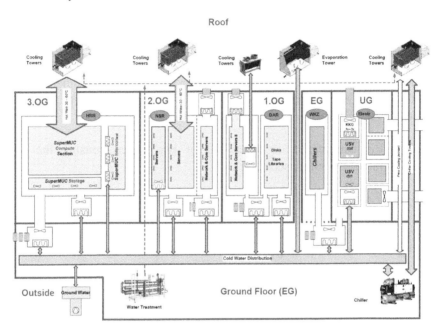

**Figure 7.5.** *LRZ cooling infrastructure overview. For a color version of this figure, see www.iste.co.uk/brochard/energy.zip*

The hot water loop is exclusively used for the compute nodes of the supercomputers on the third floor and of the CoolMUC systems on the second floor, and the cold water loop for the remaining elements.

### 7.2.2.3. *LRZ supercomputing systems*

LRZ supercomputers from 2012 to 2018 are named SuperMUC.

SuperMUC Phase 1 was installed in 2012. It is composed of 9216 IBM iDataPlex dx360M4 nodes of two sockets Intel Xeon E5-2680 processors (SandyBridge architecture) and 32GB of memory per compute node. It has a peak performance of 3.2 PFlops and was ranked number 4 in the June 2012

Top500 (Top500 Lists n.d.) with 2.987 PFlops. IBM iDataPlex was a DWC node design with inlet water temperature ranging from 20°C to 45°C and a heat-to-water ratio of about 85% depending on the ambient air temperature.

SuperMUC Phase 2 was installed in 2015. It is composed of 3072 Lenovo NeXtScale nx360M5 nodes with two sockets Intel Xeon E5-2697v3 processors (Haswell architecture) and 64GB of memory per compute node. It has a peak performance of 3.6 PFlops and was ranked number 20 in June 2015 Top500 (Top500 Lists n.d.) with 2.8 PFlops. Lenovo NeXtScale is a DWC node design with inlet water temperature ranging from 20°C to 45°C and a heat-to-water ratio of about 75% depending on the ambient air temperature.

From 2012 up to the present, LRZ buildings are heated reusing waste heat from SuperMUC.

In 2015, LRZ installed another but smaller hot-water cooled system, named CoolMUC-2, to further explore waste heat reuse. It is composed of 384 Lenovo NeXtScale nx360M5 nodes with two sockets Intel Xeon E5-2697v3 processors (Haswell architecture). It has a peak performance of 466 TFlops and was ranked number 252 in the November 2015 Top500 (Top500 Lists n.d.) with 366 TFlops. To help LRZ conduct its waste heat reuse project, Lenovo NeXtScale supported inlet water temperature up to 50°C. In 2017, 70 similar compute nodes were added to CoolMUC-2 leading to a configuration with 454 Lenovo NeXtScale nx360M5 nodes with two sockets Intel Xeon E5-2697v3 processors.

In 2018, LRZ is installing a new supercomputer named SuperMUC-NG ("Next Generation"), which will replace SuperMUC. It is composed of 6480 Lenovo ThinkSystem SD650 nodes with two sockets Intel Xeon 8174 processors (Skylake architecture) and 96GB of memory per thin compute node and 768GB for the fat compute nodes.

The Skylake 8174 is an off-roadmap SKU, which is a derivative of the 8168 (see Table 7.1).

| SKU | Cores | LLC (MB) | TDP (W) | Base non-AVX Core Frequency (GHz) | Max. non-AVX Core Turbo Frequency (GHz) all cores active | Base AVX2 Core Frequency (GHz) | Max. AVX2 Core Turbo Frequency (GHz) all cores | Base AVX-512 Core Frequency (GHz) | Max. AVX-512 Core Turbo Frequency (GHz) with all cores active |
|---|---|---|---|---|---|---|---|---|---|
| 8168 | 24 | 33.0 | 205 | 2.7 | 3.4 | 2.3 | 3.0 | 1.9 | 2.5 |
| 8174 | 24 | 33.0 | 249 | 3.1 | 3.8 | 2.7 | 3.2 | 2.3 | 2.8 |

**Table 7.1.** *Xeon 8168 and 8174 TDP and frequencies*

SuperMUC-NG has a peak performance of 22.4 PFlops and is ranked number 8 in November 2018 Top500 (Top500 Lists n.d.) with 19.5 PFlops. HPL power consumption of SuperMUC-NG is 4.0 MW when the 8174 is run with Turbo ON. As LRZ is focusing on energy-efficient computing, the 8174 will run in production at lower frequencies controlled by EAR (see section 6.3.2).

The Lenovo SD650 is the last generation of DWC node with inlet water temperature ranging from 20°C to 50°C and a heat-to-water ratio of about 85% depending of the ambient air temperature. SD650 cooling has been addressed in section 3.5. As discussed in sections 3.4 and 3.5, such a performance and power consumption per socket is only possible in a dense server with DWC.

### 7.2.2.4. *LRZ PUE and ERE*

Figure 7.6 presents the measured PUE of SuperMUC during the year 2015.

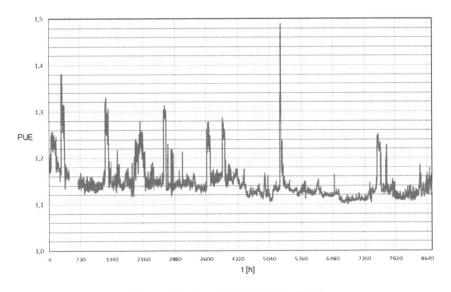

**Figure 7.6.** *SuperMUC PUE for 2015*

On this graph, PUE peaks are due to the system maintenances, which lead to a much lower IT power consumption while the cooling energy is about constant. On average for the year, PUE has been around 1.16. It should be noted that due to the efficiency of the dynamic UPS systems alone the PUE cannot be better than 1.10.

Figures 7.7–7.9 present CoolMUC-2 power consumption, its heat transfer to the adsorption chiller and the cold water produced based on the hot water outlet temperature of 50°C during one week in 2016.

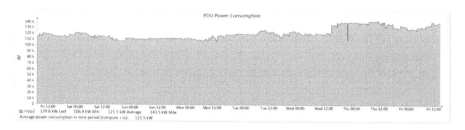

**Figure 7.7.** *CoolMUC-2 power consumption in 2016*

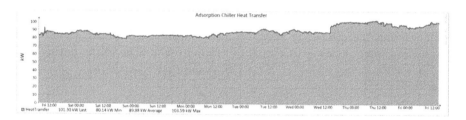

**Figure 7.8.** *CoolMUC-2 heat transfer to the absorption chiller in 2016*

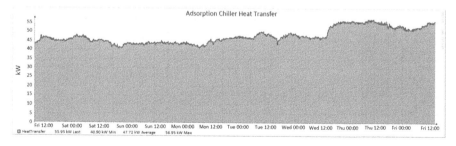

**Figure 7.9.** *CoolMUC-2 cold water generated by the absorption chiller in 2016*

On average CoolMUC-2 power consumption was 121.5 kW with a maximum of 143.5 kW and minimum of 106.9 kW. This is what we would we expect from a 384 nodes system based on two sockets 2697v3 (145 W

TDP), 64GB of memory and one Mellanox FDR adapter, knowing it is expected HPL performance consumption for a water cooled configuration is 147 kW. On average, the heat output into the hot water loop was 90 kW (heat-to-hot-water = 74%) and the average cold water generated by the adsorption chillers was 47.7 kW. Therefore, during this period, COP = 0.53 [3.2], ERE = 0.36 [I.3] and ERE_DC = PUEERE_DC = 0.71 [7.4].

Figure 7.10 presents the power consumption, heat transfer of the hot water loop (HT) to the adsorption chiller, the cold water produced (LT) and the electricity saved by the adsorption chillers by CoolMUC-2 during summer 2017 based on the hot water outlet temperature of 50°C.

On average CoolMUC-2 power consumption during summer 2017 was 142 kW, average heat output into the hot water loop was 92 kW (heat-to-hot-water transfer = 65%) and the average cold water generated by the adsorption chillers was 54 kW. The operation of the adsorption chillers saved on average 18 kW of electricity, which is computed as the electricity LRZ would have spent to generate the chilled water with the compression chillers minus the electricity spent on the adsorption chillers, its pumps and the cooling tower leading to a total of around 6 kW. Therefore, during this period, COP = 0.58 [3.2], ERE = 0.51 [I.3] and ERE_DC = PUEERE_DC = 0.77 [7.4].

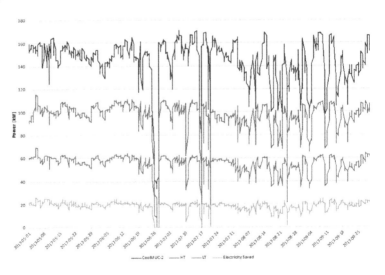

**Figure 7.10.** *CoolMUC-2 operations 05/2017–09/2017.For a color version of this figure, see www.iste.co.uk/brochard/energy.zip*

A detailed analysis of the impact of adsorptions chillers on ERE and TCO is discussed in the following section.

## 7.3. Impact of cooling on TCO with no waste heat reuse

We saw earlier that electricity price has a linear impact on the energy cost. In this section, we will analyze how cooling affects TCO by comparing the TCO of different cooling solutions with no waste heat reuse. We will use a similar methodology to the one used by Demetriou *et al.* (2016).

As all the solutions will be based on the same IT equipment, CAPEX will include only the acquisition cost of the cooling infrastructure (CRAH, RDHX, chillers, etc.) and the cooling cost of the servers (fan, heat sink, cold plate, etc.). Therefore, TCO will be very different if the data center is already equipped with cooling devices or not. A Brownfield data center is an existing data center already equipped with a cooling infrastructure, designed for air cooling since it is the defactor standard today. A Greenfield data center is a new data center being built where no cooling infrastructure has been installed. In such a situation, the cost of all cooling devices will be factored, while for a Brownfield data center air-cooling will have some obvious advantage.

For a given configuration and cooling design, total energy is computed by the addition of IT equipment energy plus the respective cooling energy. The cooling energy considers the PUE of the different cooling technologies. Based on the different ratios $f_{air}$, $f_{rdhx}$ and $f_{dwc}$ [7.14–7.16] and the number of hours in a year, an air-cooled system can use free cooling, an overall PUE is calculated [7.17] and energy cost is calculated according to [7.9] with the appropriate electricity price.

The financial analysis uses standard discounted cash flow methods (Park 2012) to compute the acquisition costs. An incremental analysis is used to compare each technology to a traditional air-cooled design. We compute the acquisition cost of each components using Table 7.2 and its annual cost $A_n$ using the following capital recovery formula:

$$A_n = P_0 \left( \frac{i(1+i)^n}{(1+i)^n - 1} \right) \qquad [7.20]$$

where $P_0$ is the present cost at installation time, $n$ is the number of years (1–5) and $i$ is the discount rate per year, which is set to 5%. Electricity price is set constant over the 5 years.

| Cooling Infrastructure Costs (excludes installation, service, plumbing, external pumps, etc..) | | |
|---|---|---|
| Chiller (0.5kW/Ton) | $120 | per kW |
| Tower, Evap cooler | $36 | per kW |
| Dry-cooler | $120 | per kW |
| In-Row Cooler CW | $600 | per kW |
| RDHX | $241 | per kW |
| CDU | $100 | per kW |
| CRAH | $270 | per kW |
| CRAC | $486 | per kW |

| Node Cooling Costs (fan, heat sink, cold plate, manifold ..) | | |
|---|---|---|
| Air | $54 | per node |
| DWC | $294 | per node |
| Hybrid | $204 | per node |
| RDHX | $54 | per node |

**Table 7.2.** *Acquisition Costs of the different cooling components*

It should be noted that our installation cooling infrastructure costs are realistic but excludes installation, service, plumbing and external pumps, which have a financial impact but are too much data center dependent to be taken into account here. That is why a specific TCO analysis will have to be done before making a decision on which technology to use for a data center.

The IT equipment we consider is composed of 32 racks with 72 nodes per rack. Each node has two central processing unit (CPU) sockets, 12 DIMMs, one HDD and one high-performance network adapter, very similar to the nodes we have used in Chapter 5 to measure power and performance of workloads. In our analysis, the base TDP SKU will be 150 W but some variations will be calculated with 200 W and 250 W TDP SKU. With a 150 W TDP SKU, DC node power is assumed to be 335 W for an air-cooled node, which leads to 768 kW for the 32 racks. This node power consumption, as we have seen in section 5.1.6, is representative of the power consumption of real workloads on a two-socket node with a 150 W TDP SKU. We assume, as did Demetriou *et al.* (2016), that the cooling technology will only affect the power consumption of the servers and not their performance, which is a choice the data center can select as described in Chapter 4.

We compare four different data center cooling designs based on three different cooling technologies of the IT equipment.

The three cooling technologies for the IT equipment are air cooling (Air), direct water cooling and hybrid cooling (Hybrid).

In an air-cooled node, 100% of the heat load is removed to air using the nodes internal fans. The maximum inlet air temperature is 25°C since at this temperature the processor has the same performance as the DWC node. The water-cooled (DWC) node is the server similar to the one described in section 3.5.5, where the most power consuming components of the node (CPU, memory, network device and voltage regulators) are directly cooled by water through conductive plate and heat pipes. With latest generation of DWC servers about 90% of the node's heat is removed directly to water and 10% being rejected to the data center using the power supply fans. Latest generation DWC server can support up to 50°C and inlet air up to 25°C. In a hybrid-cooled node, as described in section 3.7.3, water removes only the CPU heat with a conductive plate. With Hybrid cooling, about 60% of heat goes to water and 40% to the data center air. We assume the thermal characteristic of DWC servers result in about 10% reduction of the overall node power consumption compared to an equivalent air-cooled node with 7% due to the removal of internal fans and 3% due to the node power reduction resulting from a decreased processor leakage power. Under the same assumptions, the power consumption of the hybrid node is reduced by 6% due fan power and power leakage reductions.

All the above parameters are used for illustrative purposes since they will vary depending on the workloads, the specific processor, the node and data center characteristics.

The four data center cooling designs are an air cooled (Air), a DWC, a hybrid cooled (Hybrid) and an extension of air cooled called RDHX.

In an air-cooled data center (Air), CRAH are supplied with 10°C chilled water from a water-cooled chiller. A plate and frame heat exchanger allows for free cooling when the cooling tower supply water is lower than the data center return water temperature. The Hybrid cooling data center uses a combination of low-density rear door exchanger (RDHX) capable of removing 15 kW for the heat going to air and direct cold plate cooling for the heat going to water. RDHX are supplied via cooling distribution units (CDUs). CDUs are feed via a compression chiller with 10°C supply. The cold plate removes the majority of the load and is fed using the return water from the RDHX. In a DWC data center, evaporative coolers provide chilled liquid to the CDUs, which remove 90% of the IT equipment heat. Water-cooled direct expansion (DX) in-row cooling units cool the 10% of IT equipment heat rejected to the data center. Forth scenario (RDHX) is similar to the air-cooled design except RDHX are introduced on all racks to extract the heat in place of less efficient CRAH units. These RDHX are fed with CDUs, which receive 10°C water from compression chillers. Water economizer operation is provided using plate and frame heat exchangers.

In our analysis of the different data center cooling designs, the individual PUEs extracted from Table 7.3 will be used. We take these values as examples, and other data centers will have higher or lower individual PUEs, which will impact the overall PUE of the cooling design.

|                 | Air | RDHX | DWC | free cooling |
|-----------------|-----|------|-----|--------------|
| individual PUEs | 1.6 | 1.3  | 1.1 | 1.06         |

**Table 7.3.** *Individual PUEs of the different cooling solutions*

The set of figures in the following sections present the percentage of incremental cumulative discounted cash flow over 5 years for each of the cooling solutions (DWC, Hybrid and RDHX) with respect to air cooling. A negative value means air cooling is a better financial alternative. A positive value means DWC, Hybrid or RDHX design is a better choice. When the DWC, Hybrid or RDHX curve crosses the 0% value, it shows the number of years needed for the solution to pay back versus an air-cooled solution.

Figure 7.11 presents the impact of electricity on project payback with three different electricity prices ($0.10, $0.15 and $0.20 per kWh), 20% of free air-cooling ratio and a 150 W processor TDP. Figure 7.12 presents the impact of processor TDP with an electricity price set to $0.15/kWh and the same free air-cooling ratio of 20%. Figure 7.13 presents the impact of three free air-cooling ratios (10%, 20% and 30%) on the project payback with an electricity price of $0.15/kWh and a 150 W processor TDP.

### 7.3.1. *Impact of electricity price on TCO*

Tables 7.4 and 7.5 present the overall PUE [7.10] of each cooling solution, the cooling infrastructure cost, the servers cooling cost, the total installation cost and the energy cost after 5 years.

In a Greenfield data center (see Table 7.4), for RDHX the installation cost is about the same as Air and the 5-year energy costs are much higher than the total installation cost at every electricity price. For Hybrid and DWC, the cooling infrastructure cost is lower than Air and RDHX, while the server cooling costs are much higher. The 5-year energy costs are much higher than the total installation costs only for high electricity prices ($0.15/kWh and above).

| Greenfield | Air | RDHX | Hybrid | DWC |
|---|---|---|---|---|
| overall PUE | 1.49 | 1.25 | 1.16 | 1.12 |
| Cooling infra cost | $326,653 | $381,497 | $238,714 | $171,161 |
| Servers cooling cost | $124,416 | $124,416 | $470,016 | $677,376 |
| Total Installation cost | $451,069 | $505,913 | $708,730 | $848,537 |
| 5 year Energy cost at $0.20 | $10,035,362 | $8,421,095 | $7,339,213 | $6,750,866 |
| 5 year Energy cost at $0.15 | $7,526,521 | $6,315,821 | $5,504,409 | $5,063,150 |
| 5 year Energy cost at $0.10 | $5,017,681 | $4,210,547 | $3,669,606 | $3,375,433 |

**Table 7.4.** *Greenfield costs and PUE of the different designs and electricity price*

In a Brownfield data center (see Table 7.5), the cooling infrastructure cost for Air is zero and therefore much less than for RDHX, Hybrid or DWC. Server cooling costs are identical to Greenfield. The energy costs are the same for Brownfield and Greenfield data centers, which are proportional to their respective overall PUEs.

| Brownfield | Air | RDHX | Hybrid | DWC |
|---|---|---|---|---|
| overall PUE | 1.49 | 1.25 | 1.16 | 1.12 |
| Cooling infra cost | $0 | $261,937 | $193,759 | $171,161 |
| Servers cooling cost | $124,416 | $124,416 | $470,016 | $677,376 |
| Total Installation cost | $124,416 | $386,353 | $663,775 | $848,537 |
| 5 year Energy cost at $0.20 | $10,035,362 | $8,421,095 | $7,339,213 | $6,750,866 |
| 5 year Energy cost at $0.15 | $7,526,521 | $6,315,821 | $5,504,409 | $5,063,150 |
| 5 year Energy cost at $0.10 | $5,017,681 | $4,210,547 | $3,669,606 | $3,375,433 |

**Table 7.5.** *Brownfield costs and PUE of the different designs and electricity price*

Figure 7.11 shows that for a Greenfield data center, all three cooling solutions (RDHX, Hybrid and DWC) present a positive payback compared to Air after only 1 year regardless of the electricity price, except for DWC at $0.10/kWh. When electricity price is $0.15/kWh, RDHX has a 10% payback ratio after 1 year while DWC and Hybrid have a better payback than RDHX after 2 years. At $0.20/kWh, DWC provides a 20% payback ratio after 5 years. For a Brownfield data center, due to the low installation cost of Air, when electricity price is $0.10/kWh, RDHX has a positive payback after 3 years, Hybrid after 5 years and DWC has no financial benefit even after 5 years. At $0.20/kWh, RDHX has a positive payback after 1 year and a payback ratio of 9% after 5 years, while Hybrid and DWC have a positive payback after 2 years and a payback ratio of 13% and 15% after 5 years.

### 7.3.2. *Impact of node power on TCO*

Another important factor for TCO is the power consumed by the IT equipment and what will happen as servers use higher TDP SKU.

Figure 7.12 presents the same analysis as presented in Figure 7.11 with a constant price of electricity of $0.15 kW/h and three different node powers (333, 413 and 493 W) representing the typical power consumption of a workload running on the two-socket node we described earlier with a processor TDP of 150, 200 and 250 W.

Figure 7.12 shows that higher power consumption improves the attractiveness of DWC and Hybrid for both Greenfield and Brownfield data centers. For Greenfield data centers, DWC and Hybrid have positive payback ratios after 1 year and which increase up to 20% after 5 years for SKU TDP of 200 W and higher. For Brownfield data centers, with a 200 W TDP SKU, all three cooling solutions have a positive payback after 2 years while DWC and Hybrid have payback ratios of 10% after 5 years. With a 250 W SKU TDP, DWC and Hybrid have a payback ratio of 13% and 15% after 5 years. We note the SKU TDP has nearly no influence on RDHX payback versus Air.

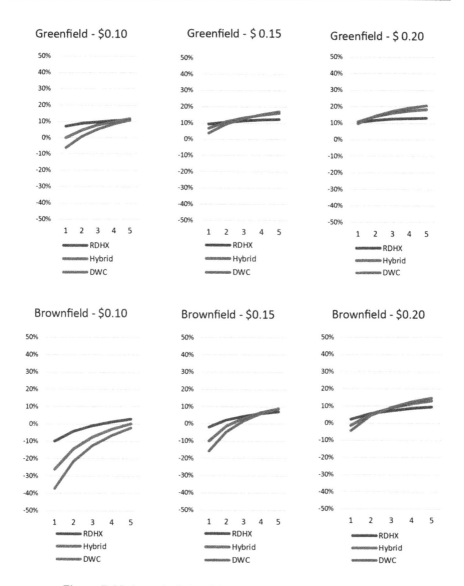

**Figure 7.11.** *Impact of electricity on project payback. For a color version of this figure, see www.iste.co.uk/brochard/energy.zip*

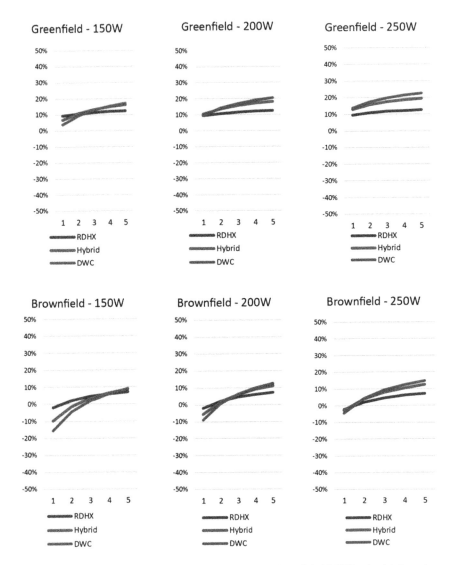

**Figure 7.12.** *Impact of SKU TDP on project payback at $ 0.15/kWh electricity price. For a color version of this figure, see www.iste.co.uk/brochard/energy.zip*

Table 7.6 shows that for a Greenfield data center, the cooling infrastructure costs increase with the SKU TDP as more cooling equipment has to be installed. It shows energy cost is also increasing with SKU TDP to a point where energy cost overwhelms the installation cost.

| Greenfield | Air | RDHX | Hybrid | DWC |
|---|---|---|---|---|
| overall PUE | 1.49 | 1.25 | 1.16 | 1.12 |
| Cooling infra cost at 250W | $483,483 | $564,659 | $353,324 | $253,337 |
| Servers cooling cost | $124,416 | $124,416 | $212,312 | $677,376 |
| Total Installation cost at 250W | $607,899 | $689,075 | $565,636 | $930,713 |
| 5 year Energy cost at 250W | $11,140,093 | $9,348,121 | $8,147,141 | $7,494,027 |
| 5 year Energy cost at 200W | $9,333,307 | $7,831,971 | $6,825,775 | $6,278,588 |
| 5 year Energy cost at 150W | $7,526,521 | $6,315,821 | $5,504,409 | $5,063,150 |

**Table 7.6.** *Greenfield costs and PUE of the different designs and SKU TDP*

### 7.3.3. *Impact of free cooling on TCO*

Figure 7.13 presents the same analysis as presented in Figure 7.11 with a constant price of electricity of $0.15 kW/h, a 333 W node power (corresponding to the typical power of an air-cooled node with a 150 W SKU TDP) and three different free air-cooling ratios of 10%, 20% and 30%, which represent the ratio of number of free cooling hours per year versus the total number of hours per year (8,670 h).

As shown in Table 7.7 and Figure 7.13, free-air cooling's impact depends greatly on the data center cooling design. It has a big impact on the Air design, a bit less on the RDHX design, much less on the Hybrid design and close to marginal on the DWC design. This is due to the fact that with the Air and RDHX cooling designs, 100% of heat is extracted to air and with a high PUE (respectively, 1.6 and 1.3), which is higher than the free-cooling PUE (1.06). On the contrary, the DWC design has only 10% of heat extracted to air and 90% of heat is extracted with a PUE of 1.1 comparable to the free-cooling PUE. The Hybrid design is in between with 60% of heat extracted by water and 40% with RDHX.

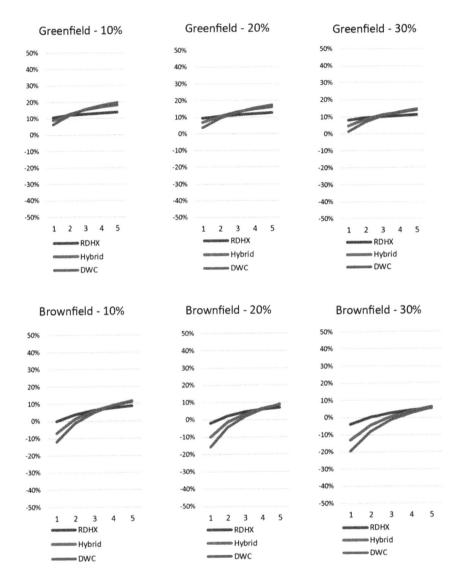

**Figure 7.13.** *Impact of free cooling ratio on project payback at $0.15 electricity price. For a color version of this figure, see www.iste.co.uk/brochard/energy.zip*

| Greenfield | Air | RDHX | Hybrid | DWC |
|---|---|---|---|---|
| overall PUE at 10% | 1.55 | 1.28 | 1.17 | 1.12 |
| overall PUE at 20% | 1.49 | 1.25 | 1.16 | 1.12 |
| overall PUE at 30% | 1.44 | 1.23 | 1.15 | 1.11 |
| Cooling infra cost | $326,653 | $381,497 | $238,714 | $171,161 |
| Servers cooling cost | $124,416 | $124,416 | $470,016 | $677,376 |
| Total Installation cost | $451,069 | $505,913 | $708,730 | $848,537 |
| 5 year Energy cost at 10% | $7,798,929 | $6,436,891 | $5,549,932 | $5,074,046 |
| 5 year Energy cost at 20% | $7,526,521 | $6,315,821 | $5,504,409 | $5,063,150 |
| 5 year Energy cost at 30% | $7,254,114 | $6,194,751 | $5,458,887 | $5,052,253 |

**Table 7.7.** *Greenfield costs and PUEs of different designs and free air-cooling ratios*

This explains why air-cooled data center can be very efficient in terms of overall PUE and TCO when they are located in geographies with a large number of free air-cooling hours per year and when the air PUE is low due to a careful design of the data center. That is the case with the data centers of cloud providers such as Microsoft, which can achieve overall average PUE of ~1.25 with air-cooled data centers (Data Center Knowledge 2010), and with the Google data centers, which can achieve overall average PUE of ~1.15 (Google n.d.).

In geographies where the outside environmental conditions do not provide a large number of free air-cooling hours, other cooling design than Air may have to be used like RDHX or "Hot Hut" (Kava 2012), which provide a much better individual PUE than CRAH. A complementary approach is to increase the room temperature up to 27–35°C to maximize the use of free air-cooling.

Under such circumstances, the DWC and Hybrid designs show little benefit even though the payback can be slightly positive with a Greenfield data center and more positive as the electricity price is increasing. This conclusion will change when waste heat reuse is taken into account as we will see in the following section.

## 7.4. Emerging technologies and their impact on TCO

We present now the impact of emerging technologies on TCO. The two technologies we discuss are waste heat reuse and electricity generation. They both address a different aspect of the power cycle and therefore can be complementary.

### 7.4.1. *Waste heat reuse*

We discussed in section 3.7 the different ways to reuse waste heat. We will focus here on the PUE and TCO impact of reusing waste heat to produce cold water with adsorption chillers as described in section 3.7.2 and with the CoolMUC-2 use case presented in section 7.2.2.3.

To evaluate the impact of such a technology on TCO, we reuse the same framework as we did in section 7.3 and instead of comparing DWC, Hybrid and RDHX designs to the Air design, we compare DWC, DWC with adsorption chillers (which we will call DWC + ERE) and RDHX designs to the Air design.

#### 7.4.1.1. *Ideal scenario of hot water reuse*

Figures 7.15 presents the relative payback ratios for the scenario DCW + ERE with a 150 W SKU TDP, a free cooling ratio of 20% and various electricity prices ($0.10/kWh, $ 0.15/kWh and $ 0.20/kWh) as in Figure 7.13 but with a COP of 50%. We call it the "ideal scenario" for reasons we will explain later.

Energy cost with reused energy is calculated according to [7.18] and the energy reused by the data center is calculated by:

$$Energy\_DCreused = \text{COP} * Energy\_hot\,water \qquad [7.21]$$

where COP as defined by [3.2] is set to 50% and Energy_hotwater is calculated as 90% of the IT power of a node (333 W × 0.90) times 72 × 32 nodes leading to 622 kW of Energy_hotwater and 311 kW of reused Energy_DCreused.

Table 7.8 presents the costs and overall PUEs of the different cooling designs. It should be noted that for DWC + ERE design, PUE is $PUE_{ERE\_DC} = 0.62$ and equal to $ERE\_DC$.

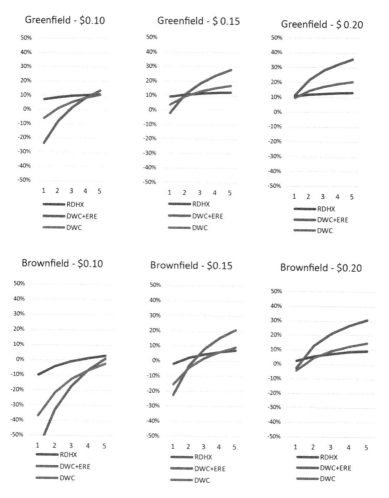

**Figure 7.14.** *Impact of hot water reuse on project payback and different electricity price. For a color version of this figure, see www.iste.co.uk/brochard/energy.zip*

| Greenfield | Air | RDHX | DWC+ERE | DWC |
|---|---|---|---|---|
| overall PUE | 1.49 | 1.25 | ERE=0,62 | 1.12 |
| Cooling infra cost | $326,653 | $381,497 | $706,469 | $171,161 |
| Servers cooling cost | $124,416 | $124,416 | $677,376 | $677,376 |
| Total Installation cost | $451,069 | $505,913 | $1,383,845 | $848,537 |
| 5 year Energy cost at $0.20 | $10,035,362 | $8,421,095 | $3,754,382 | $6,750,866 |
| 5 year Energy cost at $0.15 | $7,526,521 | $6,315,821 | $2,815,787 | $5,063,150 |
| 5 year Energy cost at $0.10 | $5,017,681 | $4,210,547 | $1,877,191 | $3,375,433 |

**Table 7.8.** *Greenfield costs and PUE of the different designs*

Figure 7.14 shows that, although DWC + ERE installation costs are high, the payback is important. For a Greenfield data center, even at low electricity price of $0.10/kWh, payback happens after 3 years but is barely better than RDHX after 5 years. When electricity price increases, payback is important and fast and the DWC + ERE design has the best payback of all designs. For a Brownfield data center, at low electricity price a slight positive payback is reached after 5 years. With an increased electricity price, the DWC + ERE payback is important and fast with a 13% payback ratio after 2 years and 31% payback ratio after 5 years.

As said earlier, we should emphasize that installation costs do not take into account installation service and plumbing costs that can be important, shifting by 1 or 2 years the payback return our analysis is showing.

Finally, it should be noted that with this DWC + ERE scenario we assume that $Energy_{-DCreused} = Energy_{-produced}$ meaning all the energy produced is exactly reused by the data center. This energy is used either for cooling the building or for cooling the 10% of heat going to air from the DWC servers since there is no air-cooled equipment such as air-cooled servers, storage or networks in this configuration.

This is not the usual situation in a data center and why we call it an "ideal" scenario. We will analyze a more realistic scenario in the following section with a mix of water-cooled and air-cooled IT devices.

### 7.4.1.2. *Realistic scenario of hot water reuse*

In this scenario, the configuration is composed of the same DWC servers as above with additional air-cooled IT devices, which consume 20%, 30% and 40% of the DWC servers power consumption leading to a configuration with a total power consumption of 1.2, 1.3 and 1.4 times the power of the configuration analyzed in the previous section. To simplify the calculation of the servers cooling cost, we assume the air-cooled devices are storage. The other parameters are unchanged: electricity price of $0.15/ kWh, free air-cooling ratio of 20%, COP of 50%. We compare the Air, RDHX, DWC and DWC + ERE designs. The Air design uses CRAH to extract the heat going to air with a PUE of 1.6. The RDHX design uses RDHX with a PUE of 1.3 to extract the 100% of heat going to air. The DWC design uses RDHX to extract the 10% of heat going to air of the DWC servers and 100% of the heat of the air-cooled devices. The DWC + ERE design uses the same cooling as the DWC design but reuses the hot water produced by the DWC servers to produce by adsorption chillers the cold water needed to cool all the air-cooled devices.

Table 7.9 presents the overall PUE of the different cooling designs with the various air to water power ratio configurations (20%, 30% and 40%); the cold-water energy produced, needed and used by each configuration of the DWC + ERE cooling design; and the corresponding ERF value.

| | over all PUE | | |
|---|---|---|---|
| AIR vs DWC power ratio | 20% | 30% | 40% |
| DWC | 1.14 | 1.15 | 1.16 |
| RDHx | 1.25 | 1.25 | 1.25 |
| Air | 1.49 | 1.49 | 1.49 |
| DWC + ERE | 0.80 | 0.78 | 0.81 |
| | Cold water balance | | |
| produced kW | 311 | 311 | 311 |
| needed kW | 289 | 389 | 489 |
| used kW | 289 | 311 | 311 |
| yearly Energy Cost reused | $380,362 | $449,473 | $449,473 |
| Energy Recovery Factor (%) | 30.1% | 32.3% | 29.6% |

**Table 7.9.** *Cold water balance and PUE of the different power ratio configurations*

We note that with an air to water power ratio of 20%, the DWC servers produce more cold water than the capacity needed by the air-cooled devices (311 kW vs. 289 kW). With air to power ratios of 30% and 40%, the DWC servers produce less cold water capacity than needed (respectively, 311kW vs. 389kW and 311 kW vs. 489 kW) leading to a constant energy cost reused value. The overall PUEs of the Air and RDHX designs are unchanged versus Table 7.8, since these cooling designs have no energy reuse. The only difference between the ideal and realistic scenario for the Air and RDHX designs is found in Table 7.10 where we see an increased total power and energy cost versus Table 7.8. For the DWC design, the overall PUE is increasing with the air to water power ratio since the amount of heat to air is increasing and cooled by RDHX with a PUE of 1.3. For the DWC + ERE design, ERE_DC (which is equal to $PUE_{ERE\_DC}$) is less than 1 but varies depending on the air to water power ratios. With a power ratio of 20%, the servers produce more cold water than needed while with power ratios of 30% and 40%, they produce less cold water than needed. The optimal ERE_DC value of 0.77 would be achieved with a power ratio of 23% when cold water generated is equal to the cold water needed. This optimal ERE_DC value of 0.77 for the realistic scenario is below the ERE_DC value of 0.63 of the ideal scenario (see Table 7.8) since for the same amount of cold water generated by the DWC servers there are additional air-cooled IT devices while there were none in the ideal scenario. This behavior is shown by the PUE, which varies between 1.14 and 1.16 in Table 7.9 while PUE is 1.12 in Table 7.8. ERF as defined in [7.2] is computed by dividing the 5-year energy cost reused in Table 7.9 by the 5-year energy cost of the DWC design in Table 7.10. ERF value is quite high and varies with the PUE. ERF is maximum with the 30% air to power ratio and the ERE_DC of 0.78. We note that ERE_DC (which is equal to $PUE_{ERE\_DC}$), $PUE_{DWC}$ and ERF verify [7.1].

Table 7.10 presents the cooling infrastructure cost for a power ratio of 40%, the servers cooling cost and the energy cost after 5 years with power ratios of 20%, 30% and 40% for each cooling design for a Greenfield data center as presented in Table 7.8.

| Greenfield | Air | RDHX | DWC+ERE | DWC |
|---|---|---|---|---|
| Cooling infra cost at 40% | $457,314 | $534,096 | $859,068 | $323,759 |
| Servers cooling cost | $124,416 | $124,416 | $677,376 | $677,376 |
| Total Installation cost | $581,730 | $658,512 | $1,536,444 | $1,001,135 |
| 5 year Energy cost at 40% | $10,537,130 | $8,842,149 | $5,342,115 | $7,589,478 |
| 5 year Energy cost at 30% | $9,784,478 | $8,210,567 | $4,710,533 | $6,957,896 |
| 5 year Energy cost at 20% | $9,031,826 | $7,578,985 | $4,424,505 | $6,326,314 |

**Table 7.10.** *Greenfield costs of the different designs*

In Table 7.10, we note a significant difference of costs between the DWC and DWC + ERE designs due to the additional cost of adsorption chillers.

From an energy saving perspective, Table 7.10 shows that the energy savings between the DWC + ERE design and the Air design for all power ratios are around 50%, and are around 40% compared with the RDHX design.

Figure 7.15 presents the same relative payback ratio over time of RDHX, DWC and DWC + ERE versus Air as in Figure 7.14 but with a varying air to water power ratio.

Although the realistic scenario is financially less attractive than the ideal scenario with a lower payback after 5 years, the DWC + ERE design provides a rather important relative payback ratio of 22%, 25% and 24% for a Greenfield data center and of 15%, 18% and 17% for a Brownfield data center with the 20%, 30% and 40% power ratios. It shows also the DWC + ERE design has a much better payback than the RDHX design for Greenfield and Brownfield data centers.

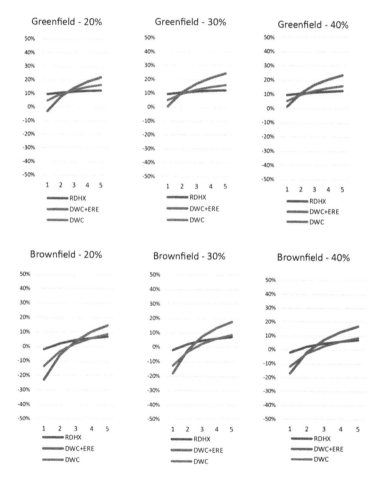

**Figure 7.15.** *Impact of hot water energy reused on project payback with various air to water power ratios, $0.15/kWh electricity price, 20% free air-cooling ratio and 50% COP. For a color version of this figure, see www.iste.co.uk/brochard/energy.zip*

## 7.4.2. *Renewable electricity generation*

So far, we discussed how to minimize the total power consumption and how to reuse waste heat generated by a data center, which are essential to minimize the data center energy cost. Once we reduced the energy needed, it is important to look for solutions to reduce the amount of electricity needed to power the system. This section presents how renewable electricity generation can be used to produce "free" electricity for the data center through photovoltaic panels (PV) and wind turbines.

In section 7.2.1, we analyzed how NREL is reducing its data center load by optimizing the design of the RSF air-cool data center and reusing waste heat. NREL has also conducted other research in the area of renewable electricity generation.

Hootman *et al.* (2012) describe an expansion of the RSF data center to build a net-zero energy high-performance building based, among other technologies, on PV located on the RSF and RSF expansion roofs as well as the RSF visitor and staff parking roofs. The total PV size (theoretical power capacity) is 2.5 MW. NREL built a model of the energy generated by such PV over 1 year: 3.4 GWh per year with a split of 606 MWh for RSF roof, 551 MWh for the RSF expansion roof, 707 MWh for the visitor parking and 1,560 MWh for the staff parking. A comparison with the measured energy shows the error is just a few percent. As the RSF data center has an energy consumption of 935 MWh per year (Sheppy *et al.* 2011), this shows PV electricity generated by the RSF roof itself would cover about two-thirds of RSF data center energy needs while adding the PV energy produced by the visitor parking (707 MWh) would cover 100% of the data center energy.

But as shown in Figure 7.1, NREF data center energy needs are not constant over the year. Similarly, PV production varies a lot depending on the season and the time of the day while the data center consumption is about constant. Table 7.11 summarizes the RSF data center power consumption variations and the variations of the energy produced by NREL PVs installed on the RSF data center roof.

| RSF DC Min Power consumption (kWh) | RSF DC Max Power consumption (kWh) | Golden, CO PV efficiency | RSF PV Avg. Power production (kWh) | RSF PV Min Power production (kWh) | RSF PV Max Power production (kWh) |
|---|---|---|---|---|---|
| 90.0 | 130.0 | 15.7% | 69.2 | 11.3 | 116.3 |

**Table 7.11.** *RSF data center power consumption and PV power production*

RSF power consumption estimations are based on Figure 7.1. RSF PV power production is based on NREL measured data, including the PV efficiency (ratio of peak vs. produced kWh), while the minimum and maximum have been estimated using a simple tool (Wattuneed n.d.). As expected, PV production varies considerably and if on average PV can cover two-thirds of RSF data center need, there are times when PV will cover only a 1/10 and times when it could cover 100% or more. Table 7.12 present the same results taking into account that all PVs installed on NREL RSF premises (RSF roof, RSF visitor parking, RSF staff parking) are used at the exception of the PVs installed on the RSF expansion roof.

| RSF DC Min Power consumption (kWh) | RSF DC Max Power consumption (kWh) | Golden CO PV efficiency | "All" PV Avg. Power production (kWh) | "All" PV Min Power production (kWh) | "All" PV Max Power production (kWh) |
|---|---|---|---|---|---|
| 90.0 | 130.0 | 15.7% | 328.1 | 53.4 | 551.5 |

**Table 7.12.** *RSF data center power consumption and all PV power production*

With this PV capacity, there are periods when PVs produce more power than needed and also be periods when PVs will not produce enough capacity to power the data center. The following section will address the technologies to store excess PV energy and retrieve it to cover the shortage periods.

Wind Turbines are also another way to provide renewable energy for data centers (Dykes *et al.* 2017). With this program called "System Management of Atmospheric Resource through technology" (SMART), NREL researchers are able to accurately model the behavior of wind flow into and through a wind plant at a level of resolution that illustrates the full flow physics. Scientists will apply supercomputing to high-fidelity physics models (HFMs) of complex flows and will use "Big Data" along with data science to manage extensive measurements that provide formal validation of supercomputing models.

Wind turbine companies like Vestas are also using "Big Data" to model the effectiveness of a wind turbine to select the location where wind turbines will be built and then manage their production in real time (Vestas n.d.).

The latest example is a new data center built by Google in Denmark (Kava 2018) using at large scale similar techniques as NREL's RSF data center in order to reduce PUE and use 100% carbon-free electricity, which will come from onshore and offshore wind and PVs.

### 7.4.3. *Storing excess energy for later reuse*

Electrolysis (Energy.gov n.d.) can produce hydrogen from water when DC current is applied causing water to split into oxygen and hydrogen:

$$2H_2O = 2H_2 + O_2 \hspace{3cm} [7.22]$$

A fuel cell is an electrochemical cell that converts the energy from a fuel (like hydrogen) into electricity through an electrochemical reaction of the hydrogen fuel with oxygen. A proton exchange membrane (PEM) fuel cell (PEMFC)[1] is a specific type of fuel cell using PEM as electrolyte with a response time of about 1 s, which makes it usable in the context of energy generation in a data center. Figure 7.16 presents the schematics of a PEMFC.

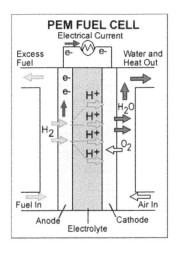

**Figure 7.16.** *PEMFC diagram. For a color version of this figure, see www.iste.co.uk/brochard/energy.zip*

On the anode side, hydrogen is split into protons ($H^+$) and electrons ($e^-$). The protons permeate through the polymer electrolyte membrane to the

_____

1    Available    at:    https://en.wikipedia.org/wiki/Proton-exchange_membrane_fuel_cell# Efficiency [Accessed April 30, 2019].

cathode side. The electrons travel through the external circuit to the cathode side. At the cathode side oxygen molecules react with the protons permeating and the electrons arriving through the external circuit to form water molecules [7.22].

Zao *et al.* (2014) show that a 10 kW PEMFC can reliably be used to power servers in a data center with efficiency between 40 and 60%. Duan *et al.* (2019) present a reversible protonic ceramic electrochemical cell with above 97% overall electric-to-hydrogen energy conversion efficiency and a repeatable round-trip efficiency (electricity-to-hydrogen-to-electricity) efficiency of above 75% and stable operation.

Therefore, $H_2$ electrolysis coupled with PEM is becoming an effective way to use excess electricity to produce hydrogen through water electrolysis, which can be stored and used later to produce electricity as shown in Figure 7.17.

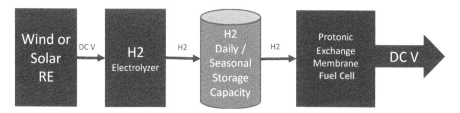

**Figure 7.17.** *Storing and reusing excess energy with PEMFC. For a color version of this figure, see www.iste.co.uk/brochard/energy.zip*

### 7.4.4. *Toward a net-zero energy data center*

The different technologies we presented in this book can minimize the data center total energy consumption by reducing both the IT energy and the cooling energy. By introducing renewable energy in the data center and storing excess energy for later reuse, solutions exists that can lead to net-zero energy data centers.

Figure 7.18 presents a schema of a carbon free data center with a net-zero energy goal. For the sake of simplicity, it does not draw the N+1 generators, UPS, static switches and batteries to provide uninterruptable power.

In this data center, servers are hot-water cooled and waste heat generated is reused by adsorption chillers to produce cold water for the data center air-cooled devices. As we have seen, others with low PUE solutions exist but they do not address waste heat reusability within the data center. Such a solution does minimize the data center energy needs.

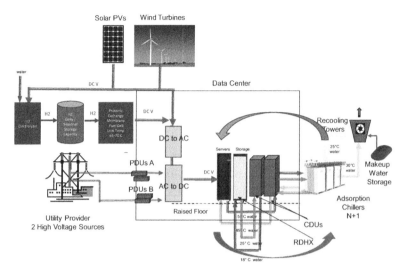

**Figure 7.18.** *Toward a net-zero energy data center. For a color version of this figure, see www.iste.co.uk/brochard/energy.zip*

PVs and/or wind turbines are used in conjunction with PEMFC to provide as much as possible renewable energy to the data center. As it is unlikely that the local grid will produce 100% of the data center energy 100% of the time, coexistence of classic electrical power supply, distributed power generation and the associated AC/DC/AC converters are still needed. In a perfect net-zero energy data center, those AC/DC/AC converters would be removed.

# Conclusion

After describing the major IT components in a data center and their power consumption, we presented how servers are cooled and the challenge of air-cooling dense servers with the trend of increasing power of processors and accelerators leading to higher heat capacity per rack. We presented various cooling solutions for the data center leveraging air cooling and water cooling and how waste heat can be reused to cool the IT devices in the data center. We showed, through the recent evolution of processors and accelerators, that higher performance is still delivered every generation, but at the expense of an increased power consumption, an increasing number of cores and the introduction of more specialized processors.

We analyzed the power, temperature and performance of a server when running various workloads. We showed that the two major application characteristics to influence its power consumption are CPI (cycle per instructions) and GBS (total memory bandwidth), while the processor frequency is the major system characteristic. We analyzed the impact of cooling on power, temperature and frequency, and showed water cooling allows processors to run at lower temperature due to the high heat capacity of water, enabling servers to either consume lower power or run at higher frequency, leading to potential higher performance.

As accurate measurements of the of the IT devices power and performance is critical for the data center, we presented the low-level sensors and APIs to measure the server power and performance, and compared their accuracy and granularity. We showed different techniques exist to model power and performance for predicting the impact of a frequency change on the server energy or of a cooling change on the data center PUE. We also presented different software to manage and optimize the system energy or the data center operations.

After presenting the example of an air-cooled and a water-cooled data center and how they can achieve low PUE and ERE, we analyzed and compared PUE and TCO of various cooling designs. We analyzed the TCO of these various cooling designs under various circumstances (existing or new data center, electricity price, free cooling ratio, server power load). Introducing ERE in the TCO calculation, we showed that waste heat generated by hot water-cooled servers and reused by adsorption chillers to produce cold water to cool the air-cooled IT devices in the data center can reduce the data center energy by 40–50% and has a tremendous impact on TCO, with a payback ratio between 15% and 25% over an air-cooled design making this solution highly attractive even for existing data centers.

We presented how renewable energy through PV and wind turbines can be effective to produce the energy still required by the data center, leading to reduced $CO_2$ emission and toward a net-zero energy data center. As renewable energy production is highly variable, we presented how hydrogen electrolysis and PEMFC can store the excess energy and retrieve it when needed. Although these technologies are still being prototyped, we have seen the technologies are available and can provide the data center energy through a local grid without the losses of high voltage AC lines. In this self-sufficient data center running on DC power, AC to DC power conversion is also becoming useless improving again the energy efficiency and simplifying the data center infrastructure.

Looking back to a legacy data center as presented in Figure C.1 where electricity losses are numerous and where 100% of the heat generated by the data center is going to the sky, we described available and affordable technology improvements to reduce the data centers energy consumption and carbon footprint.

Figure C.2 shows such a data center running smart software to reduce the energy need through the integration and optimization of the building and the IT management infrastructures with the job scheduler and system resource manager. Hot water is used to cool the dense servers and cold water with RDHX for the remaining IT devices. The hot water is reused to generate through adsorption chillers the cold water for the RDHX; renewable electricity is produced and stored locally, and used when appropriate to cover the remaining data center electricity needs, leading to a net-zero energy data center.

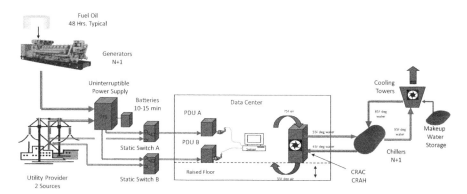

**Figure C.1.** *Power and heat flow of legacy air-cooled data center*

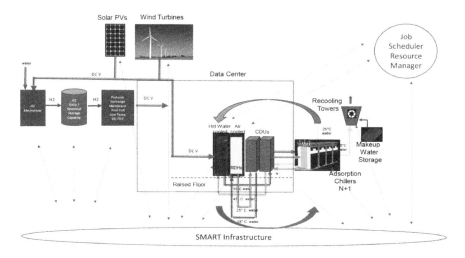

**Figure C.2.** *A net-zero energy and smart data center*

# References

80 Plus (2011). Energy-efficient computers run with 80 PLUS. Brochure. Available at: https://www.plugloadsolutions.com/docs/broch/80PLUS_brochurepages.pdf [Accessed April 29, 2019].

ACPI (2014). Advanced Configuration and Power Interface [Online]. Available at: http://www.acpi.info [Accessed April 29, 2019].

Alibaba Group (2018). Immersion cooling for green computing. Presentation at OCP summit, March 20–21, 2018. Available at: https://www.opencompute.org/files/Immersion-Cooling-for-Green-Computing-V1.0.pdf [Accessed April 29, 2019].

Archer, D.W., Deverell, D.R., Fox, T.F., Gronowski, P.E., Jain, A.K., Leary, M., Miner, D.G., Olesin, A., Persels, S.D., Rubinfeld, P.I., Supnik R.M. (1987). A CMOS VAX microprocessor with on-chip cache and memory management. *IEEE Journal of Solid-State Circuits*, 22(5), 849–852.

ARM (n.d.). Arm Processors for the Widest Range of Devices—from Sensors to Servers [Online]. Available at: https://www.arm.com/products/silicon-ip-cpu [Accessed April 29, 2019].

Artman, P. (2018). The benefits of Lenovo thermal transfer module technology in ThinkSystem SD530 servers [Online]. Available at: https://lenovopress.com/lp0922.pdf [Accessed April 29, 2019].

ASHRAE TC 9.9 (2015). Data center storage equipment – Thermal guidelines, issues, and best practices. White paper. Available at: https://tc0909.ashraetcs.org/documents/ASHRAE_Storage_White_Paper_2015.pdf [Accessed April 29, 2019].

Aucun, B., Miller, P., Kale, L.V. (2016). Variation among processors under turbo boost in HPC systems. Working paper, University of Illinois at Urbana-Champaign. Available at: http://charm.cs.illinois.edu/newPapers/16-08/paper.pdf [Accessed April 29, 2019]

Auweter, A., Bode, A., Brehm, M., Brochard, L., Hammer, N., Huber, H., Panda, R., Thomas, F., Wilde, T. (2014). A case study of energy aware scheduling on SuperMUC. In *Supercomputing: ISC 2014*, J.M. Kunkel, T. Ludwig, H.W. Meuer (eds). Lecture Notes in Computer Science, Springer, Cham, 8488, 394–409.

Benini, L. (2018). Scaling performance in power limited HPC system. Presentation at the MAX Conference in Trieste, Italy, January 21. Available at: http://indico. ictp.it/event/8004/session/107/contribution/222 [Accessed April 29, 2019].

BLAS3 Level Routines (2018). Developer Reference for Intel Math Kernel Library—Fortran [Online]. Available at: https://software.intel.com/en-us/mkl-developer-reference-fortran-blas-level-3-routines.

Blodgett, A.J., Barbour, D.R. (1982). Thermal conduction module: A high-performance multilayer ceramic package. *IBM Journal of Research and Development*, 26(1), 30–36.

Bonfa, P., Affinito, F., Cavazzoni C. (2018). Performance prediction for Quantum ESPRESSO on GPU accelerated systems. Presentation at the MAX Conference in Trieste, Italy, January 21, 2018. Available at: http://indico.ictp.it/event/ 8004/session/107/contribution/223 [Accessed April 29, 2019].

Boyer, E. (2017). *TCO Model, 2017:* Total cost of ownership and HPC system procurement SC17: Birds of feather. Presentation at SC17 in Denver, CO, November 14, 2017. Available at: https://eehpcwg.llnl.gov/assets/sc17_bof_ tco_procurement.pdf.

Brochard, L. (1989). Efficiency of some parallel numerical algorithms on distributed systems. *Parallel Computing*, 12(1), 21–44.

Brochard, L, Panda, R., Vemuganti, S. (2010). Optimizing performance and energy of HPC applications on POWER7. *Computer Science – Research and Development*, 25(3), 135–140.

Brochard L., Panda R., DeSota D., Thomas F., Bell R. (2011). Power and energy-aware processor scheduling. ACM SIGSOFT Software Engineering Notes, 36(40).

BSC (n.d.). Software & Apps: EAR: Energy management framework for HPC. Available at: https://www.bsc.es/research-and-development/software-and-apps/ software-list/energy-aware-runtime-ear [Accessed April 30, 2019].

Coles, H., Herrlin, M. (2016). Immersion cooling of electronics in DoD installations. Lawrence Berkley National Laboratory report LBNL-1005666. Available at: https://datacenters.lbl.gov/sites/all/files/ImmersionCooling2016.pdf    [Accessed April 30, 2019].

Corbalán, J., Brochard, L. (2019). EAR: Energy management framework for supercomputers. Working paper, Barcelona Supercomputing Center (BSC). Available at: https://www.bsc.es/sites/default/files/public/bscw2/content/ software-app/ technical-documentation/ear.pdf [Accessed April 30, 2019].

CEA (1996). Cray T90 [Online]. Available at: http://www-hpc.cea.fr/en/complexe/pages/15-crayT90.htm [Accessed April 30, 2019].

CGG (2012). Case Study: Cooling with oil. Available at: https://www.cgg.com/en/Sustainability/Case-Studies/Cooling-With-Oil [Accessed April 30, 2019].

Danilak, R. (2017). Why energy is a big and rapidly growing problem for data centers. Forbes Technology Council CommunityVoice, Dec 15, 2017. Available at: https://www.forbes.com/sites/forbestechcouncil/2017/12/15/why-energy-is-a-big-and-rapidly-growing-problem-for-data-centers/#6965d8615a30 [Accessed April 30, 2019].

Data Center Knowledge (2010). Largest data centers: i/o data centers, Microsoft. Available at: https://www.datacenterknowledge.com/special-report-the-worlds-largest-data-centers/largest-data-centers-io-data-centers-microsoft [Accessed April 30, 2019].

DCDB (n.d.). The DataCenter DataBase [Online]. Available at: http://dcdb.it [Accessed April 30, 2019].

Demetriou, D., Kamath, V., Mahaney, H. (2016). A holistic evaluation of data center water cooling total cost of ownership. *ASME Journal of Electronic Packaging*, 138(1), 11.

Dennard, R. H., Gaensslen, F., Yu, H., Rideout, L., Bassous, E., LeBlanc, A. (1974). Design of ion-implanted MOSFET's with very small physical dimensions. *IEEE Journal of Solid State Circuits*, October, 256–268.

DMTF (n.d.). Redfish API [Online]. Available at: https://www.dmtf.org/standards/redfish [Accessed April 30, 2019].

Duan, C., Kee, R., Zhu, H., Sullivan, N., Zhu, L., Bian, L., Jennings, D., O'Hayre R. (2019). Highly efficient reversible protonic ceramic electrochemical cells for power generation and fuel production. *Nature Energy*, 4, 230–240.

Dykes, K., Hand, M., Stehly, T., Veers, P., Robinson, M., Lantz, E., Tusing, R. (2017). Enabling the SMART wind power plant of the future through science-based innovation. NREL Technical Report NREL/TP-5000-68123.

Eastep, J., Sylvester, S., Cantalupo, C., Geltz, B., Ardanaz, F., Al-Rawi, A., Livingston, K., Keceli, F, Maiterth, M., Jana S. (2017). Global extensible open power manager: A vehicle for HPC community collaboration on co-designed energy management solutions. In *High Performance Computing - 32nd International Conference, ISC High Performance 2017*, 394–412, Springer, Frankfurt, Germany.

Economou, D., Rivoire, S., Kozyrakis, C, Ranganathan, P. (2006). Full-system power analysis and modeling for server environments. In: *Workshop on Modeling, Benchmarking and Simulation, MoBS 2006, 33rd Annual International Symposium on Computer Architecture.* Available at: www-mount.ece.umn.edu/~jjyi/MoBS/2006/program/3A-Economou.pdf    [Accessed May 7, 2019]

Efi Rotem, E., Naveh, A., Rajwan, D., Ananthakrishnan, A., Weissmann E. (2011) Power management of the 2nd generation Intel core microarchitecture, formerly codenamed Sandy Bridge. Presentation at Hot Chips 2011, August. Available at: https://www.hotchips.org/wp-content/uploads/hc_archives/hc23/HC23.19.9-Desktop-CPUs/HC23.19.921.SandyBridge_Power_10-Rotem-Intel.pdf   [Accessed April 30, 2019].

Energy.gov (2018). Hydrogen production: Electrolysis [Online]. Available at: https://www.energy.gov/eere/fuelcells/hydrogen-production-electrolysis [Accessed April 30, 2019].

Etinski, M., Corbalan, J., Labarta, J., Valero, M., Veidenbaum A. (2009). Power-aware load balancing of large scale MPI applications. In: *2009 IEEE International Symposium on Parallel & Distributed Processing,* Rome, May 23–29. Available at: http://ieeexplore.ieee.org/stamp/stamp.jsp?tp=&arnumber=5160973&isnumber=5160846 [Accessed May 1, 2019].

Eurostat    (n.d.).    Electricity    price    statistics    [Online].    Available    at: https://ec.europa.eu/eurostat/statistics-explained/index.php/Electricity_price_statistics #Electricity_prices_for_non-household_consumers [Accessed April 26, 2019].

Ferro, M., Yokoyama, A., Kloh, V., Silva, G., Gandra, R., Braganc, R., Bulcao, A., Schulze, B. (2017). Analysis of GPU power consumption using internal sensors. In *XXXVII Congresso da Sociedade Brasileira de Computação,* 1698–1711. Available at: http://csbc2017.mackenzie.br/public/files/16-wperformance/completos/7.pdf [Accessed April 30, 2019].

Fröhlich, D. Pantatosaki, E., Kolokathis, P.D., Markey, K, Reinsch, H., Baumgartner, M., ver der Veen, M.A., De Vos, D.E., Stock, N., Papdopoulos, G.K., Henninger, S.K., Janiak, C. (2016). Water adsorption behavior of CAU-10-H: a thorough investigation of its structure–property relationships. *Journal of Material Chemistry A*, 4(30), 11859–11869.

Gao, J. (2014). Machine learning applications for data center optimization. Working paper, Google. Available at: https://docs.google.com/a/google.com/viewer?url=www.google.com/about/datacenters/efficiency/internal/assets/machine-learning-applicationsfor-datacenter-optimization-finalv2.pdf [Accessed April 30, 2019].

GPU Database (n.d.). GPU Specs Database [Online]. TechPowerup. Available at: https://www.techpowerup.com/gpudb [Accessed April 30, 2019].

Gennady, F., Shaojuan Z. (2018). Math Kernel Library Benchmarks (Intel MKL Benchmarks). Intel Developer Done, updated May 29. Available at: https://software.intel.com/en-us/articles/intel-mkl-benchmarks-suite  [Accessed April 30, 2019].

Google (n.d.). Data Centers [Online]. Available at: https://www.google.com/about/datacenters [Accessed April 30, 2019].

Grant, R.E., Levenhagen, M., Olivier, S.L., DeBonis, D., Pedretti, K.T., Laros, J.H. III (2016). Standardizing power monitoring and control at exascale. *Computer*, 49(10), 38–46.

Guardian, The (2017). Tsunami of data could consume one fifth of global electricity by 2025 [Online]. Available at: https://www.theguardian.com/environment/2017/dec/11/tsunami-of-data-could-consume-fifth-global-electricity-by-2025 [Accessed April 29, 2019].

Haar, T.R., Nakamura, Y., Stuben, H. (2017). Berlin QCD user manual. Available at:        https://www.rrz.uni-hamburg.de/services/hpc/bqcd/files/bqcd5-manual.pdf [Accessed April 30, 2019].

Hackenberg, D., Ilsche, T., Schuchart, J., Schöne, R., Nagel, W.E., Simon, M., Georgiou, Y. (2014). HDEEM: High definition energy efficiency monitoring. In: *Energy Efficient Supercomputing Workshop (E2SC@SC 2014)*, 1–10

Hootman, T., Okada, D., Pless, S., Sheppy, M., Torcellini, P. (2012). Net-zero blueprint. In: *High Performing Buildings*, ASHRAE, 20–33. Available at: http://www.hpbmagazine.org/attachments/article/12170/12F-Department-of-Energys-National-Renewable-Energy-Laboratory-Research-Support-Facility-Golden-CO.pdf [Accessed April 30, 2019].

Hu, Z., Brooks, D., Zyuban, V., Bose P. (2003). Microarchitecture-level power-performance simulators: Modelling, validation, and impact on design. Tutorial, Harvard University. Available at: https://www.eecs.harvard.edu/~dbrooks/micro36_tutorial.htm [Accessed April 30, 2019].

IBM Icons (n.d.). Blue Gene [Online]. Available at: www-03.ibm.com/ibm/history/ibm100/us/en/icons/bluegene [Accessed April 29, 2019].

IBM Knowledge Center (n.d.) LoadLeveler V5.1 using and administering: Energy aware job support. Available at: https://www.ibm.com/support/knowledgecenter/SSFJTW_5.1.0/com.ibm.cluster.loadl.v5r1.load100.doc/am2xx_energyawarejob support.htm [Accessed April 30, 2019].

IBM Newsroom (2012). First commercial IBM hot-water cooled supercomputer to consume 40% less energy: Leibniz's "SuperMUC" named Europe's fastest supercomputer [Online]. Available at: https://www-03.ibm.com/press/us/en/press release/38065.wss [Accessed April 30, 2019].

IBM Systems Reference Library (1974). IBM System/360 installation manual – physical planning [Online]. Available at: http://www.bitsavers.org/pdf/ibm/360/fe/GC22-6820-12_System_360_Installation_Manual_Physical_Planning. pdf [Accessed April 29, 2019].

Ilsche, T. (2016). Integrated performance and energy measurements. Tutorial presentation at the 45th SPEEDUP Workshop on High-Performance Computing, University of Basel, Switzerland, September 15–16. Available at: http://www.speedup.ch/workshops/w45_2016/presentations/Monitoring/06_Energy.pdf [Accessed April 30, 2019].

Indium Corporation (2008). Indium foil: A thermal interface material [Online]. Available at: https://www.indium.com/blog/indium-foil-a-thermal-interface-material.php [Accessed April 30, 2019].

Intel (2017). Intel 64 and IA 32 architectures performance monitoring events. Document number 335279-001, rev. 1.0, December. Available at: https://software.intel.com/sites/default/files/managed/8b/6e/335279_performance_monitoring_events_guide.pdf [Accessed April 30, 2019].

Intel (2012). Intel Xeon Processor E5-2600 product family uncore performance monitoring guide. Ref. no. 327043-001, March. Available at: https://www.intel.com/content/dam/www/public/us/en/documents/design-guides/xeon-e5-2600-uncore-guide.pdf [Accessed April 30, 2019].

Intel (2018). Intel Xeon Processor Scalable Family: Thermal mechanical specifications and design guide. Ref. no. 336064-003US, January. Available at: https://www.intel.com/content/dam/www/public/us/en/documents/guides/xeon-scalable-thermal-guide.pdf [Accessed April 29, 2019].

IPMI (2009). Using IPMItool to view system information. In: *Sun Blade X6275 Server Mobile Diagnostics Guide*, Chapter 7. Available at: https://docs.oracle.com/cd/E19464-01/820-6850-11/IPMItool.html#50602039_99299.

Jones, N. (2018). How to stop data centres from gobbling up the world's electricity [Online]. *Nature* news feature (September 12). Available at: https://www.nature.com/articles/d41586-018-06610-y [Accessed April 29, 2019].

Jouppi, N.P. Young, C., Patil, N., Patterson, D. *et al.* (2017). In-datacenter performance analysis of a tensor processing unit. Google presentation at the 44th International Symposium on Computer Architecture (ISCA), Toronto, Canada, June 26. Available at: https://arxiv.org/pdf/1704.04760 [Accessed April 30, 2019].

Kava, J. (2012). Cooling the cloud: A look inside Google's Hot Huts [Online]. Available at: https://green.googleblog.com/2012/10/cooling-cloud-look-inside-googles-hot.html [Accessed April 30, 2019].

Kava, J. (2018). Breaking ground for Google's first data center in Denmark [Online]. *The Keyword*, November 20. Available at: https://blog.google/inside-google/infrastructure/breaking-ground-googles-first-data-center-denmark [Accessed April 30, 2019].

Keyes, D., Gropp, W. (1986). A comparison of domain decomposition techniques for elliptic partial differential equations and their parallel implementation. Research report, Yale University, December 1985. Available at: https://apps.dtic.mil/dtic/tr/fulltext/u2/a165996.pdf [Accessed April 30, 2019].

LAPACK (n.d.). LAPACK: Linear Algebra PACKage 3.8.0, subroutine degemm(). Available at: http://www.netlib.org/lapack/explore-html/d1/d54/group__double__blas__level3_gaeda3cbd99c8fb834a60a6412878226e1.html [Accessed April 30, 2019].

Lenovo (n.d.). Lenovo ThinkSystem SD530 server (Xeon SP Gen 1) product guide [Online]. Available at: https://lenovopress.com/lp0635.pdf [Accessed April 30, 2019].

Libri, A., Bartolini, A., Beneventi, F., Borghesi, A., Benini, L. (2018). Out-of-band high resolution HPC power and performance monitoring for big-data analysis. Presentation at EETHPC Workshop, Frankfurt, Germany, June 28. Available at: http://eethpc.net/wp-content/uploads/2018/05/ISC2018_EETHPC_AL.pdf [Accessed April 30, 2019].

Lim, M.Y., Free, V.W., Lowenthal D.K. (2006). Adaptive, transparent frequency and voltage scaling of communication phases in MPI programs. In: *SC '06: Proceedings of the ACM/IEEE Conference on Supercomputing*, Tampa, USA, Nov. 11–17. Available at: https://ieeexplore.ieee.org/document/4090188 [Accessed April 30, 2019].

Marathe, A., Bailey, P.E., Lowenthal, D.K., Rountree, B., Schulz, M., de Supinski B.R. (2015). A run-time system for power-constrained HPC applications. In *High Performance Computing. ISC High Performance 2015*, Kunkel, J. and Ludwig, T. (eds). Lecture Notes in Computer Science, vol. 9137. Springer, Cham. Available at: https://e-reports-ext.llnl.gov/pdf/789054.pdf [Accessed April 29, 2019].

Marion, W., Urban, K. (1995). *User's Manual for TMY2s Typical Meteorological Years*. National Renewable Energy Laboratory, Golden, CO.

McAlpin, J.D. (2017). STREAM: Sustainable memory bandwidth in high performance computers. Website. Available at: https://www.cs.virginia.edu/stream/ [Accessed April 30, 2019].

Mei, X., Wang, Q., Chu, X. (2016). A survey and measurement study of GPU DVFS on energy conservation. *Digital Communications and Networks*, 3, 89–100.

Meyer, N. (2016). Data centre infrastructure monitoring. Working paper, Partnership for Advanced Computing in Europe. Available at: http://www.prace-ri.eu/IMG/pdf/WP226.pdf [Accessed April 30, 2019].

Moore, G.E. (1965). Cramming more components onto integrated circuits. *Electronics*, 38(8), 114.

Munroe M. (2016). How to reuse waste heat from data centers intelligently [Online]. Data Center Knowledge, May 10. Available at: https://www.datacenter knowledge.com/archives/2016/05/10/how-to-reuse-waste-heat-from-data-centers-intelligently [Accessed April 30, 2019].

Mutjaba H. (2018). AMD officially talks Zen 2 CPU architecture: Significant performance uplift with 2X throughput, doubled core density with up to 64 cores, PCIe Gen 4.0 support, aiming server EPYC Rome 7 nm CPUs first [Online]. Available at: https://wccftech.com/amd-zen-2-7nm-cpu-architecture-epyc-rome-and-ryzen-official [Accessed April 29, 2019].

NVIDIA (2015). Performance counters. In: NVIDIA Nsight visual studio edition 4.6 user guide [Online]. Available at: https://docs.nvidia.com/nsight-visual-studio-edition/4.6/Content/Analysis/Report/CudaExperiments/KernelLevel/Performance Counters.htm [Accessed April 30, 2019].

NVIDIA (2017). NVIDIA Tesla V100 GPU architecture. White paper, WP-08608-001_v1.1, August. Available at: http://images.nvidia.com/content/volta-architecture/pdf/volta-architecture-whitepaper.pdf.

NVIDIA Developer (n.d.). CUDA Math library [Online]. Available at: https://developer.nvidia.com/cuda-math-library [Accessed April 30, 2019].

NVML (2019). NVML API reference guide [Online]. Available at: https://docs.nvidia.com/deploy/nvml-api/index.html [Accessed April 30, 2019].

NVSMI (n.d.). NVIDIA system management interface [Online]. Available at: https://developer.download.nvidia.com/compute/DCGM/docs/nvidia-smi-367.38.pdf [Accessed April 30, 2019].

Official Data Foundation (2018). Prices for electricity 2000–2018 [Online]. Available at: http://www.in2013dollars.com/Electricity/price-inflation [Accessed April 26, 2019].

OLCF (n.d.). Summit user guide: system overview [Online]. Available at: https://www.olcf.ornl.gov/for-users/system-user-guides/summit/system-overview [Accessed April 30, 2019].

Park, C. (2012). *Fundamentals of Engineering Financials*, 3rd edition. Prentice Hall, New York.

Patterson, M., Tschudi, B., Vangeet, O., Azevedo, D. (2010). ERE: a metric for measuring the benefit of reuse energy from a data center. White paper #29, The Green Grid. Available at: https://eehpcwg.llnl.gov/documents/infra/06_energyreuseefficiencymetric.pdf [Accessed April 30, 2019].

PBS Works (n.d.). Green computing [Online]. Available at: https://pbsprofessional.com.br/PBSSolution.aspx?v=1&i=6&n=Green-Computing [Accessed April 30, 2019].

PDP-11 (1975). PDP-11/70 maintenance and installation manual [Online]. Available at: http://bitsavers.informatik.uni-stuttgart.de/www.computer.museum.uq.edu.au/pdf/EK-11070-MM-002%20PDP11-70%20Maintenance%20And%20Installation%20Manual.pdf [Accessed April 29, 2019].

Petitet, A., Whaley, R.C., Dongarra, J., Cleary, A. (2018). HPL – A portable implementation of high-performance Linpack for distributed memory computers, Version 2.2 [Online]. Available at: www.netlib.org/benchmark/hpl [Accessed April 30, 2019].

PRACE (n.d.). PRACE resources [Online]. Available at: http://www.prace-ri.eu/prace-resources [Accessed April 30, 2019].

Puzovic, M., Lee, E.K., Elisseev, V. (2018). A study on cross-architectural modelling of power consumption using neural networks. *Supercomputing Frontiers and Innovations*, 5(4), 24–41.

Rountree, B., Lownenthal, D.K., de Supinski, B.R., Schulz, M., Freeh, V.W., Bletsch, T. (2009). Adagio: Making DVS practical for complex HPC applications. In: *Proceedings of the 23rd International Conference on Supercomputing (ICS'09)*. ACM, New York, USA, 460–469.

Sameh, S., DeSota, D., Panda, R., Stevens, S., Taylor, V, Wu, X. (2012) SWAPP: A framework for performance projections of HPC applications using benchmarks. In: *Proceedings of the 2012 IEEE 26th International Parallel and Distributed Processing Symposium Workshops*, 1722–1731.

Shenoy, N. (2018). Innovating for the "Data-Centric" era [Online]. Intel Newsroom, August 8, 2018. Available at: https://newsroom.intel.com/editorials/data-centric-innovation-summit [Accessed April 30, 2019].

Sheppy, M., Lobato, C., Van Geet, O., Pless, S., Donovan, K., Powers, C. (2011). Reducing data center loads for a large-scale, low-energy office buildings: NREL's research support facility. Report, NREL/BK-74A40-52785. Available at: https://www.nrel.gov/docs/fy12osti/52785.pdf [Accessed April 30, 2019].

Shoukourian, H., Wilde, T., Auweter, A., Bode, A. (2014). Monitoring power data: A first step towards a unified energy efficiency evaluation toolset for HPC data centers. *Environmental Modelling & Software*, 56, 13–26.

SLURM (2018). Power adaptive computing [Online]. Available at: https://slurm.schedmd.com/SLUG16/slug16_powercap.pdf [Accessed April 30, 2019].

Snavely, A., Wolter, N., Carrington L. (2013). Modeling application performance by convolving machine signatures with application profiles [Online]. Available at: https://pdfs.semanticscholar.org/61c6/afae262b0184c249da5f378a631b96f0a017.pdf [Accessed April 30, 2019].

SPEC (2006). Standard Performance Evaluation Corporation: SPEC CPU 2006 [Online]. Available at: https://www.spec.org/cpu2006 [Accessed April 30, 2019].

SPEC (2008). Standard Performance Evaluation Corporation: SPEC Power [Online]. Available at: https://www.spec.org/power_ssj2008 [Accessed April 30, 2019].

Terpstra, D., Jagode, H., You, H., Dongarra, J. (2010). Collecting performance data with PAPI-C. In: *Tools for High Performance Computing 2009*, Springer Berlin / Heidelberg, 3rd Parallel Tools Workshop, Dresden, Germany, 157–173.

Todi, R., Gustafson, J., Prabhu, G. (1998). Application signature: An analytical technique to model system performance. Working paper. Available at: http://citeseerx.ist.psu.edu/viewdoc/download;jsessionid=4F0A64BD77510C6E B0A2BC0826742828?doi=10.1.1.543.6234&rep=rep1&type=pdf    [Accessed April 30, 2019].

Top500 Lists (n.d.). Available at: https://www.top500.org/lists/top500 [Accessed April 30, 2019].

Venkatesh, A., Vishnu, A., Hamidouche, K., Tallent, N., Panda, D., Kerbyson, D., Hoisie A. (2015). A case for application-oblivious energy-efficient MPI runtime. In: *SC '15: Proceedings of the International Conference for High Performance Computing, Networking, Storage and Analysis*, Austin, USA, November 15–20. Available at: https://ieeexplore.ieee.org/document/7832803 [Accessed April 30, 2019].

Vestas (n.d.). Company website. Available at: https://www.vestas.com [Accessed April 30, 2019].

WikiChip. (n.d.). Turbo Boost Technology (TBT) – Intel [Online]. Available at: https://en.wikichip.org/wiki/intel/turbo_boost_technology.

Wikipedia (n.d.). Radeon [Online]. Available at: https://en.wikipedia.org/wiki/ Radeon [Accessed April 29, 2019].

Wattuneed (n.d.). Size your solar kit [Online]. Available at: https:// www.wattuneed.com/en/content/56-dimensionner-votre-kit-solaire-autonomes-autoconsommation [Accessed April 30, 2019].

Wittstadt, U., Füldner, G., Vasta, S., Volmer, R., Bendix, P., Schnabel, L., Mittelbach, W. (2017). Adsorption heat pumps and chillers: Recent developments for materials and components. In: *12th IEA Heat Pump Conference* K.4.3.1. Available at: https://www.researchgate.net/publication/318653464_Adsorption_Heat_Pumps_and _Chillers_-_Recent_Developments_for_Materials_and_Components.

Zao, L., Brouwer, J., James, S., Siegler, J., Peterson, E., Kansal, A., Liui, J. (2014). Servers powered by a 10 kW in-rack proton exchange membrane fuel cell system. *Proceedings of the ASME 2014 12th International Conference on Fuel Cell Science, Engineering and Technology*, FUELCELL2014, June 30–July 2, 2014, Boston, MA.

# Index

Other titles from

in

Computer Engineering

## 2019

CLERC Maurice
*Iterative Optimizers: Difficulty Measures and Benchmarks*

TOUNSI Wiem
*Cyber-Vigilance and Digital Trust: Cyber Security in the Era of Cloud Computing and IoT*

## 2018

ANDRO Mathieu
*Digital Libraries and Crowdsourcing*
*(Digital Tools and Uses Set – Volume 5)*

ARNALDI Bruno, GUITTON Pascal, MOREAU Guillaume
*Virtual Reality and Augmented Reality: Myths and Realities*

BERTHIER Thierry, TEBOUL Bruno
*From Digital Traces to Algorithmic Projections*

CARDON Alain
*Beyond Artificial Intelligence: From Human Consciousness to Artificial Consciousness*

HOMAYOUNI S. Mahdi, FONTES Dalila B.M.M.
*Metaheuristics for Maritime Operations*
*(Optimization Heuristics Set – Volume 1)*

JEANSOULIN Robert
*JavaScript and Open Data*

PIVERT Olivier
*NoSQL Data Models: Trends and Challenges*
*(Databases and Big Data Set – Volume 1)*

SEDKAOUI Soraya
*Data Analytics and Big Data*

SALEH Imad, AMMI Mehdi, SZONIECKY Samuel
*Challenges of the Internet of Things: Technology, Use, Ethics*
*(Digital Tools and Uses Set – Volume 7)*

SZONIECKY Samuel
*Ecosystems Knowledge: Modeling and Analysis Method for Information and Communication*
*(Digital Tools and Uses Set – Volume 6)*

## 2017

BENMAMMAR Badr
*Concurrent, Real-Time and Distributed Programming in Java*

HÉLIODORE Frédéric, NAKIB Amir, ISMAIL Boussaad, OUCHRAA Salma, SCHMITT Laurent
*Metaheuristics for Intelligent Electrical Networks*
*(Metaheuristics Set – Volume 10)*

MA Haiping, SIMON Dan
*Evolutionary Computation with Biogeography-based Optimization*
*(Metaheuristics Set – Volume 8)*

PÉTROWSKI Alain, BEN-HAMIDA Sana
*Evolutionary Algorithms*
*(Metaheuristics Set – Volume 9)*

PAI G A Vijayalakshmi
*Metaheuristics for Portfolio Optimization*
*(Metaheuristics Set – Volume 11)*

## 2016

BLUM Christian, FESTA Paola
*Metaheuristics for String Problems in Bio-informatics*
*(Metaheuristics Set – Volume 6)*

DEROUSSI Laurent
*Metaheuristics for Logistics*
*(Metaheuristics Set – Volume 4)*

DHAENENS Clarisse and JOURDAN Laetitia
*Metaheuristics for Big Data*
*(Metaheuristics Set – Volume 5)*

LABADIE Nacima, PRINS Christian, PRODHON Caroline
*Metaheuristics for Vehicle Routing Problems*
*(Metaheuristics Set – Volume 3)*

LEROY Laure
*Eyestrain Reduction in Stereoscopy*

LUTTON Evelyne, PERROT Nathalie, TONDA Albert
*Evolutionary Algorithms for Food Science and Technology*
*(Metaheuristics Set – Volume 7)*

MAGOULÈS Frédéric, ZHAO Hai-Xiang
*Data Mining and Machine Learning in Building Energy Analysis*

RIGO Michel
*Advanced Graph Theory and Combinatorics*

## 2015

BARBIER Franck, RECOUSSINE Jean-Luc
*COBOL Software Modernization: From Principles to Implementation with
the BLU AGE® Method*

CHEN Ken
*Performance Evaluation by Simulation and Analysis with Applications to Computer Networks*

CLERC Maurice
*Guided Randomness in Optimization*
*(Metaheuristics Set – Volume 1)*

DURAND Nicolas, GIANAZZA David, GOTTELAND Jean-Baptiste, ALLIOT Jean-Marc
*Metaheuristics for Air Traffic Management*
*(Metaheuristics Set – Volume 2)*

MAGOULÈS Frédéric, ROUX François-Xavier, HOUZEAUX Guillaume
*Parallel Scientific Computing*

MUNEESAWANG Paisarn, YAMMEN Suchart
*Visual Inspection Technology in the Hard Disk Drive Industry*

## 2014

BOULANGER Jean-Louis
*Formal Methods Applied to Industrial Complex Systems*

BOULANGER Jean-Louis
*Formal Methods Applied to Complex Systems:*
*Implementation of the B Method*

GARDI Frédéric, BENOIST Thierry, DARLAY Julien, ESTELLON Bertrand, MEGEL Romain
*Mathematical Programming Solver based on Local Search*

KRICHEN Saoussen, CHAOUACHI Jouhaina
*Graph-related Optimization and Decision Support Systems*

LARRIEU Nicolas, VARET Antoine
*Rapid Prototyping of Software for Avionics Systems: Model-oriented Approaches for Complex Systems Certification*

## 2011

BICHOT Charles-Edmond, SIARRY Patrick
*Graph Partitioning*

BOULANGER Jean-Louis
*Static Analysis of Software: The Abstract Interpretation*

CAFERRA Ricardo
*Logic for Computer Science and Artificial Intelligence*

HOMES Bernard
*Fundamentals of Software Testing*

KORDON Fabrice, HADDAD Serge, PAUTET Laurent, PETRUCCI Laure
*Distributed Systems: Design and Algorithms*

KORDON Fabrice, HADDAD Serge, PAUTET Laurent, PETRUCCI Laure
*Models and Analysis in Distributed Systems*

LORCA Xavier
*Tree-based Graph Partitioning Constraint*

TRUCHET Charlotte, ASSAYAG Gerard
*Constraint Programming in Music*

VICAT-BLANC PRIMET Pascale *et al.*
*Computing Networks: From Cluster to Cloud Computing*

## 2010

AUDIBERT Pierre
*Mathematics for Informatics and Computer Science*

BABAU Jean-Philippe *et al.*
*Model Driven Engineering for Distributed Real-Time Embedded Systems 2009*

BOULANGER Jean-Louis
*Safety of Computer Architectures*

MONMARCHE Nicolas *et al.*
*Artificial Ants*

PANETTO Hervé, BOUDJLIDA Nacer
*Interoperability for Enterprise Software and Applications 2010*

SIGAUD Olivier *et al.*
*Markov Decision Processes in Artificial Intelligence*

SOLNON Christine
*Ant Colony Optimization and Constraint Programming*

AUBRUN Christophe, SIMON Daniel, SONG Ye-Qiong *et al.*
*Co-design Approaches for Dependable Networked Control Systems*

## 2009

FOURNIER Jean-Claude
*Graph Theory and Applications*

GUEDON Jeanpierre
*The Mojette Transform / Theory and Applications*

JARD Claude, ROUX Olivier
*Communicating Embedded Systems / Software and Design*

LECOUTRE Christophe
*Constraint Networks / Targeting Simplicity for Techniques and Algorithms*

## 2008

BANÂTRE Michel, MARRÓN Pedro José, OLLERO Hannibal, WOLITZ Adam
*Cooperating Embedded Systems and Wireless Sensor Networks*

MERZ Stephan, NAVET Nicolas
*Modeling and Verification of Real-time Systems*

PASCHOS Vangelis Th
*Combinatorial Optimization and Theoretical Computer Science: Interfaces and Perspectives*

WALDNER Jean-Baptiste
*Nanocomputers and Swarm Intelligence*

## 2007

BENHAMOU Frédéric, JUSSIEN Narendra, O'SULLIVAN Barry
*Trends in Constraint Programming*

JUSSIEN Narendra
*A TO Z OF SUDOKU*

## 2006

BABAU Jean-Philippe *et al.*
*From MDD Concepts to Experiments and Illustrations – DRES 2006*

HABRIAS Henri, FRAPPIER Marc
*Software Specification Methods*

MURAT Cecile, PASCHOS Vangelis Th
*Probabilistic Combinatorial Optimization on Graphs*

PANETTO Hervé, BOUDJLIDA Nacer
*Interoperability for Enterprise Software and Applications 2006 / IFAC-IFIP
I-ESA'2006*

## 2005

GÉRARD Sébastien *et al.*
*Model Driven Engineering for Distributed Real Time Embedded Systems*

PANETTO Hervé
*Interoperability of Enterprise Software and Applications 2005*

Printed and bound by CPI Group (UK) Ltd, Croydon, CR0 4YY

27/10/2024

14580248-0001